LIVING  LITURGY™

for Lectors

Year A • 2023

Paul-Vincent Niebauer, OSB

with
Jessie Bazan
Orin E. Johnson
Jessica Mannen Kimmet

LITURGICAL PRESS
Collegeville, Minnesota

www.litpress.org

ISSN 2831-5146 (print)   2831-5154 (ebook)

ISBN 978-0-8146-6781-1 (print)   978-0-8146-6782-8 (ebook)

Presented to

_____

in grateful appreciation
for your ministry

_____

_____
(date)

Proclaimed well, the word of God can and does change the lives of the hearers. Ah, but "proclaimed well" is sometimes the challenge. That is what I want to humbly offer: helpful insights and technique to enrich your delivery of the word of God.

I come from the theater side of the street. In selecting a play for a successful production, one must always begin with a good script. In Scripture, we have one of the best, if not *the* best, "scripts" in the history of humankind. Even though many may have heard numerous times what will be proclaimed, when proclaimed well new insights can and do occur, both for the hearer and the reader. The gospels are the living word of God. If proclaimed well we never hear them the same way twice.

Here are a few practical, technical points to be considered when proclaiming the word of God:

1. Do you have an adequate sound system? Can everyone hear and understand all the words that are being read?

   • Sound systems can be intimidating. Might there be someone in the parish who can assist in delivering the best sound your system is capable of?

   • Get as comfortable as possible with your system and microphone. If you can't hear yourself over the sound system (or even a large room without a system) then there is a very good chance few others can hear you.

2. Is your diction as good as it might be? The following are some tips.

   • When you are speaking publicly are you pronouncing the end consonants? For example, try reading the following, pronouncing the underlined letter:

   Indeed, religion with contentment is a great gain. For we brought nothing into the world, just as we shall not be able to take anything out of it. If we have food and clothing, we shall be content with that. (1 Timothy 6:6-8)

   • Often when speaking publicly we think we are sounding the end consonants but in fact we are not. Don't be afraid to exaggerate.

Finally, taking care to pronounce the end consonants will almost always make you slow down.

3. Something that nearly all of us need to do is *slow down.* I am 69 at this writing and I have heard fewer people than I can count on one hand read too slowly. The opposite is usually the case: most people read too fast. When in doubt, slow down.

4. Do you understand what you are reading? Can you verbalize the sense of the reading in your own words?

   • When addressing the above questions, Saint Paul always comes to mind. A biblical commentary is indispensable in helping to understand what Paul—or any other Scripture author—is saying. Frankly stated, if you the reader, do not understand what you are reading then how can the listener be expected to understand what you are reading?

5. Rehearsing aloud will always help improve your reading. It will also lower your nervousness and help you keep from stumbling!

6. Is the reader's tone of voice fresh and accessible for the hearer?

   • When my theater voice teacher assigned our acting class to bring our Bibles to class to do a reading, we all failed miserably! Why? We all put on this churchy sort of voice – you know, a somber, stilted, monotone sort of voice. Our professor immediately said, "That is not your own voice! Why are you speaking like that?" We said, "Well, that was the way we thought you should read from the Bible." She said, "Well yes, if you want to put your listeners to sleep!" All this is to say, use your own voice. Don't try to sound "holy." Simply be *sincere* with your reading, taking great care that the listener hears and understands the written word of the Lord. This, after all, is the bottom line.

Brother Paul-Vincent Niebauer, OSB
Saint John's Abbey
Collegeville, Minnesota

Preparing to Proclaim

Key words and phrases: "[S]tay awake! . . . you also must be prepared."

To the point: Even for those of us who believe in observing Advent before Christmas, the secular world's insistence on rushing to the latter can form our expectations. When Advent begins, we come to Mass ready for flickering flame, for slowly growing light, for tidings of comfort and joy. But this gospel snaps us back to reality: it is not Christmas yet. What is described here is rather scary and unsettling. The image of people being suddenly taken away is uncomfortable; the idea of being left behind doesn't sound great either. All this reminds us that our God is a God of surprises. For most of us, God's surprising work will be much more ordinary than vanishing neighbors, but we are still called to stay aware of God's presence and open to the unexpected ways God moves in our hearts and in our world.

Making Connections

Between the readings: Compared to the gospel, the first reading offers a more comforting and joyful vision of the end times. There is unity and inclusion rather than division; all are called to be part of the lasting peace God envisions for us. The psalmist echoes the joy of the nations streaming toward Jerusalem as he, too, heads there on pilgrimage and prays for its peace. The second reading gives us practical ways to "stay awake," through moral conduct and union with Christ.

To experience: "Staying awake" means remaining attentive to how small choices build into robust lives of faith. It means cultivating awareness of God's ongoing presence in the mundane realities of our lives. It means turning our attention toward the things that really matter and turning away from things that are distracting. Advent might be an invitation to shake off the stupor of binge watching and social media scrolling and to enter into the fully vibrant lives that God wants for us.

Prayer

God of Heaven and Earth,
you long to be our God; we long to draw near
  to you.
Show unto us the path to your holy city,
that all may cry out with joy:
"Let us go rejoicing to the house of the Lord."
Through Christ our Lord.
Amen.

First Reading (Isa 2:1-5)

A reading from the Book of the Prophet Isaiah

This is what Isaiah, son of Amoz,
  saw concerning Judah and Jerusalem.
    In days to come,
the mountain of the LORD's house
  shall be established as the highest
    mountain
  and raised above the hills.
All nations shall stream toward it;
  many peoples shall come and say:
"Come, let us climb the LORD's mountain,
  to the house of the God of Jacob,
that he may instruct us in his ways,
  and we may walk in his paths."
For from Zion shall go forth instruction,
  and the word of the LORD from
    Jerusalem.
He shall judge between the nations,
  and impose terms on many peoples.
They shall beat their swords into
    plowshares
  and their spears into pruning hooks;
one nation shall not raise the sword against
    another,
  nor shall they train for war again.
O house of Jacob, come,
  let us walk in the light of the LORD!

Pronunciation
Amoz   AY-muhz
Judah   JOU-duh
Zion   ZAI-uhn

Good times are coming!
All nations are going to
enjoy the prosperity! All
war will end with imple-
ments of war being
beaten into tools to culti-
vate the land to support
life rather than destroy
life.

Try a pause after "nor
shall they train for war
again." Then really pro-
claim: "O house of Jacob,
come . . .!"

7

Responsorial Psalm (Ps 122:1-2, 3-4, 4-5, 6-7, 8-9)

℟. Let us go rejoicing to the house of the Lord.

I rejoiced because they said to me,
    "We will go up to the house of the Lord."
And now we have set foot
    within your gates, O Jerusalem.

℟. Let us go rejoicing to the house of the Lord.

Jerusalem, built as a city
    with compact unity.
To it the tribes go up,
    the tribes of the Lord.

℟. Let us go rejoicing to the house of the Lord.

According to the decree for Israel,
    to give thanks to the name of the Lord.
In it are set up judgment seats,
    seats for the house of David.

℟. Let us go rejoicing to the house of the Lord.

Pray for the peace of Jerusalem!
    May those who love you prosper!
May peace be within your walls,
    prosperity in your buildings.

℟. Let us go rejoicing to the house of the Lord.

Because of my brothers and friends
    I will say, "Peace be within you!"
Because of the house of the Lord, our God,
    I will pray for your good.

℟. Let us go rejoicing to the house of the Lord.

Try being very measured in your delivery of the first two lines emphasizing the word *know*. Then after "You *know* the time"—you tell them what it is time to do!

Second Reading (Rom 13:11-14)

A reading from the Letter of Saint Paul to the Romans

Brothers and sisters:
You know the time;
    it is the hour now for you to awake from
        sleep.

For our salvation is nearer now than when we
   first believed;
   the night is advanced, the day is at hand.
Let us then throw off the works of darkness
   and put on the armor of light;
   let us conduct ourselves properly as in the
      day,
   not in orgies and drunkenness,
   not in promiscuity and lust,
   not in rivalry and jealousy.
But put on the Lord Jesus Christ,
   and make no provision for the desires of
      the flesh.

After the orgies, etc., which can be a bit embarrassing to read and hear, enjoy a nice pause and then say with great thoughtfulness, "But put on . . ."

Gospel (Matt 24:37-44; L1A)

A reading from the holy Gospel according
to Matthew

Jesus said to his disciples:
"As it was in the days of Noah,
   so it will be at the coming of the Son of
      Man.
In those days before the flood,
   they were eating and drinking,
   marrying and giving in marriage,
   up to the day that Noah entered the ark.
They did not know until the flood came and
      carried them all away.
So will it be also at the coming of the Son of
   Man.
Two men will be out in the field;
   one will be taken, and one will be left.
Two women will be grinding at the mill;
   one will be taken, and one will be left.
Therefore, stay awake!
For you do not know on which day your Lord
      will come.
Be sure of this: if the master of the house
   had known the hour of night when the
      thief was coming,

Try taking a longer than usual three-to-four-second pause after "A reading from the holy Gospel . . ." This is a technique used by great speakers to really arrest the listeners' attention.

Matthew is obviously drawing a parallel here between those caught unaware in the flood and those who will be caught unprepared for the coming of the Son of Man. Terrifying, isn't it? Allow a pause for listeners to ask, what shall we do? The answer follows: "Therefore, stay awake!" Be ready always!

he would have stayed awake
and not let his house be broken into.
So too, you also must be prepared,
for at an hour you do not expect, the Son of
Man will come."

Preparing to Proclaim

Key words and phrases: "Repent, for the kingdom of heaven is at hand."

To the point: This week's gospel introduces one of Advent's main characters: John the Baptist. And he is treated as a character here, given a more vivid description than many biblical figures. We are meant to picture him; we know what he wears and what he eats. He is rough. He is unkempt. He is blunt. He is, in a word, weird. And yet, people are drawn to him, listening to his preaching and going to be baptized. Throughout the Advent and Christmas seasons, we hear stories of God coming in ways we didn't expect, from this bizarre desert preacher to a literal infant born into poverty. In John the Baptist, holiness could have been overlooked because of his oddities. But the season insists on reminding us to keep our eyes open to the truth that God often comes disguised in interruption and inconvenience.

Making Connections

Between the readings: Again, a harsh-sounding gospel is paired with an Old Testament prophecy of lush comfort. At the same time, though, it echoes the gospel's promise that Jesus is not coming to bring peace alone; those who are unrepentantly wicked or ruthless should be afraid of his coming. The second reading affirms that Christ's coming is for all; it is not our background or origin that matters but our choice to follow Jesus.

To experience: Recognizing that God works through the interruptions of our lives is an ongoing challenge. Very often we are tempted to think we know best, especially if we have included God in our discernment and the making of our plans. But our plans—even the ones that seem good and holy—are up for interruption. Convenience is not a prerequisite for how God works. Prophets often appear in our midst in weird and inconvenient ways. They are there for a reason; they interrupt our too-small ways of understanding God. How often do we overlook prophets in our midst?

Prayer

God of the Lowly and Poor,
we await the coming of your son, Jesus,
who shall make everything whole.
*Justice shall flourish in his time, and fullness
    of peace forever.*
May he come to us quickly, without delay,
he who is compassion and mercy.
Amen.

Pronunciation
Gentiles   JEHN-tailz

Have you ever had a plant
that you thought was
dead and then one day
you spot a beautiful green
shoot making an appear-
ance? Wow! This is the
kind of excitement with
which you can deliver the
first line.

With the arrival of this
new being, the order of
the world will change for
the better.

First Reading (Isa 11:1-10)

A reading from the Book of the Prophet Isaiah

On that day, a shoot shall sprout from the
        stump of Jesse,
    and from his roots a bud shall blossom.
The spirit of the LORD shall rest upon him:
    a spirit of wisdom and of understanding,
a spirit of counsel and of strength,
    a spirit of knowledge and of fear of the
        LORD,
    and his delight shall be the fear of the
        LORD.
Not by appearance shall he judge,
    nor by hearsay shall he decide,
but he shall judge the poor with justice,
    and decide aright for the land's afflicted.
He shall strike the ruthless with the rod of his
        mouth,
    and with the breath of his lips he shall slay
        the wicked.
Justice shall be the band around his waist,
    and faithfulness a belt upon his hips.
Then the wolf shall be a guest of the lamb,
    and the leopard shall lie down with the kid;
the calf and the young lion shall browse
        together,
    with a little child to guide them.
The cow and the bear shall be neighbors,
    together their young shall rest;
    the lion shall eat hay like the ox.

The baby shall play by the cobra's den,
    and the child lay his hand on the adder's
        lair.
There shall be no harm or ruin on all my holy
        mountain;
    for the earth shall be filled with knowledge
        of the LORD,
    as water covers the sea.
On that day, the root of Jesse,
    set up as a signal for the nations,
the Gentiles shall seek out,
    for his dwelling shall be glorious.

Responsorial Psalm (Ps 72:1-2, 7-8, 12-13, 17)

R℣. (cf. 7) Justice shall flourish in his time, and
fullness of peace for ever.

O God, with your judgment endow the king,
    and with your justice, the king's son;
he shall govern your people with justice
    and your afflicted ones with judgment.

R℣. Justice shall flourish in his time, and
fullness of peace for ever.

Justice shall flower in his days,
    and profound peace, till the moon be no
        more.
May he rule from sea to sea,
    and from the River to the ends of the earth.

R℣. Justice shall flourish in his time, and
fullness of peace for ever.

For he shall rescue the poor when he cries out,
    and the afflicted when he has no one to
        help him.
He shall have pity for the lowly and the poor;
    the lives of the poor he shall save.

R℣. Justice shall flourish in his time, and
fullness of peace for ever.

13

May his name be blessed forever;
>as long as the sun his name shall remain.
In him shall all the tribes of the earth be
>blessed;
>all the nations shall proclaim his happiness.

R/. Justice shall flourish in his time, and
fullness of peace for ever.

Pronunciation
Gentiles JEHN-tailz

This reading is a pretty straightforward one for St. Paul. Nevertheless, read through it a number of times and out loud, if at all possible. Readings should never be done "fast."

Paul often writes in a de-clarative voice, as in this case. Try delivering this in a very determined manner.

Second Reading (Rom 15:4-9)

A reading from the Letter of Saint Paul to the Romans

Brothers and sisters:
Whatever was written previously was written
>for our instruction,
>that by endurance and by the
>>encouragement of the Scriptures
>we might have hope.
May the God of endurance and
>encouragement
>grant you to think in harmony with one
>>another,
>in keeping with Christ Jesus,
>that with one accord you may with one
>>voice
>glorify the God and Father of our Lord
>>Jesus Christ.

Welcome one another, then, as Christ
>welcomed you,
>for the glory of God.
For I say that Christ became a minister of the
>circumcised
>to show God's truthfulness,
>to confirm the promises to the patriarchs,
>but so that the Gentiles might glorify God
>>for his mercy.
As it is written:
>*Therefore, I will praise you among the*
>>*Gentiles*
>*and sing praises to your name.*

Gospel (Matt 3:1-12; L4A)

A reading from the holy Gospel according to Matthew

John the Baptist appeared, preaching in the
    desert of Judea
    and saying, "Repent, for the kingdom of
      heaven is at hand!"
It was of him that the prophet Isaiah had
    spoken when he said:
     A voice of one crying out in the desert,
     Prepare the way of the LORD,
      make straight his paths.
John wore clothing made of camel's hair
    and had a leather belt around his waist.
His food was locusts and wild honey.
At that time Jerusalem, all Judea,
    and the whole region around the Jordan
    were going out to him
    and were being baptized by him in the
      Jordan River
    as they acknowledged their sins.

When he saw many of the Pharisees and
    Sadducees
    coming to his baptism, he said to them,
      "You brood of vipers!
Who warned you to flee from the coming
    wrath?
Produce good fruit as evidence of your
    repentance.
And do not presume to say to yourselves,
    'We have Abraham as our father.'
For I tell you,
    God can raise up children to Abraham
      from these stones.
Even now the ax lies at the root of the trees.
Therefore every tree that does not bear good
    fruit
    will be cut down and thrown into the fire.

Pronunciation
Judea   jou-DEE-uh
Pharisees   FEHR-ih-seez
Sadducees   SAD-joo-seez

What a wonderfully theatrical writing (in the best sense) we have been given here! At the beginning you are describing one of the Bible's most colorful prophets—one who I don't think I would like to meet in a dark alley by myself! Yet the people are flocking to him; it's amazing.

Notice that there is arguably a crescendo in this reading. It begins gently, albeit not without substance, and builds straight through to the last line. Don't be afraid to give this reading the same energy that John the Baptist would.

I am baptizing you with water, for repentance,
     but the one who is coming after me is
          mightier than I.
I am not worthy to carry his sandals.
He will baptize you with the Holy Spirit and
     fire.
His winnowing fan is in his hand.
He will clear his threshing floor
     and gather his wheat into his barn,
          but the chaff he will burn with
               unquenchable fire."

Preparing to Proclaim
Key words and phrases: "Go and tell John what you hear and see."

To the point: In this gospel, Jesus instructs John's disciples to serve as witnesses. Witnesses are people who have seen something firsthand and who share what they have seen for the benefit of those who could not be there. Their presence at the scene of what's happening gives their testimony a certain privilege. Witnesses are important; we trust what they say. Jesus instructs these witnesses in what they are to say: most elements are familiar aspects of ancient prophecies, but he throws a twist in at the end. He brings healing not only for those who are blind, lame, deaf, or ill; he restores to life even those who have died. Jesus is the fulfillment of the Old Testament prophecies, but he is also something completely new. The work Jesus is beginning is beyond anyone's wildest hopes or imaginings.

Making Connections
Between the readings: The future tense of the first reading transforms into present tense in the gospel. With Jesus's coming, the blind *do* see, the deaf *do* hear, here and now. Jesus's presence is effecting healing and change as his earthly ministry begins. It is still effecting healing now as his presence continues with us in countless harder-to-see ways. And yet Advent is also our season of waiting; the second reading reminds us that we are still waiting for Christ's healing work to be accomplished in its fullness. The transformation of our world has yet to be complete.

To experience: We don't often see the grand miracles that Jesus enumerates here, but we, too, are called to witness to God's work of healing and giving life. Jesus usually slips in quietly, blessing us with subtle strength and slow growth that we might fail to notice. Very often in our lives, we have to train our eyes to see it.

Prayer

Voice of the Oppressed,
you are divine power to those in need,
the oppressed, the hungry, the captive.
Bring your healing, bring your justice;
come to reign over us forever.
Lord, come and save us,
we who patiently await your coming.
Amen.

Pronunciation
Lebanon LEH-buh-nuhn
Carmel KAHR-muhl
Zion ZAI-uhn

What great news! The barren, dusty earth will *bloom*! Even better, those who are sick and weak will be made well again. Better yet, all of the Lord's people will be crowned with *everlasting* joy!

Try reading this with real energy, from the very beginning. Everything you read here is great news.

First Reading (Isa 35:1-6a, 10)

A reading from the Book of the Prophet Isaiah

The desert and the parched land will exult;
    the steppe will rejoice and bloom.
They will bloom with abundant flowers,
    and rejoice with joyful song.
The glory of Lebanon will be given to them,
    the splendor of Carmel and Sharon;
they will see the glory of the LORD,
    the splendor of our God.
Strengthen the hands that are feeble,
    make firm the knees that are weak,
say to those whose hearts are frightened:
    Be strong, fear not!
Here is your God,
    he comes with vindication;
with divine recompense
    he comes to save you.
Then will the eyes of the blind be opened,
    the ears of the deaf be cleared;
then will the lame leap like a stag,
    then the tongue of the mute will sing.

Those whom the LORD has ransomed will
        return
    and enter Zion singing,
    crowned with everlasting joy;
they will meet with joy and gladness,
    sorrow and mourning will flee.

Responsorial Psalm (Ps 146:6-7, 8-9, 9-10)

℟. (cf. Isaiah 35:4) Lord, come and save us.
or: ℟. Alleluia.

The LORD God keeps faith forever,
    secures justice for the oppressed,
    gives food to the hungry.
The LORD sets captives free.

℟. Lord, come and save us. *or:* ℟. Alleluia.

The LORD gives sight to the blind;
    the LORD raises up those who were bowed
        down.
The LORD loves the just;
    the LORD protects strangers.

℟. Lord, come and save us. *or:* ℟. Alleluia.

The fatherless and the widow he sustains,
    but the way of the wicked he thwarts.
The LORD shall reign forever;
    your God, O Zion, through all generations.

℟. Lord, come and save us. *or:* ℟. Alleluia.

Second Reading (Jas 5:7-10)

A reading from the Letter of Saint James

Be patient, brothers and sisters,
    until the coming of the Lord.
See how the farmer waits for the precious
        fruit of the earth,
    being patient with it
    until it receives the early and the late rains.
You too must be patient.
Make your hearts firm,
    because the coming of the Lord is at hand.
Do not complain, brothers and sisters, about
        one another,
    that you may not be judged.
Behold, the Judge is standing before the gates.

The first sentence of any Scripture passage is always important, but the first sentence here says *exactly* what the whole passage is about. Take your time really declaring that first sentence.

The word "patient" appears three times in the first half of the reading. Give it its due, emphasizing it each time.

Take as an example of hardship and patience,
    brothers and sisters,
    the prophets who spoke in the name of the
        Lord.

Gospel (Matt 11:2-11; L7A)

A reading from the holy Gospel according
to Matthew

When John the Baptist heard in prison of the
    works of the Christ,
    he sent his disciples to Jesus with this
        question,
    "Are you the one who is to come,
    or should we look for another?"
Jesus said to them in reply,
    "Go and tell John what you hear and see:
    the blind regain their sight,
    the lame walk,
    lepers are cleansed,
    the deaf hear,
    the dead are raised,
    and the poor have the good news
        proclaimed to them.
And blessed is the one who takes no offense
    at me."

As they were going off,
    Jesus began to speak to the crowds about
        John,
    "What did you go out to the desert to see?
A reed swayed by the wind?
Then what did you go out to see?
Someone dressed in fine clothing?
Those who wear fine clothing are in royal
    palaces.
Then why did you go out? To see a prophet?
Yes, I tell you, and more than a prophet.
This is the one about whom it is written:

Here is another really colorful and dramatic reading about John the Baptist. The first half confirms to John that Jesus is the Messiah, and the second talks about confirming John as the prophet who is preparing the way of the Lord. Be sure to break in tone or in some other way differentiate these two parts of this great news.

The kicker, of course, is the last sentence and that is a distinct part 3 to the reading. Make it stand out as such.

Be careful to deliver the last word of each section with energy—"takes no offense at me," "prepare your way before you," "greater than he."

*Behold, I am sending my messenger
    ahead of you;*
    he will prepare your way before you.
Amen, I say to you,
    among those born of women
    there has been none greater than John the
        Baptist;
    yet the least in the kingdom of heaven is
        greater than he."

Preparing to Proclaim
Key words and phrases: "*[T]hey shall name him Emmanuel, /* which means 'God is with us.'"

To the point: Here we have Joseph's side of the story—mostly a story about being left out of a very big decision. Joseph's exclusion is challenging and confusing for him, but it is important; it affirms that Jesus's origins are not natural but supernatural. There is no human father responsible for this son. He is the Son of God, and at the same time, son of Mary, fully human. He enters into human life with all its greatness and littleness, all its joys and sorrows. He is God with us, Emmanuel. He shares in our human experience, even in neediness. And although he was left out of the main event, Joseph does have a decision to make here, and he chooses radical hospitality for the stranger in need that is God in disguise. He accepts this woman into his home and her child as his own. Jesus will even share Joseph's lineage; it is through his foster father that he is a descendant of David.

Making Connections
Between the readings: Isaiah's prophecy is so extraordinary that it is not recognized as a sign when it finally occurs in Mary; the presumption is that this virgin's conception is not God's work but a very ordinary moment of human sin and weakness. Our Advent theme continues: this is a God who defies expectations and comes in ways for which we are not ready. In the second reading, Paul packs a lot of theology into the opening of his letter, echoing the idea of Christ's dual origin: fully human, fully divine.

To experience: Have you ever asked for a sign from God? God does work through signs at times, but they are very rarely the signs we would have chosen. Often, God works in places we never would have thought to look. Advent is about training our eyes, about paying attention, about noticing what once we would have ignored—the panhandler, the criminal, the child—and learning to see God there.

Prayer

God of Power and Might,
you choose the lowly among us to bring to
    birth
your words of justice and peace.
You chose Mary, the *highest honor of our
    race*, to bring to birth
your Word: Jesus, justice and peace incarnate.
May we also embody such holiness in all we
    say and do.
Amen.

First Reading (Isa 7:10-14)

A reading from the Book of the Prophet Isaiah

The LORD spoke to Ahaz, saying:
    Ask for a sign from the LORD, your God;
    let it be deep as the netherworld, or high as
        the sky!
But Ahaz answered,
    "I will not ask! I will not tempt the LORD!"
Then Isaiah said:
    Listen, O house of David!
Is it not enough for you to weary people,
    must you also weary my God?
Therefore the Lord himself will give you this
    sign:
    the virgin shall conceive, and bear a son,
    and shall name him Emmanuel.

Responsorial Psalm (Ps 24:1-2, 3-4, 5-6)

R̝. (7c and 10b) Let the Lord enter; he is king
of glory.

The LORD's are the earth and its fullness;
    the world and those who dwell in it.
For he founded it upon the seas
    and established it upon the rivers.

R̝. Let the Lord enter; he is king of glory.

Pronunciation
Ahaz   AY-haz
Emmanuel
    eh-MAN-yoo-ehl

Sometimes God sends us
signs whether we want
them or not. The second
part of what Isaiah is saying here is that God is
going to send the *greatest
sign of all*!

Any prophet is going as-
sume you are listening,
but when Isaiah actually
says "Listen!" then you
know he is going to say
something important. So,
of course, hit that word
with energy.

Remember that Emman-
uel means "God with us,"
so say "Emmanuel" with
that in mind.

23

Who can ascend the mountain of the LORD?
>   or who may stand in his holy place?
One whose hands are sinless, whose heart is
>   clean,
>   who desires not what is vain.

R̸. Let the Lord enter; he is king of glory.

He shall receive a blessing from the LORD,
>   a reward from God his savior.
Such is the race that seeks for him,
>   that seeks the face of the God of Jacob.

R̸. Let the Lord enter; he is king of glory.

Pronunciation
Gentiles   JEHN-tailz

Here comes Paul, so read this a number of times out loud. Of course, the first two parts are *two long sentences*, which is so typical of Paul's writing.

Make sure you know what he is saying, being careful that you communicate when he is pausing (noted by a comma or semicolon) and when he has finished a sentence.

Second Reading (Rom 1:1-7)

A reading from the Letter of Saint Paul to the Romans

Paul, a slave of Christ Jesus,
>   called to be an apostle and set apart for the
>   gospel of God,
>   which he promised previously through his
>   prophets in the holy Scriptures,
>   the gospel about his Son, descended from
>   David according to the flesh,
>   but established as Son of God in power
>   according to the Spirit of holiness
>   through resurrection from the dead, Jesus
>   Christ our Lord.
Through him we have received the grace of
>   apostleship,
>   to bring about the obedience of faith,
>   for the sake of his name, among all the
>   Gentiles,
>   among whom are you also, who are called
>   to belong to Jesus Christ;
>   to all the beloved of God in Rome, called to
>   be holy.
Grace to you and peace from God our Father
>   and the Lord Jesus Christ.

Gospel (Matt 1:18-24; L10A)

A reading from the holy Gospel according to Matthew

This is how the birth of Jesus Christ came
    about.
When his mother Mary was betrothed to
    Joseph,
    but before they lived together,
    she was found with child through the Holy
        Spirit.
Joseph her husband, since he was a righteous
    man,
    yet unwilling to expose her to shame,
    decided to divorce her quietly.
Such was his intention when, behold,
    the angel of the Lord appeared to him in a
        dream and said,
    "Joseph, son of David,
    do not be afraid to take Mary your wife
        into your home.
For it is through the Holy Spirit
    that this child has been conceived in her.
She will bear a son and you are to name him
    Jesus,
    because he will save his people from their
        sins."
All this took place to fulfill what the Lord had
    said through the prophet:
    Behold, the virgin shall conceive and bear a
        son,
    and they shall name him Emmanuel,
    which means "God is with us."
When Joseph awoke,
    he did as the angel of the Lord had
        commanded him
    and took his wife into his home.

Pronunciation
Emmanuel
    eh-MAN-yoo-ehl

This is one of the gospel passages we have heard so many times that it may be hard for the listener to really hear it afresh. That being said, right after the rather short but amazing opening sentence, we are told in the next sentence that Mary is pregnant before being with Joseph. Then, in the next sentence, we hear that Joseph is going to divorce her. What??!!

Of course, everyone—or at least the great majority of your listeners—know how this is going to work out. But here's the effort: read the first few sentences as though your listeners are hearing it for the first time! Make sure they don't miss a word, as every word is so important.

Now, read the rest of the gospel with the same energy.

Preparing to Proclaim

Key words and phrases: "Do not be afraid; for behold, I proclaim to you good news of great joy that will be for all the people."

To the point: The Christmas readings radiate joy and peace. Even so, we continue to live in a world where injustice, suffering, and death is commonplace. While it is important to convey hope in your proclamation, for Jesus Christ is indeed Hope of the World, we cannot forget the reality so many people face. War, famine, and poverty are just some of these realities. The birth of Emmanuel, "God is with us," is simultaneously a celebration and a call to action.

Making Connections

The shepherds drop everything to go and see the Christ child—the one who the Lord revealed. Imagine how different their lives would have been had they stayed in the fields, deciding that they were "too busy" to change course. Our God is a God of interruptions. God works in unexpected ways and in unexpected times. In the busyness of this Christmas season, let us be open to holy interruptions.

Holiness appears in the messy realties of daily life. God's messengers appear to the shepherds in the fields. Mary and Joseph experience the most sacred night of their lives inside a stable meant for barn animals. The gospel writer leaves out the exact details of Mary's delivery, but we can be sure it was messy and painful like every other human birth. Nativity sets and Christmas cards often depict a pristine manger scene—likely a far cry from that night's realities. Holiness is not clean and tidy. Instead, God meets us in the mess.

Prayer

God of Isaiah, Jesse, David, and Mary,
you draw near to us today, in kindness and in truth.
Generations have awaited you;
in this moment let each heart cry out:
Forever I will sing the goodness of the Lord.
You are Emmanuel, "God is With Us."
Remain with us, now and always.
Amen.

Vigil Mass Readings

First Reading (Isa 62:1-5)

A reading from the Book of the Prophet Isaiah

For Zion's sake I will not be silent,
    for Jerusalem's sake I will not be quiet,
until her vindication shines forth like the
    dawn
    and her victory like a burning torch.

Nations shall behold your vindication,
    and all the kings your glory;
you shall be called by a new name
    pronounced by the mouth of the LORD.
You shall be a glorious crown in the hand
    of the LORD,
    a royal diadem held by your God.
No more shall people call you "Forsaken,"
    or your land "Desolate,"
but you shall be called "My Delight,"
    and your land "Espoused."
For the LORD delights in you
    and makes your land his spouse.
As a young man marries a virgin,
    your Builder shall marry you;
and as a bridegroom rejoices in his bride
    so shall your God rejoice in you.

Responsorial Psalm (Ps 89:4-5, 16-17, 27, 29)

R̷. (2a) For ever I will sing the goodness of the Lord.

I have made a covenant with my chosen one,
    I have sworn to David my servant:
forever will I confirm your posterity
    and establish your throne for all
        generations.

R̷. For ever I will sing the goodness of the Lord.

Pronunciation
Zion   ZAI-uhn

In this reading we have a 180-degree turnaround for Zion and Jerusalem, going from "Forsaken" to "My Delight"!

The words in the quotes should absolutely stand out, and at the same time contrast the first two descriptions with the next two. You can absolutely *smile* when you say, "My Delight" and "Espoused."

Espoused means "to take up and support as a cause; become attached to."

Blessed the people who know the joyful shout;
in the light of your countenance, O LORD,
they walk.
At your name they rejoice all the day,
and through your justice they are exalted.

R̸. For ever I will sing the goodness of the Lord.

He shall say of me, "You are my father,
my God, the Rock, my savior."
Forever I will maintain my kindness toward
him, .
and my covenant with him stands firm.

R̸. For ever I will sing the goodness of the Lord.

Pronunciation
Antioch   AN-tih-ahk
Pisidia   pih-SIH-dih-uh

Paul is giving a major
catechism class here, trac-
ing the progression of the
Old Testament into the beginning of the New Testa-
ment. Wow! Imagine the
confidence and directness
with which Paul spoke
these words.

Make sure you are well rehearsed with this reading,
as Paul is not always easily read.

Second Reading (Acts 13:16-17, 22-25)

A reading from the Acts of the Apostles

When Paul reached Antioch in Pisidia and
entered the synagogue,
he stood up, motioned with his hand, and
said,
"Fellow Israelites and you others who are
God-fearing, listen.
The God of this people Israel chose our
ancestors
and exalted the people during their sojourn
in the land of Egypt.
With uplifted arm he led them out of it.
Then he removed Saul and raised up David as
king;
of him he testified,
'I have found David, son of Jesse, a man
after my own heart;
he will carry out my every wish.'
From this man's descendants God, according
to his promise,
has brought to Israel a savior, Jesus.
John heralded his coming by proclaiming a
baptism of repentance
to all the people of Israel;

and as John was completing his course, he
would say,
'What do you suppose that I am? I am not he.
Behold, one is coming after me;
I am not worthy to unfasten the sandals of
his feet.'"

Gospel (Matt 1:1-25 [or Matt 1:18-25]; L13ABC)

A reading from the holy Gospel according
to Matthew

The book of the genealogy of Jesus Christ,
the son of David, the son of Abraham.

Abraham became the father of Isaac,
Isaac the father of Jacob,
Jacob the father of Judah and his brothers.
Judah became the father of Perez and Zerah,
whose mother was Tamar.
Perez became the father of Hezron,
Hezron the father of Ram,
Ram the father of Amminadab.
Amminadab became the father of Nahshon,
Nahshon the father of Salmon,
Salmon the father of Boaz,
whose mother was Rahab.
Boaz became the father of Obed,
whose mother was Ruth.
Obed became the father of Jesse,
Jesse the father of David the king.

David became the father of Solomon,
whose mother had been the wife of Uriah.
Solomon became the father of Rehoboam,
Rehoboam the father of Abijah,
Abijah the father of Asaph.
Asaph became the father of Jehoshaphat,
Jehoshaphat the father of Joram,
Joram the father of Uzziah.
Uzziah became the father of Jotham,
Jotham the father of Ahaz,

Pronunciation

Judah   JOU-duh
Perez   PEE-rehz
Zerah   ZEE-ruh
Tamar   TAY-mer
Hezron   HEHZ-ruhn
Amminadab
  ah-MIHN-uh-dab
Nahshon   NAY-shuhn
Salmon   SAL-muhn
Boaz   BO-az
Rahab   RAY-hab
Obed   O-behd
Solomon   SAH-lo-muhn
Uriah   you-RAI-uh
Rehoboam
  ree-ho-BO-am
Abijah   uh-BAI-juh
Asaph   AY-saf
Jehoshaphat
  jee-HAHSH-uh-fat
Joram   JO-ram
Uzziah   yoo-ZAI-uh
Jotham   JO-thuhm
Ahaz   AY-haz
Hezekiah
  heh-zeh-KAI-uh
Manasseh   man-AS-eh
Josiah   jo-SAI-uh
Jechoniah   jehk-o-NAI-uh
Shealtiel   shee-AL-tih-ehl
Zerubbabel
  zeh-RUH-buh-behl
Abiud   uh-BAI-uhd
Eliakim   ee-LAI-uh-kihm
Azor   AY-sawr

29

Zadok   ZAY-dahk
Achim   AY-kihm
Eliud   ee-LAI-uhd
Eleazar   ehl-ee-AY-zer
Matthan   MAT-than
Babylonian
   bab-ih-LO-nih-uhn
Emmanuel
   eh-MAN-yoo-ehl

How can you deliver the genealogy of Jesus in an interesting manner— without using a giant image of Jesus's family tree, of course? It is a long genealogy and it is traceable: That is at least part of your subtext for how to deliver this reading.

I would certainly give extra energy to those names that you know will probably be familiar to your listeners, and move along those that probably are not. Make sure you rehearse the unfamiliar names out loud, even writing the phonetic spelling on a piece of paper when you read, if necessary.

Ahaz the father of Hezekiah.
Hezekiah became the father of Manasseh,
   Manasseh the father of Amos,
   Amos the father of Josiah.
Josiah became the father of Jechoniah and his brothers
   at the time of the Babylonian exile.

After the Babylonian exile,
   Jechoniah became the father of Shealtiel,
   Shealtiel the father of Zerubbabel,
   Zerubbabel the father of Abiud.
Abiud became the father of Eliakim,
   Eliakim the father of Azor,
   Azor the father of Zadok.
Zadok became the father of Achim,
   Achim the father of Eliud,
   Eliud the father of Eleazar.
Eleazar became the father of Matthan,
   Matthan the father of Jacob,
   Jacob the father of Joseph, the husband of Mary.
Of her was born Jesus who is called the Christ.

Thus the total number of generations
   from Abraham to David
   is fourteen generations;
   from David to the Babylonian exile,
   fourteen generations;
   from the Babylonian exile to the Christ,
   fourteen generations.

Now [this is how the birth of Jesus Christ came about.
When his mother Mary was betrothed to Joseph,
   but before they lived together,
      she was found with child through the Holy Spirit.
Joseph her husband, since he was a righteous man,
      yet unwilling to expose her to shame,
      decided to divorce her quietly.

Such was his intention when, behold,
    the angel of the Lord appeared to him in a
        dream and said,
    "Joseph, son of David,
    do not be afraid to take Mary your wife
        into your home.
For it is through the Holy Spirit
    that this child has been conceived in her.
She will bear a son and you are to name him
    Jesus,
    because he will save his people from their
        sins."
All this took place to fulfill
    what the Lord had said through the prophet:
    Behold, the virgin shall conceive and bear
        a son,
        and they shall name him Emmanuel,
    which means "God is with us."
When Joseph awoke,
    he did as the angel of the Lord had
        commanded him
    and took his wife into his home.
He had no relations with her until she bore a
    son,
    and he named him Jesus.]

Mass at Midnight Readings

First Reading (Isa 9:1-6)

A reading from the Book of the Prophet Isaiah

The people who walked in darkness
    have seen a great light;
upon those who dwelt in the land of gloom
    a light has shone.
You have brought them abundant joy
    and great rejoicing,
as they rejoice before you as at the harvest,
    as people make merry when dividing spoils.

Pronunciation
Midian   MIH-dih-uhn

It doesn't get much more joyful than this! Christ has been born to the human race. God is finally with us in person.

Simply proclaim this reading as joyfully as you can.

31

Think of this passage as three parts. Pause after "dividing spoils" and "day of Midian." How do the three parts contrast with each other? Deliver them accordingly.

For the yoke that burdened them,
    the pole on their shoulder,
and the rod of their taskmaster
    you have smashed, as on the day of
        Midian.
For every boot that tramped in battle,
    every cloak rolled in blood,
    will be burned as fuel for flames.
For a child is born to us, a son is given us;
    upon his shoulder dominion rests.
They name him Wonder-Counselor, God-Hero,
    Father-Forever, Prince of Peace.
His dominion is vast
    and forever peaceful,
from David's throne, and over his kingdom,
    which he confirms and sustains
by judgment and justice,
    both now and forever.
The zeal of the LORD of hosts will do this!

Responsorial Psalm (Ps 96:1-2, 2-3, 11-12, 13)

℟. (Luke 2:11) Today is born our Savior,
Christ the Lord.

Sing to the LORD a new song;
    sing to the LORD, all you lands.
Sing to the LORD; bless his name.

℟. Today is born our Savior, Christ the Lord.

Announce his salvation, day after day.
    Tell his glory among the nations;
    among all peoples, his wondrous deeds.

℟. Today is born our Savior, Christ the Lord.

Let the heavens be glad and the earth rejoice;
    let the sea and what fills it resound;
    let the plains be joyful and all that is in
        them!
Then shall all the trees of the forest exult.

℟. Today is born our Savior, Christ the Lord.

They shall exult before the Lord, for he comes;
   for he comes to rule the earth.
He shall rule the world with justice
   and the peoples with his constancy.

R̅. Today is born our Savior, Christ the Lord.

Second Reading (Titus 2:11-14)

A reading from the Letter of Saint Paul to Titus

Beloved:
The grace of God has appeared, saving all
   and training us to reject godless ways and
      worldly desires
   and to live temperately, justly, and devoutly
      in this age,
   as we await the blessed hope,
   the appearance of the glory of our great
      God
   and savior Jesus Christ,
   who gave himself for us to deliver us from
      all lawlessness
   and to cleanse for himself a people as his
      own,
   eager to do what is good.

Pronunciation
Titus   TAI-tuhs

Of course, this is Paul writing and it is all *one* sentence, so make sure to rehearse it out loud so that you don't accidentally put a period where there isn't one.

Gospel (Luke 2:1-14; L14ABC)

A reading from the holy Gospel according
to Luke

In those days a decree went out from Caesar
      Augustus
   that the whole world should be enrolled.
This was the first enrollment,
   when Quirinius was governor of Syria.
So all went to be enrolled, each to his own town.
And Joseph too went up from Galilee from the
      town of Nazareth
   to Judea, to the city of David that is called
      Bethlehem,
   because he was of the house and family of
      David,

Pronunciation
Caesar   SEE-zer
Augustus
   uh-GUHS-tuhs
Quirinius
   kwai-RIHN-ih-uhs
Galilee   GAL-ih-lee
Judea   jou-DEE-uh

A good approach to any of the well-known Scripture readings is to deliver it as though it is brand new. Imagine what your own emotions would be like if you were hearing it for the first time.

33

THE NATIVITY OF THE LORD

Pay attention to the parts of the reading that signal a shift in topic—beginning with "While they were there, the time came . . .," "Now there were shepherds in that region . . .," "And suddenly there was a multitude . . ." A corresponding shift in your tone and emotion would absolutely be appropriate here.

to be enrolled with Mary, his betrothed,
who was with child.
While they were there,
the time came for her to have her child,
and she gave birth to her firstborn son.
She wrapped him in swaddling clothes and
laid him in a manger,
because there was no room for them in the
inn.

Now there were shepherds in that region
living in the fields
and keeping the night watch over their
flock.
The angel of the Lord appeared to them
and the glory of the Lord shone around
them,
and they were struck with great fear.
The angel said to them,
"Do not be afraid;
for behold, I proclaim to you good news of
great joy
that will be for all the people.
For today in the city of David
a savior has been born for you who is
Christ and Lord.
And this will be a sign for you:
you will find an infant wrapped in
swaddling clothes
and lying in a manger."
And suddenly there was a multitude of the
heavenly host with the angel,
praising God and saying:
"Glory to God in the highest
and on earth peace to those on whom
his favor rests."

Mass at Dawn Readings

First Reading (Isa 62:11-12)

A reading from the Book of the Prophet Isaiah

See, the LORD proclaims
    to the ends of the earth:
say to daughter Zion,
    your savior comes!
Here is his reward with him,
    his recompense before him.
They shall be called the holy people,
    the redeemed of the LORD,
and you shall be called "Frequented,"
    a city that is not forsaken.

Responsorial Psalm (Ps 97:1, 6, 11-12)

R̄. A light will shine on us this day: the Lord is born for us.

The LORD is king; let the earth rejoice;
    let the many isles be glad.
The heavens proclaim his justice,
    and all peoples see his glory.

R̄. A light will shine on us this day: the Lord is born for us.

Light dawns for the just;
    and gladness, for the upright of heart.
Be glad in the LORD, you just,
    and give thanks to his holy name.

R̄. A light will shine on us this day: the Lord is born for us.

Second Reading (Titus 3:4-7)

A reading from the Letter of Saint Paul to Titus

Beloved:
When the kindness and generous love
    of God our savior appeared,
not because of any righteous deeds we had done
    but because of his mercy,

Pronunciation
Zion   ZAI-uhn

This is Isaiah speaking, so it is a proclamation. Pay close attention to the commas and other punctuation, taking a good pause for each one.

For example:
"See," (*pause*)
"the LORD proclaims to the ends of the earth:" (*pause*) (What does the Lord proclaim? It is rather significant!)
"say to daughter Zion," (*pause*)
"your savior comes!"

Pronunciation
Titus   TAI-tuhs

Once again this reading is one complete sentence. Can you paraphrase Paul's writing? This is a great way to make sure

35

you are delivering the reading intelligently.

Take a nice pause after his opening, "Beloved." It is always a good idea to read Paul slowly not only for your "safety" but also for the listeners, as his sentences are often complex.

he saved us through the bath of rebirth
    and renewal by the Holy Spirit,
whom he richly poured out on us
    through Jesus Christ our savior,
so that we might be justified by his grace
    and become heirs in hope of eternal life.

This seems to be all about some shepherds finding the Holy Family—except the first two lines of the last part:

"And Mary kept all these things,
reflecting on them in her heart."

These lines stand out in close reading and should also stand out in your delivery. The shepherds are literally covering a lot of ground. Mary, on the other hand, is not. How might this be communicated in your delivery?

Gospel (Luke 2:15-20; L15ABC)

A reading from the holy Gospel according to Luke

When the angels went away from them to
        heaven,
    the shepherds said to one another,
    "Let us go, then, to Bethlehem
    to see this thing that has taken place,
    which the Lord has made known to us."
So they went in haste and found Mary and
        Joseph,
    and the infant lying in the manger.
When they saw this,
    they made known the message
    that had been told them about this child.
All who heard it were amazed
    by what had been told them by the
        shepherds.
And Mary kept all these things,
    reflecting on them in her heart.
Then the shepherds returned,
    glorifying and praising God
    for all they had heard and seen,
    just as it had been told to them.

Mass during the Day Readings

First Reading (Isa 52:7-10)

A reading from the Book of the Prophet Isaiah

How beautiful upon the mountains
    are the feet of him who brings glad tidings,
announcing peace, bearing good news,
    announcing salvation, and saying to Zion,
    "Your God is King!"

Hark! Your sentinels raise a cry,
    together they shout for joy,
for they see directly, before their eyes,
    the LORD restoring Zion.
Break out together in song,
    O ruins of Jerusalem!
For the LORD comforts his people,
    he redeems Jerusalem.
The LORD has bared his holy arm
    in the sight of all the nations;
all the ends of the earth will behold
    the salvation of our God.

Responsorial Psalm (Ps 98:1, 2-3, 3-4, 5-6)

℟. (3c) All the ends of the earth have seen the
saving power of God.

Sing to the LORD a new song,
  for he has done wondrous deeds;
his right hand has won victory for him,
    his holy arm.

℟. All the ends of the earth have seen the
saving power of God.

The LORD has made his salvation known:
    in the sight of the nations he has revealed
        his justice.
He has remembered his kindness and his
    faithfulness
    toward the house of Israel.

℟. All the ends of the earth have seen the
saving power of God.

Pronunciation
Zion   ZAI-uhn

I can't help hearing the first lines of this reading without hearing them sung in Handel's *Messiah*! This reading is like a fever breaking. All that was ruined is now restored forever.

Pay attention to the white space with a good pause. Savor the good news. Hit the verbs and keep the energy up through to the end of every sentence.

Finally *"all the ends of the earth will behold the salvation of our God."* It doesn't get any better than this.

All the ends of the earth have seen
    the salvation by our God.
Sing joyfully to the LORD, all you lands;
    break into song; sing praise.

R̸. All the ends of the earth have seen the
saving power of God.

Sing praise to the LORD with the harp,
    with the harp and melodious song.
With trumpets and the sound of the horn
    sing joyfully before the King, the LORD.

R̸. All the ends of the earth have seen the
saving power of God.

Refulgence means to radiate light.

The author of this letter is a good teacher.

In the first part of this reading, he describes God's reign before Christ and then the arrival of Christ on earth. In the second part, which begins with, "When he had accomplished . . . ," Christ does all the Father has asked of him and takes his seat next to his Father. And in the third part, Christ is the absolute Son of God.

Might your tone reflect the three parts of the reading?

Second Reading (Heb 1:1-6)

A reading from the Letter to the Hebrews

Brothers and sisters:
In times past, God spoke in partial and
    various ways
    to our ancestors through the prophets;
in these last days, he has spoken to us
    through the Son,
    whom he made heir of all things
    and through whom he created the universe,
    who is the refulgence of his glory,
        the very imprint of his being,
    and who sustains all things by his mighty
        word.
    When he had accomplished purification
        from sins,
    he took his seat at the right hand of the
        Majesty on high,
    as far superior to the angels
    as the name he has inherited is more
        excellent than theirs.

For to which of the angels did God ever say:
    You are my son; this day I have begotten you?
Or again:

I will be a father to him, and he shall be a
son to me?
And again, when he leads the firstborn into
    the world, he says:
Let all the angels of God worship him.

Gospel (John 1:1-18 [or John 1:1-5, 9-14]; L16ABC)

A reading from the holy Gospel according
to John

[In the beginning was the Word,
    and the Word was with God,
    and the Word was God.
He was in the beginning with God.
All things came to be through him,
    and without him nothing came to be.
What came to be through him was life,
    and this life was the light of the human
        race;
the light shines in the darkness,
    and the darkness has not overcome it.]
A man named John was sent from God.
He came for testimony, to testify to the light,
    so that all might believe through him.
He was not the light,
    but came to testify to the light.
[The true light, which enlightens everyone,
    was coming into the world.
He was in the world,
    and the world came to be through him,
    but the world did not know him.
He came to what was his own,
    but his own people did not accept him.

But to those who did accept him
    he gave power to become children of God,
    to those who believe in his name,
    who were born not by natural generation
    nor by human choice nor by a man's decision
    but of God.

The Prologue of John's Gospel, which we read today, is surely one of his more amazing writings. Don't rush this at all, for in ten lines John is giving us the story of the incarnation of Jesus.

Note the wonderful back and forth between the Word becoming flesh and John's foretelling of the coming of Jesus. Might you read these two narratives by using a different tone for each?

Then there's the real moment at the end: in Jesus we now have literally seen God!

And the Word became flesh
and made his dwelling among us,
and we saw his glory,
the glory as of the Father's only Son,
full of grace and truth.]
John testified to him and cried out, saying,
"This was he of whom I said,
'The one who is coming after me ranks
ahead of me
because he existed before me.'"
From his fullness we have all received,
grace in place of grace,
because while the law was given through
Moses,
grace and truth came through Jesus Christ.
No one has ever seen God.
The only Son, God, who is at the Father's side,
has revealed him.

Preparing to Proclaim

Key words and phrases: "[R]eflecting . . . in her heart."

To the point: This gospel is an active one; the shepherds go in haste and then turn around to share what they have seen. The story is dynamic, full of praise and proclamation of the good news. Mary, though, contrasts with this action. She is, perhaps, somewhat cocooned in her postpartum experience; mothers of newborns often enclose themselves with their infants for a while as they focus on breastfeeding, diapering, and soothing. Her reaction to the great things she is witnessing is different from that of the shepherds. Rather than hastening out to share the news, she keeps these things in her heart, reflecting on and pondering all that she has seen. Others are rightfully celebrating the amazing thing that has happened, and she is quietness in the midst of all this. Both these responses are good. Both are necessary. All of us are called to both at different points in our lifelong journeys of encountering Jesus.

Making Connections

Between the readings: The words with which Aaron blesses the Israelites are fulfilled in the gospel. Now that God is incarnate, God has a face—a literal one. It is shining on us as God-made-flesh takes in the fullness of the human condition and transforms it into something greater. The second reading reminds us that we share in Jesus's status as a child of God; all of us, through him, have received the privilege of calling God our Father.

To experience: The shepherds work with animals; they know mangers. A contemporary equivalent to this scene would be an office worker visiting someone else's office and finding that someone has given birth on a desk. The extraordinary has entered the very mundane, the very ordinary. God has really truly entered into *this* life. *Our* life. And God remains with us, here and now, present in our midst.

Prayer

Divine Compassion,
you who free us from our sins
and make us heirs to your love and life,
hear our prayer today: *May God bless us in his mercy.*
Look upon us and bless us;
enter our hearts and dwell within us,
you who are God for ever and ever.
Amen.

This is certainly one of the most beautiful Scripture blessings we have! Read it slowly, savoring every word, especially emphasizing the verbs.

First Reading (Num 6:22-27)

A reading from the Book of Numbers

The LORD said to Moses:
    "Speak to Aaron and his sons and tell them:
    This is how you shall bless the Israelites.
Say to them:
    The LORD bless you and keep you!
    The LORD let his face shine upon
        you, and be gracious to you!
    The LORD look upon you kindly and
        give you peace!
So shall they invoke my name upon the
        Israelites,
    and I will bless them."

Responsorial Psalm (Ps 67:2-3, 5, 6, 8)

R̸. (2a) May God bless us in his mercy.

May God have pity on us and bless us;
    may he let his face shine upon us.
So may your way be known upon earth;
    among all nations, your salvation.

R̸. May God bless us in his mercy.

May the nations be glad and exult
    because you rule the peoples in equity;
    the nations on the earth you guide.

R̸. May God bless us in his mercy.

May the peoples praise you, O God;
    may all the peoples praise you!
May God bless us,
    and may all the ends of the earth fear him!

R̞. May God bless us in his mercy.

Second Reading (Gal 4:4-7)

A reading from the Letter of Saint Paul to
the Galatians

Brothers and sisters:
When the fullness of time had come, God sent
    his Son,
    born of a woman, born under the law,
    to ransom those under the law,
    so that we might receive adoption as sons.
As proof that you are sons,
    God sent the Spirit of his Son into our
        hearts,
    crying out, "Abba, Father!"
So you are no longer a slave but a son,
    and if a son then also an heir, through God.

Pronunciation
Galatians
    guh-LAY-shih-uhnz

Paul is using his familiar logical approach here: "If this, then that!" Every phrase in the first part is so important, as it is part of his opening argument.

The second part proves that Jesus was the Son of God. Finally, the last two lines define our own standing in the argument and "seal the deal" for our salvation.

Gospel (Luke 2:16-21; L18ABC)

A reading from the holy Gospel according
to Luke

The shepherds went in haste to Bethlehem
    and found Mary and Joseph,
    and the infant lying in the manger.
When they saw this,
    they made known the message
    that had been told them about this child.
All who heard it were amazed
    by what had been told them by the
        shepherds.
And Mary kept all these things,
    reflecting on them in her heart.

We already heard this account earlier in the Christmas season, so why are we hearing it again? Well, it's an incredible event and certainly worth repeating. It should be read with a sense of both prior knowledge as well as profound amazement and gratefulness.

"And Mary kept all these things,
reflecting on them in her heart."

43

If these events are mind-blowing for us, what were they for Mary? Verbs are always important but in this reading they are very important. Pay close attention to them.

Then the shepherds returned,
    glorifying and praising God
    for all they had heard and seen,
    just as it had been told to them.

When eight days were completed for his
        circumcision,
    he was named Jesus, the name given him
        by the angel
    before he was conceived in the womb.

Preparing to Proclaim
Key words and phrases: "We saw."

To the point: The magi see a new star and are the very few who see and correctly interpret its meaning. They saw the star because they were paying attention; they were scholars who studied the stars. When they started their study, the magi could not have imagined themselves bearing witness to such a hugely unique event. Only once in history will this happen. The birth of Jesus changes the universe in ways far more significant than the appearance of a new celestial body. For the magi, a lifetime of cultivating knowledge and attentiveness culminated in this exceptional moment. They were called to come pay homage to a newborn king. For us, too, our interests and skills can become places of encounter with the God who made all things and who gave us the talents we have.

Making Connections
Between the readings: The gospel has a clear fulfillment of the first reading's prophecy; the magi from faraway lands are following light to Jerusalem. But there is a dark turn; Herod's wicked jealousy makes Jerusalem an unsafe place even for the newborn king, and the magi must move on to Bethlehem as their ultimate destination. Isaiah's prophecy has yet to be achieved in its fullness. Even still, the magi rejoice at what the star reveals to them; even if the story is not yet complete, this is a moment of God's word being fulfilled.

To experience: The magi found signs of God's saving work in their study of astronomy, an interest and talent that was itself a gift from God. God endows us with an astonishing variety of passions and gifts, and all of these can reveal God to the world in different ways. The fact that our interests vary is precisely why we are given each other; we each reveal a different facet of God's infinite goodness and beauty.

Prayer

God, Radiant Splendor,
all peoples bow down before you,
every nation on earth will adore you.
Reveal to us the fulness of your promises,
and show us the ways of your truth.
Shepherd us, keep us safe.
We make this prayer though your son,
Christ, Lord for ever and ever.
Amen.

Pronunciation
dromedaries
    DRAH-muh-dher-eez
Midian   MIH-dih-uhn
Ephah   EE-fuh
Sheba   SHEE-buh
frankincense
    FRANGK-ihn-sehns

This is great news! Jerusalem has been chosen above all other cities and nations on earth.

There are three parts here, each more amazing than the previous one:
    1. The whole world is in darkness but upon Jerusalem the Lord shines.
    2. All other nations will come to you.
    3. Wealth from the whole world will be given you.

There can easily be a crescendo of excitement building all the way through this reading until the absolute final phrase:

First Reading (Isa 60:1-6)

A reading from the Book of the Prophet Isaiah

Rise up in splendor, Jerusalem! Your light has
        come,
    the glory of the Lord shines upon you.
See, darkness covers the earth,
    and thick clouds cover the peoples;
but upon you the LORD shines,
    and over you appears his glory.
Nations shall walk by your light,
    and kings by your shining radiance.
Raise your eyes and look about;
    they all gather and come to you:
your sons come from afar,
    and your daughters in the arms of their
        nurses.

Then you shall be radiant at what you see,
    your heart shall throb and overflow,
for the riches of the sea shall be emptied out
        before you,
    the wealth of nations shall be brought to
        you.
Caravans of camels shall fill you,
    dromedaries from Midian and Ephah;
all from Sheba shall come
    bearing gold and frankincense,
    and proclaiming the praises of the LORD.

Responsorial Psalm (Ps 72:1-2, 7-8, 10-11, 12-13)

℟. (cf. 11) Lord, every nation on earth will adore you.

O God, with your judgment endow the king,
and with your justice, the king's son;
he shall govern your people with justice
and your afflicted ones with judgment.

℟. Lord, every nation on earth will adore you.

Justice shall flower in his days,
and profound peace, till the moon be no more.
May he rule from sea to sea,
and from the River to the ends of the earth.

℟. Lord, every nation on earth will adore you.

The kings of Tarshish and the Isles shall offer gifts;
the kings of Arabia and Seba shall bring tribute.
All kings shall pay him homage,
all nations shall serve him.

℟. Lord, every nation on earth will adore you.

For he shall rescue the poor when he cries out,
and the afflicted when he has no one to help him.
He shall have pity for the lowly and the poor;
the lives of the poor he shall save.

℟. Lord, every nation on earth will adore you.

"proclaiming the praises of the LORD"

Second Reading (Eph 3:2-3a, 5-6)

A reading from the Letter of Saint Paul to the Ephesians

Brothers and sisters:
You have heard of the stewardship of God's grace
that was given to me for your benefit,

Pronunciation
Ephesians
eh-FEE-zhuhnz
Gentiles   JEHN-tailz

Paul reminds us that we are a New Testament people. The Gentiles are

47

now coheirs of the people of God.

In the first part, Paul reminds the listener that Christ's message was made known to him through revelation. In the second part, Paul teaches that Christ included the Gentiles in his teachings.

"It was not made known to people in other generations as it has now been revealed . . ."; this refers to the New Testament. Don't drop the final phrase, "through the gospel."

Pronunciation
Judea   jou-DEE-uh
Herod   HEHR-uhd
Judah   JOU-duh
frankincense
   FRANGK-ihn-sehns
myrrh   mer

What a great story, filled with suspense!

Three kings are looking for the newborn king to pay him homage. They ask King Herod of his whereabouts, but of course Herod wants him dead. The kings find the child and present precious gifts to him. Because of a dream, upon their return

namely, that the mystery was made known to me by revelation.
It was not made known to people in other generations
as it has now been revealed
to his holy apostles and prophets by the Spirit:
that the Gentiles are coheirs, members of the same body,
and copartners in the promise in Christ Jesus through the gospel.

Gospel (Matt 2:1-12; L20ABC)

A reading from the holy Gospel according to Matthew

When Jesus was born in Bethlehem of Judea, in the days of King Herod,
   behold, magi from the east arrived in Jerusalem, saying,
   "Where is the newborn king of the Jews?
We saw his star at its rising
   and have come to do him homage."
When King Herod heard this,
   he was greatly troubled,
   and all Jerusalem with him.
Assembling all the chief priests and the scribes of the people,
   he inquired of them where the Christ was to be born.
They said to him, "In Bethlehem of Judea,

for thus it has been written through the
  prophet:
  And you, Bethlehem, land of Judah,
    are by no means least among the rulers
      of Judah;
  since from you shall come a ruler,
    who is to shepherd my people Israel."
Then Herod called the magi secretly
  and ascertained from them the time of the
    star's appearance.
He sent them to Bethlehem and said,
  "Go and search diligently for the child.
When you have found him, bring me word,
  that I too may go and do him homage."
After their audience with the king they set
    out.
And behold, the star that they had seen at its
    rising preceded them,
  until it came and stopped over the place
    where the child was.
They were overjoyed at seeing the star,
  and on entering the house
  they saw the child with Mary his mother.
They prostrated themselves and did him
    homage.
Then they opened their treasures
  and offered him gifts of gold, frankincense,
    and myrrh.
And having been warned in a dream not to
    return to Herod,
  they departed for their country by another
    way.

home they do not let Herod know where the newborn king is. In the midst of incredible joy great evil lurks.

I would read this as mentioned above—a story of great suspense that is finally resolved in the closing sentence.

Preparing to Proclaim
Key words and phrases: "Behold, the Lamb of God, who takes away the sin of the world."

To the point: John the Baptist had a central role during Advent; as we move on to Ordinary Time, he reminds us often that he is not the main character. In this gospel he cedes the stage to Jesus, who is beginning his active ministry. In one last testimony, he reminds us of the prophecies we heard during Advent and recounts the baptism of Jesus. He's been saying all along that he's not the real deal; here he steps aside for this one who ranks ahead of him. John also gives us the line we hear before Communion at every Mass: "Behold the Lamb of God, who takes away the sin of the world." Blessed are we who are called to the supper of this Lamb. May we join with John in bearing witness to the one we encounter there.

Making Connections
Between the readings: It is easy to see foreshadowing of John the Baptist in Isaiah's reference to himself as one "formed as [God's] servant from the womb." After all, we see John's first moment of action when he leaps in Elizabeth's womb, recognizing Jesus in joy even before either of their faces was visible. The second reading is also about callings, both Paul's particular calling as an apostle and the universal call to holiness that his entire audience—including us—shares.

To experience: There will be a lot of light imagery in the coming weeks; this week is about becoming light for others. For those of us in the Northern hemisphere, this echoes the slow but sure lengthening of days we see in the early months of the year (while in the Southern half of the world, these light images can serve as reassurance as days begin to grow shorter).

Prayer

Servant God,
you who inspire in us a desire to share
your light and your good news,
inspire in us also fervent prayer and patient
　　hearts,
that, when we pray, *"Here am I, Lord; I come
　　to do your will,"*
our desire is sincere and our focus is always
　　you and you alone.

Amen.

First Reading (Isa 49:3, 5-6)

A reading from the Book of the Prophet Isaiah

The LORD said to me: You are my servant,
　　Israel, through whom I show my glory.
Now the LORD has spoken
　　who formed me as his servant from the
　　　　womb,
that Jacob may be brought back to him
　　and Israel gathered to him;
and I am made glorious in the sight of the LORD,
　　and my God is now my strength!
It is too little, the LORD says, for you to be my
　　servant,
　　to raise up the tribes of Jacob,
　　and restore the survivors of Israel;
I will make you a light to the nations,
　　that my salvation may reach to the ends of
　　　　the earth.

Isaiah is foretelling something wondrous here. God has *chosen* Israel! And then Isaiah goes on to tell how. This is great news. Proclaim it as such.

There are two parts to this reading. Emphasize this with a nice pause after "God is now my strength!"

Responsorial Psalm (Ps 40:2, 4, 7-8, 8-9, 10)

R℣. (8a and 9a) Here am I, Lord; I come to do
your will.

I have waited, waited for the LORD,
　　and he stooped toward me and heard my cry.
And he put a new song into my mouth,
　　a hymn to our God.

R℣. Here am I, Lord; I come to do your will.

Sacrifice or offering you wished not,
    but ears open to obedience you gave me.
Holocausts or sin-offerings you sought not;
    then said I, "Behold I come."

R̸. Here am I, Lord; I come to do your will.

"In the written scroll it is prescribed for me,
to do your will, O my God, is my delight,
    and your law is within my heart!"

R̸. Here am I, Lord; I come to do your will.

I announced your justice in the vast assembly;
    I did not restrain my lips, as you, O LORD,
        know.

R̸. Here am I, Lord; I come to do your will.

Pronunciation
Corinthians
    kawr-IHN-thee-uhnz
Sosthenes
    SAHS-thee-neez
Corinth   KAWR-ihnth

This whole reading is simply a greeting by Paul to the Corinthians. Pretty fancy, eh? Clearly, Paul loves the people of the young church at Corinth. Read his greeting accordingly.

Second Reading (1 Cor 1:1-3)

A reading from the first Letter of Saint Paul
to the Corinthians

Paul, called to be an apostle of Christ Jesus
        by the will of God,
    and Sosthenes our brother,
    to the church of God that is in Corinth,
    to you who have been sanctified in Christ
        Jesus,
        called to be holy,
    with all those everywhere who call upon
        the name of our Lord
    Jesus Christ, their Lord and ours.
Grace to you and peace from God our Father
    and the Lord Jesus Christ.

What an incredible testimony John the Baptist is giving in this reading. I would read this with great confidence and energy.

Pause nicely before "John testified further . . .,"

Gospel (John 1:29-34; L64A)

A reading from the holy Gospel according
to John

John the Baptist saw Jesus coming toward
        him and said,
    "Behold, the Lamb of God, who takes away
        the sin of the world.

He is the one of whom I said,
  'A man is coming after me who ranks
    ahead of me
  because he existed before me.'
I did not know him,
  but the reason why I came baptizing with
    water
  was that he might be made known to
    Israel."
John testified further, saying,
  "I saw the Spirit come down like a dove
    from heaven
  and remain upon him.
I did not know him,
  but the one who sent me to baptize with
    water told me,
  'On whomever you see the Spirit come
    down and remain,
  he is the one who will baptize with the
    Holy Spirit.'
Now I have seen and testified that he is the
  Son of God."

which should be read with even more confidence and energy.

Preparing to Proclaim

Key words and phrases: "Come after me, and I will make you fishers of men."

To the point: Three verbs at the end of the gospel summarize Jesus's ministry: teaching, proclaiming, curing. This gives us a preview of his years of active work; this is what we can expect of Jesus's ministry. Names are also important in this gospel: these place names remind us that Jesus's ministry took place in the real world, in a place with a history and a people. New characters are also identified by name: Simon who is called Peter, his brother Andrew; James and John, the sons of Zebedee. These are real people in real places. They have family ties and daily tasks. And Jesus calls them by name. He comes to them right where they are, in all the realness and fullness of their lives, and he calls them to something greater.

Making Connections

Between the readings: The beginning of Jesus's preaching is the fulfillment of Isaiah's prophecy: Jesus himself is the great light for those who are dwelling in darkness. This must have been evident to Simon, Andrew, James, and John; Jesus's invitation is an odd interruption in their daily work, but they find themselves compelled to drop everything, leave their livelihoods and families behind, and follow him.

To experience: For the apostles called in this gospel, following Jesus meant giving up the concrete realities of their lives and careers and communities. We are given the specific place names of these events to remind us that they are real. They affect real, specific, complex people with stories and families. For us, too, specific places form part of our story. Some serve as homes and comforts; others are special places of brief encounter with God. Some places become places to settle; others are left behind. God is present in all of them, working in each of our specific contexts.

Prayer

God who Rescues,
your light breaks through the gloom
and shines on all with warmth and joy.
Bring each human soul into your luminous
    presence,
that all may rightly say, *"The Lord is my light
    and my salvation."*
May your light help us see human divisions
and a clear path to unity and peace.
Amen.

First Reading (Isa 8:23–9:3)

A reading from the Book of the Prophet Isaiah

First the LORD degraded the land of Zebulun
    and the land of Naphtali;
        but in the end he has glorified the seaward
            road,
        the land west of the Jordan,
        the District of the Gentiles.

Anguish has taken wing, dispelled is
        darkness:
    for there is no gloom where but now
        there was distress.
The people who walked in darkness
        have seen a great light;
upon those who dwelt in the land of gloom
        a light has shone.
You have brought them abundant joy
        and great rejoicing,
as they rejoice before you as at the harvest,
        as people make merry when dividing
            spoils.
For the yoke that burdened them,
        the pole on their shoulder,
    and the rod of their taskmaster
        you have smashed, as on the day of
            Midian.

Pronunciation
Zebulun   ZEH-byoo-luhn
Naphtali   NAF-tuh-lai
Gentiles   JEHN-tailz
Midian   MIH-dih-uhn

This is great news! Take a nice pause before and after the sentence that begins, "Anguish has taken wing . . ."

The following passage is a familiar one that Handel used in his *Messiah*:

"The people who walked in darkness
    have seen a great light;
    upon those who dwelt
    in the land of gloom a
    light has shone."

Read this passage with great care, as it sums up the entire reading.

Responsorial Psalm **(Ps 27:1, 4, 13-14)**

R̸. (1a) The Lord is my light and my
salvation.

The LORD is my light and my salvation;
    whom should I fear?
The LORD is my life's refuge;
    of whom should I be afraid?

R̸. The Lord is my light and my salvation.

One thing I ask of the LORD;
    this I seek:
to dwell in the house of the LORD
    all the days of my life,
that I may gaze on the loveliness of the LORD
    and contemplate his temple.

R̸. The Lord is my light and my salvation.

I believe that I shall see the bounty of the
    LORD
    in the land of the living.
Wait for the LORD with courage;
    be stouthearted, and wait for the LORD.

R̸. The Lord is my light and my salvation.

Pronunciation
Corinthians
    kawr-IHN-thee-uhnz
Chloe   KLO-ee
Apollos   uh-PAH-luhs
Cephas   SEE-fuhs

Paul's reading is no less
appropriate for today's
world than it was for his.

Take great care in delivering this reading; make it
slow and deliberate. Paul
really loves the people in
Corinth, and he addresses
them twice as brothers

Second Reading **(1 Cor 1:10-13, 17)**

A reading from the first Letter of Saint Paul
to the Corinthians

I urge you, brothers and sisters, in the name
    of our Lord Jesus Christ,
    that all of you agree in what you say,
    and that there be no divisions among you,
    but that you be united in the same mind
        and in the same purpose.
For it has been reported to me about you, my
        brothers and sisters,
    by Chloe's people, that there are rivalries
        among you.
I mean that each of you is saying,
    "I belong to Paul," or "I belong to Apollos,"

or "I belong to Cephas," or "I belong to
    Christ."
Is Christ divided?
Was Paul crucified for you?
Or were you baptized in the name of Paul?
For Christ did not send me to baptize but to
    preach the gospel,
    and not with the wisdom of human
        eloquence,
    so that the cross of Christ might not be
        emptied of its meaning.

Gospel (Matt 4:12-23 [or Matt 4:12-17]; L67A)

A reading from the holy Gospel according
to Matthew

[When Jesus heard that John had been
    arrested,
    he withdrew to Galilee.
He left Nazareth and went to live in
    Capernaum by the sea,
    in the region of Zebulun and Naphtali,
    that what had been said through Isaiah the
        prophet
    might be fulfilled:
        Land of Zebulun and land of Naphtali,
            the way to the sea, beyond the Jordan,
            Galilee of the Gentiles,
        the people who sit in darkness have seen
            a great light,
        on those dwelling in a land overshadowed
            by death
        light has arisen.
From that time on, Jesus began to preach and
    say,
    "Repent, for the kingdom of heaven is at
        hand."]

As he was walking by the Sea of Galilee, he
    saw two brothers,

and sisters. But this does
not soften his point.

Take pauses after "in the
same purpose" and "I be-
long to Christ," and also
after each question mark.

Pronunciation
Galilee   GAL-ih-lee
Capernaum
    kuh-PERR-nay-uhm
Zebulun   ZEH-byoo-luhn
Naphtali   NAF-tuh-lai
Gentiles   JEHN-tailz
Zebedee   ZEH-beh-dee

The two remarkable mo-
ments in this text occur
when the future disciples,
in both cases, immediately
drop what they are doing
and follow Jesus. Your delivery needs to convey
these remarkable
moments.

Simon who is called Peter, and his brother
Andrew,
casting a net into the sea; they were
fishermen.
He said to them,
"Come after me, and I will make you fishers
of men."
At once they left their nets and followed him.
He walked along from there and saw two
other brothers,
James, the son of Zebedee, and his brother
John.
They were in a boat, with their father
Zebedee, mending their nets.
He called them, and immediately they left
their boat and their father
and followed him.
He went around all of Galilee,
teaching in their synagogues, proclaiming
the gospel of the kingdom,
and curing every disease and illness
among the people.

Preparing to Proclaim

Key words and phrases: "Rejoice and be glad, for your reward will be great in heaven."

To the point: When hashtags started becoming popular on social media, the hashtag "blessed" quickly turned sarcastic. It is used most often to make fun of the few who do use it sincerely, because it seems that they are often those who habitually overshare or who attribute their life's luxuries to the blessing of God. We know, deep down, that having pretty, Instagramable things is not actually a sign of God's blessing. Here, Jesus also turns around what "blessed" means, but he does it in all sincerity. He affirms that those who practice hard spiritual disciplines, whose lives may not appear "blessed" in an earthly sense, are in fact those favored by God. Jesus reminds us that what we see is not always the truth of the matter; God is up to something greater than that which we can perceive.

Making Connections

Between the readings: In the first reading, righteous people are instructed to seek humility. This is a funny command, because it seems that in this life humility often finds us without us trying. We make mistakes often and our very human condition reminds us not to think too highly of ourselves. Humility doesn't always feel good, but it is the thing that saves us; it is another of the reversals that Jesus preaches. The second reading affirms God's reversal of human values. Those whom the world considers foolish, weak, and lowly are chosen and called by God.

To experience: We know that God's values are not our own; we hear this repeatedly in Scripture. But, saturated in a culture that values other things, we forget very easily. We put our time and attention into gathering money and security and social capital, even when we know this is not what Jesus asks of us. Consider the Beatitudes this week and how God might be using them to invite you into letting go of one of these false values.

Prayer

God of Paradox,
in you there is light in the darkness,
strength in weakness, new life in death.
How *[b]lessed are the poor in spirit; the
    kingdom of heaven is theirs!*
Help us to love you, your mystery,
your ways which are beyond all human
    understanding.
Amen.

Pronunciation
Zephaniah
    zeh-fuh-NAI-uh

This is a relatively short
reading with a powerful
message. The first part
basically states the point,
while the following part
goes into more detail.

Those who are the Lord's
should brag and put down
others? Quite the opposite!
The Lord's people are to
be humble and just, and if
they are, perhaps they
may be sheltered on the
day of the Lord's
judgment.

Read the first part slowly
with this in mind. Then,
taking a nice pause, de-
liver the second half,
going into more detail
about what was meant by
the first part of the
reading.

First Reading (Zeph 2:3; 3:12-13)

A reading from the Book of the Prophet
Zephaniah

Seek the LORD, all you humble of the earth,
    who have observed his law;
seek justice, seek humility;
    perhaps you may be sheltered
    on the day of the LORD's anger.

But I will leave as a remnant in your midst
    a people humble and lowly,
who shall take refuge in the name of the LORD:
    the remnant of Israel.
They shall do no wrong
    and speak no lies;
nor shall there be found in their mouths
    a deceitful tongue;
they shall pasture and couch their flocks
    with none to disturb them.

Responsorial Psalm (Ps 146:6-7, 8-9, 9-10)

℞. (Matt 5:3) Blessed are the poor in spirit; the
kingdom of heaven is theirs! *or:* ℞. Alleluia.

The LORD keeps faith forever,
    secures justice for the oppressed,
    gives food to the hungry.
The LORD sets captives free.

℞. Blessed are the poor in spirit; the kingdom of heaven is theirs! *or:* ℞. Alleluia.

The LORD gives sight to the blind;
the LORD raises up those who were bowed
down.
The LORD loves the just;
the LORD protects strangers.

℞. Blessed are the poor in spirit; the kingdom of heaven is theirs! *or:* ℞. Alleluia.

The fatherless and the widow the LORD
sustains,
but the way of the wicked he thwarts.
The LORD shall reign forever;
your God, O Zion, through all generations.
Alleluia.

℞. Blessed are the poor in spirit; the kingdom of heaven is theirs! *or:* ℞. Alleluia.

Second Reading (I Cor 1:26-31)

A reading from the first Letter of Saint Paul to the Corinthians

Consider your own calling, brothers and
sisters.
Not many of you were wise by human
standards,
not many were powerful,
not many were of noble birth.
Rather, God chose the foolish of the world to
shame the wise,
and God chose the weak of the world to
shame the strong,
and God chose the lowly and despised of
the world,
those who count for nothing,
to reduce to nothing those who are
something,
so that no human being might boast before
God.

Pronunciation
Corinthians
kawr-IHN-thee-uhnz

What a great second reading to follow the first. The point? None of us had better boast except in the Lord.

Note the contrasting descriptive words in the first part:
foolish vs. wise;
weak vs. strong;
to reduce to nothing vs. those who are something.

Be generous with your verbal emphasis in these comparisons.

It is due to him that you are in Christ Jesus,
    who became for us wisdom from God,
    as well as righteousness, sanctification,
       and redemption,
    so that, as it is written,
    "Whoever boasts, should boast in the Lord."

How can you give "newness" to a very familiar reading?

Jesus is speaking to the common people. He is taking their familiar world and totally flipping it over. The vast majority of people who are listening to Jesus are poor and downtrodden, seemingly the eternal losers. Yet in his speaking, they are the eternal winners! Wow.

Proclaim this reading slowly and deliberately, but in the speaking knowingly read it as though you are totally aware that this is going to blow the minds of your listeners.

Gospel (Matt 5:1-12a; L70A)

A reading from the holy Gospel according to Matthew

When Jesus saw the crowds, he went up the
    mountain,
    and after he had sat down, his disciples
      came to him.
He began to teach them, saying:
    "Blessed are the poor in spirit,
      for theirs is the kingdom of heaven.
    Blessed are they who mourn,
      for they will be comforted.
    Blessed are the meek,
      for they will inherit the land.
    Blessed are they who hunger and thirst for
      righteousness,
      for they will be satisfied.
    Blessed are the merciful,
      for they will be shown mercy.
    Blessed are the clean of heart,
      for they will see God.
    Blessed are the peacemakers,
      for they will be called children of God.
    Blessed are they who are persecuted for the
      sake of righteousness,
      for theirs is the kingdom of heaven.
    Blessed are you when they insult you and
      persecute you
    and utter every kind of evil against you
      falsely because of me.
    Rejoice and be glad,
      for your reward will be great in heaven."

Preparing to Proclaim

Key words and phrases: "[Y]ou are the light of the world."

To the point: This week, our light imagery shifts a bit. We've been hearing for weeks about God being light for those who walk in darkness. Here, Jesus tells us that we, too, can become light for others. Our participation in God's will—in enacting justice and compassion—allows us to also participate in the beauty of God. We don't create anything new here; the light is not our own. Rather, we reflect God's light out to the world, amplifying it and making it more visible. We spread God's goodness to corners it may not have reached. We see this image clearly at baptism, when a light from the paschal candle is handed to the newly baptized. We are charged with carrying Christ's light into the world wherever we go, thus giving others reason to glorify God.

Making Connections

Between the readings: The first reading shares the light imagery of the gospel, and gives us more explicit instructions for becoming light to the world. We are to provide food, shelter, and clothing for those in need. In readings of the previous weeks, this has been identified as God's work, as God's special area of interest. When we perform these deeds, we participate in God's preferential love for those who are poor. And we share in the beauty that God is continuously bestowing on the world in God's infinite generosity.

To experience: Performing works of mercy does not always look or feel good. This work is very often thankless, unglamorous, and inconvenient. The light we become is not the literal kind others can see; it takes practiced eyes of faith to see this sort of light. God reassures us, though, that these good deeds are beautiful in God's eyes and are worthy of our time.

Prayer

God of Justice,
you use each of us, gifted, called, and sent,
to work together in building your reign on
        earth.
When we do what is just, we are *a light in
        darkness to the upright.*
Help us to heed the voices of your prophets,
who speak your truth and call us always to
        greater holiness.
Amen.

Vindication is proof that someone or something is right, reasonable, or justified.

There are three distinct parts here; be sure to give a nice pause after "turn your back on your own" and "Here I am!" to emphasize these parts.

"Thus says the LORD . . ." is a powerful line. Be careful not to read it in a matter-of-fact way. What follows is also powerful and no less important today than it was in Isaiah's time.

First Reading (Isa 58:7-10)

A reading from the Book of the Prophet Isaiah

Thus says the LORD:
    Share your bread with the hungry,
        shelter the oppressed and the homeless;
    clothe the naked when you see them,
        and do not turn your back on your own.
    Then your light shall break forth like the
        dawn,
        and your wound shall quickly be healed;
    your vindication shall go before you,
        and the glory of the LORD shall be your
            rear guard.
    Then you shall call, and the LORD will
        answer,
        you shall cry for help, and he will say:
            Here I am!
    If you remove from your midst
        oppression, false accusation and malicious
            speech;
    if you bestow your bread on the hungry
        and satisfy the afflicted;
    then light shall rise for you in the darkness,
        and the gloom shall become for you like
            midday.

Responsorial Psalm (Ps 112:4-5, 6-7, 8-9)

℟. (4a) The just man is a light in darkness to the upright. *or:* ℟. Alleluia.

Light shines through the darkness for the
    upright;
  he is gracious and merciful and just.
Well for the man who is gracious and lends,
  who conducts his affairs with justice.

℟. The just man is a light in darkness to the upright. *or:* ℟. Alleluia.

He shall never be moved;
  the just one shall be in everlasting
      remembrance.
An evil report he shall not fear;
  his heart is firm, trusting in the LORD.

℟. The just man is a light in darkness to the upright. *or:* ℟. Alleluia.

His heart is steadfast; he shall not fear.
  Lavishly he gives to the poor;
his justice shall endure forever;
  his horn shall be exalted in glory.

℟. The just man is a light in darkness to the upright. *or:* ℟. Alleluia.

Second Reading (1 Cor 2:1-5)

A reading from the first Letter of Saint Paul to the Corinthians

When I came to you, brothers and sisters,
    proclaiming the mystery of God,
  I did not come with sublimity of words or
      of wisdom.
For I resolved to know nothing while I was
    with you
  except Jesus Christ, and him crucified.
I came to you in weakness and fear and much
    trembling,
  and my message and my proclamation

Pronunciation
Corinthians
    kawr-IHN-thee-uhnz

Sublimity is of such excellence, grandeur, or beauty as to inspire great admiration or awe.

Paul is being very humble here. He is simply (or maybe not so simply!) saying that the glory and wisdom of his words are due to Christ and not him.

65

were not with persuasive words of
    wisdom,
but with a demonstration of Spirit and
    power,
so that your faith might rest not on human
    wisdom
but on the power of God.

In directing a recent production of the Broadway musical *Godspell*, I found that even the very bright high school students had no idea what a bushel basket was. (Imagine a woven basket, like what you might see apples carried in.) Jesus's followers would have known of bushel baskets and lampstands, but we dare not assume that listeners today know all the terms mentioned in a particular reading. We must, however, know what we are proclaiming. If you are unsure of what a word means, do not hesitate to look it up. Context clues are also helpful.

Gospel (Matt 5:13-16; L73A)

A reading from the holy Gospel according to Matthew

Jesus said to his disciples:
    "You are the salt of the earth.
But if salt loses its taste, with what can it be
    seasoned?
It is no longer good for anything
    but to be thrown out and trampled
        underfoot.
You are the light of the world.
A city set on a mountain cannot be hidden.
Nor do they light a lamp and then put it under
    a bushel basket;
    it is set on a lampstand,
    where it gives light to all in the house.
Just so, your light must shine before others,
    that they may see your good deeds
    and glorify your heavenly Father."

Preparing to Proclaim
Key words and phrases: "Let your 'Yes' mean 'Yes,' and your 'No' mean 'No.'"

To the point: This gospel can feel damning and demanding. Jesus affirms that the commands of Mosaic Law still stand, and also reveals that by-the-book obedience to them is not enough. Righteousness is not just a checklist we can tick off; it is, unfortunately, not a measurable accomplishment. The orientation of our hearts matters more than the externals of our actions. This is challenging. But really, Jesus is issuing a loving invitation. He is calling us to health and wholeness as we live out God's Law. Changing our hearts is hard to measure, but it helps us more than it helps anyone else. Leaving behind sinful actions is one thing, but when we are able to move past the anger and lust that motivate such actions we are able to live in fuller freedom and joy.

Making Connections
Between the readings: The first reading affirms that God's commands are trustworthy and true; obeying them is a source of life and goodness. The Law is not an obligation to be lived in begrudging obedience; it is a gift from God, an assurance that goodness and righteousness are within our reach. The second reading acknowledges that God's wisdom is distinct from human wisdom; it often seems to us to be mysterious and hidden. Even so, it is worthy of trust.

To experience: Many of us at some time or another struggle with the moral teachings of the church, especially when leaders teach them without integrity. It is demoralizing to receive challenging teachings from people who themselves are not able to live by them. But what Jesus really wants for us is healing and freedom from the things that hold us back from the fullness of life with him. As you read this gospel, can you hear Jesus reissuing these teachings not as a way to control but as a loving invitation?

Prayer

God of Law, God of Love,
your son, love incarnate, fulfilled the law
and showed us how to live as your people.
*Blessed are they who follow the law of the
Lord!*
Help us to listen for your voice still today,
you who are still speaking, you who are still
perfect love.
Amen.

Pronunciation
Sirach   SAI-rak

Just in case we think that
we can blame anyone
other than ourselves for
our sins, we are the ones
who are totally respon-
sible. The first line really
says it all. Deliver it with
conviction.

This reading begs a nice
pause after every line.
Give the listeners time for
the words to sink in.

First Reading (Sir 15:15-20)

A reading from the Book of Sirach

If you choose you can keep the
        commandments, they will save you;
    if you trust in God, you too shall live;
he has set before you fire and water;
    to whichever you choose, stretch forth your
        hand.
Before man are life and death, good and evil,
    whichever he chooses shall be given him.
Immense is the wisdom of the Lord;
    he is mighty in power, and all-seeing.
The eyes of God are on those who fear him;
    he understands man's every deed.
No one does he command to act unjustly,
    to none does he give license to sin.

Responsorial Psalm (Ps 119:1-2, 4-5, 17-18, 33-34)

R̚. (1b) Blessed are they who follow the law of
the Lord!

Blessed are they whose way is blameless,
    who walk in the law of the LORD.
Blessed are they who observe his decrees,
    who seek him with all their heart.

R̚. Blessed are they who follow the law of the
Lord!

You have commanded that your precepts
   be diligently kept.
Oh, that I might be firm in the ways
   of keeping your statutes!

R̂. Blessed are they who follow the law of the
Lord!

Be good to your servant, that I may live
   and keep your words.
Open my eyes, that I may consider
   the wonders of your law.

R̂. Blessed are they who follow the law of the
Lord!

Instruct me, O LORD, in the way of your
      statutes,
   that I may exactly observe them.
Give me discernment, that I may observe your
      law
   and keep it with all my heart.

R̂. Blessed are they who follow the law of the
Lord!

Second Reading (1 Cor 2:6-10)

A reading from the first Letter of Saint Paul
to the Corinthians

Brothers and sisters:
We speak a wisdom to those who are mature,
   not a wisdom of this age,
      nor of the rulers of this age who are
         passing away.
Rather, we speak God's wisdom, mysterious,
      hidden,
   which God predetermined before the ages
      for our glory,
   and which none of the rulers of this age
      knew;
   for, if they had known it,
      they would not have crucified the Lord of
         glory.

Pronunciation
Corinthians
   kawr-IHN-thee-uhnz

The wisdom of humans
has nothing to do with the
wisdom of God!

Make sure you know what
you are reading when you
deliver the italicized passage. Deliver it as slowly
and thoughtfully as you
can.

Be careful not to deliver
the final sentence of the
reading in a matter-of-fact
style. It is profound.

69

But as it is written:

What eye has not seen, and ear has not heard,

and what has not entered the human heart,

what God has prepared for those who love him,

this God has revealed to us through the Spirit.

For the Spirit scrutinizes everything, even the depths of God.

Pronunciation

Pharisees FEHR-ih-seez

Raqa RA-kuh

Sanhedrin
  san-HEE-drihn

Gehenna geh-HEHN-uh

This is a rather long reading with a lot of examples of what to do and what not to do. It might be nice to organize the whole of your delivery in sections.

For example, the first two sections are similar. Read them as such and follow with a nice long pause before beginning the third part, and so on.

Gospel (Matt 5:17-37 [Matt 5:20-22a, 27-28, 33-34a, 37]; L76A)

A reading from the holy Gospel according to Matthew

[Jesus said to his disciples:]
    "Do not think that I have come to abolish the law or the prophets.
I have come not to abolish but to fulfill.
Amen, I say to you, until heaven and earth pass away,
    not the smallest letter or the smallest part of a letter
    will pass from the law,
    until all things have taken place.
Therefore, whoever breaks one of the least of these commandments
    and teaches others to do so
    will be called least in the kingdom of heaven.
But whoever obeys and teaches these commandments
    will be called greatest in the kingdom of heaven.
[I tell you, unless your righteousness surpasses
    that of the scribes and Pharisees,
    you will not enter the kingdom of heaven.

"You have heard that it was said to your
ancestors,
*You shall not kill; and whoever kills will be
liable to judgment.*
But I say to you,
whoever is angry with his brother
will be liable to judgment;]
and whoever says to his brother, 'Raqa,'
will be answerable to the Sanhedrin;
and whoever says, 'You fool,'
will be liable to fiery Gehenna.
Therefore, if you bring your gift to the altar,
and there recall that your brother
has anything against you,
leave your gift there at the altar,
go first and be reconciled with your
brother,
and then come and offer your gift.
Settle with your opponent quickly while on
the way to court.
Otherwise your opponent will hand you over
to the judge,
and the judge will hand you over to the
guard,
and you will be thrown into prison.
Amen, I say to you,
you will not be released until you have paid
the last penny.

["You have heard that it was said,
You shall not commit adultery.
But I say to you,
everyone who looks at a woman with lust
has already committed adultery with her in
his heart.]
If your right eye causes you to sin,
tear it out and throw it away.
It is better for you to lose one of your
members
than to have your whole body thrown into
Gehenna.

And if your right hand causes you to sin,
cut it off and throw it away.
It is better for you to lose one of your
members
than to have your whole body go into
Gehenna.

"It was also said,
*Whoever divorces his wife must give her a
bill of divorce.*
But I say to you,
whoever divorces his wife—unless the
marriage is unlawful—
causes her to commit adultery,
and whoever marries a divorced woman
commits adultery.

["Again you have heard that it was said to
your ancestors,
Do not take a false oath,
but make good to the Lord all that you vow.
But I say to you, do not swear at all;]
not by heaven, for it is God's throne;
nor by the earth, for it is his footstool;
nor by Jerusalem, for it is the city of the
great King.
Do not swear by your head,
for you cannot make a single hair white or
black.
[Let your 'Yes' mean 'Yes,' and your 'No' mean
'No.'
Anything more is from the evil one."]

Preparing to Proclaim
Key words and phrases: "[L]ove your enemies."

To the point: Like last week, Jesus explains to his disciples that being his followers will ask more of them than a literal reading of the law they have always been taught. They are called not to an approach of compliance with minimum requirements, but to a life of radical generosity that imitates the love of God, whose love spills forth and gives us life. They are called to offer forgiveness and love that is not deserved by the recipients. "Be perfect" is an intimidating instruction, but it may help to think of "perfect" in the sense of whole or complete. The life to which Jesus calls us is one of integrity, one where our hearts and minds and actions are all in alignment with each other. Living as Jesus asks is healing. It brings us to wholeness. It enables us to follow him with our whole hearts.

Making Connections
Between the readings: Jesus's gospel teachings are not the first time God has given commandments to love profoundly: "[L]ove your neighbor as yourself" is already pretty radical. As in the gospel, this love is commanded in imitation of God; we are to strive for the holiness and perfection that characterizes God's very self. The second reading also reminds us of our dignity and our call to holiness; here, the image of the temple is used to illustrate how God dwells within us. The psalm offers an important counterbalance to the commands of the other readings: even when we fail in our quest for holiness, God is ready to greet us with mercy.

To experience: This gospel can be very much misused in cases of abuse; victims are not morally required to continuously turn the other cheek to one who has hurt them. An important mark of maturity in Christian life is the ability to discern between suffering we are called to accept and suffering we are called to resist. Remember that God wants justice for the oppressed and is always on the side of those who are downtrodden.

Prayer

Holy One,
you who *is kind and merciful,*
you teach us to love our neighbors as
　　ourselves,
and to pray for our enemies.
Especially when your lessons are hard,
give to us a spirit of trust and of
　　perseverance,
that we may ever strive to be one holy people,
one in your love and truth.
Amen.

Pronunciation
Leviticus
　　leh-VIH-tih-kous

Can you imagine the Lord
literally speaking to
Moses? What might the
Lord's voice sound like?
On top of this thought,
here we have one of the
major teachings of the
Christian faith. It's not a
trite message!

Proclaim this reading
slowly and deliberately.
Seal it with the final sentence: "I am the Lord."

First Reading (Lev 19:1-2, 17-18)

A reading from the Book of Leviticus

The LORD said to Moses,
　"Speak to the whole Israelite community
　　and tell them:
　Be holy, for I, the LORD, your God, am holy.

"You shall not bear hatred for your brother or
　　sister in your heart.
Though you may have to reprove your fellow
　　citizen,
　do not incur sin because of him.
Take no revenge and cherish no grudge
　　against any of your people.
You shall love your neighbor as yourself.
I am the LORD."

Responsorial Psalm (Ps 103:1-2, 3-4, 8, 10, 12-13)

R︎. (8a) The Lord is kind and merciful.

Bless the LORD, O my soul;
　　and all my being, bless his holy name.
Bless the LORD, O my soul,
　　and forget not all his benefits.

R︎. The Lord is kind and merciful.

74

He pardons all your iniquities,
>heals all your ills.
He redeems your life from destruction,
>crowns you with kindness and compassion.

R̸. The Lord is kind and merciful.

Merciful and gracious is the LORD,
>slow to anger and abounding in kindness.
Not according to our sins does he deal with us,
>nor does he requite us according to our
>>crimes.

R̸. The Lord is kind and merciful.

As far as the east is from the west,
>so far has he put our transgressions from us.
As a father has compassion on his children,
>so the LORD has compassion on those who
>>fear him.

R̸. The Lord is kind and merciful.

Second Reading (1 Cor 3:16-23)

A reading from the first Letter of Saint Paul
to the Corinthians

Brothers and sisters:
Do you not know that you are the temple of
>God,
>and that the Spirit of God dwells in you?
If anyone destroys God's temple, God will
>destroy that person;
>for the temple of God, which you are, is
>>holy.

Let no one deceive himself.
If any one among you considers himself wise
>in this age,
>let him become a fool, so as to become wise.
For the wisdom of this world is foolishness in
>the eyes of God,
>for it is written:

Pronunciation
Corinthians
>kawr-IHN-thee-uhnz
Apollos   uh-PAH-luhs
Cephas   SEE-fuhs

A *ruse* is an action intended to deceive someone.

There are three rather distinct parts here, so let there be a nice pause before "Let no one deceive himself . . ." and "So let no one boast . . ."

The final phrase really wraps up the whole reading. Deliver it with strength and conviction.

God catches the wise in their own ruses,
and again:
> *The Lord knows the thoughts of the
> wise,*
> *that they are vain.*

So let no one boast about human beings, for
everything belongs to you,
Paul or Apollos or Cephas,
or the world or life or death,
or the present or the future:
all belong to you, and you to Christ, and
Christ to God.

Gospel (Matt 5:38-48; L79A)

A reading from the holy Gospel according
to Matthew

Jesus said to his disciples:
"You have heard that it was said,
An eye for an eye and a tooth for a tooth.
But I say to you, offer no resistance to one
who is evil.
When someone strikes you on your right
cheek,
turn the other one as well.
If anyone wants to go to law with you over
your tunic,
hand over your cloak as well.
Should anyone press you into service for one
mile,
go for two miles.
Give to the one who asks of you,
and do not turn your back on one who
wants to borrow.

"You have heard that it was said,
*You shall love your neighbor and hate your
enemy.*
But I say to you, love your enemies
and pray for those who persecute you,

I suspect this reading is no more easily heard by congregations today as it was when Jesus first taught this!

Matthew gives many examples of what exactly he is speaking about. I would let each example stand apart on its own a bit. It is almost like an examination of conscience.

The final sentence is the real challenge, however.

that you may be children of your heavenly
    Father,
for he makes his sun rise on the bad and
    the good,
and causes rain to fall on the just and the
    unjust.
For if you love those who love you, what
    recompense will you have?
Do not the tax collectors do the same?
And if you greet your brothers only,
    what is unusual about that?
Do not the pagans do the same?
So be perfect, just as your heavenly Father is
    perfect."

Preparing to Proclaim
Key words and phrases: "Get away, Satan!"

To the point: Jesus demonstrates his sinlessness in this gospel as he responds to the devil's temptations with strength and confidence, rebuffing his advances without missing a beat. These temptations are perhaps relatable; all of them encourage Jesus to put something—food, safety, power—ahead of his relationship with God. The middle temptation is particularly chilling, as we hear the devil himself quote Scripture to support a twisted agenda that is not of God. This one can be confusing; it seems that the devil is asking Jesus to trust in God, which is surely a good thing. But trusting God does not mean treating God like a vending machine that will dispense favors at our command; in fact, telling God what he ought to do for us stands in direct opposition to true trust in his providence. Fortunately, Jesus knows better than the devil's most clever tricks; his relationship with God is built on a loving trust that will carry him all the way to the cross.

Making Connections
Between the readings: Jesus's response to the devil stands in contrast to Adam and Eve's; he outsmarts temptation at every turn where their naivete caused them to cave immediately. Unfortunately, this is not enough to undo the consequences of sin; this work will be continued all the way to Calvary. The second reading affirms Jesus as the mirror image of Adam. Through Adam we inherit sin and death; from Jesus we inherit freedom and life.

To experience: The temptations the devil throws at Jesus are versions of those we encounter all the time. Food and power and security are constantly present in our lives; they are not bad in and of themselves, but when we allow them to take the place in our hearts that ought to belong only to God, they keep us from living the fullness of life that comes only from union with God.

Prayer

Creator God,
you made everything good and holy.
Sometimes we stray from your path,
tempted by this world's desires.
Be merciful, O Lord, for we have sinned.
Help us recognize the gift of Jesus Christ,
the pinnacle of your creation,
and his sacrifice, his salvation, his grace.
Amen.

First Reading (Gen 2:7-9; 3:1-7)

A reading from the Book of Genesis

The LORD God formed man out of the clay of
the ground
and blew into his nostrils the breath of life,
and so man became a living being.

Then the LORD God planted a garden in Eden,
in the east,
and placed there the man whom he had
formed.
Out of the ground the LORD God made various
trees grow
that were delightful to look at and good for
food,
with the tree of life in the middle of the
garden
and the tree of the knowledge of good and
evil.

Now the serpent was the most cunning of all
the animals
that the LORD God had made.
The serpent asked the woman,
"Did God really tell you not to eat
from any of the trees in the garden?"
The woman answered the serpent:
"We may eat of the fruit of the trees in the
garden;
it is only about the fruit of the tree

Pronunciation
Genesis   JEHN-uh-sihs

There are three distinct
parts to this reading:
   1. The creation of man
   and the setting of the
   garden.
   2. The serpent's tempt-
   ing of the woman, and
   the woman and man
   eating the forbidden
   fruit.
   3. The eyes of the
   woman and man are
   opened.

Obviously, the most exciting or colorful part of the
reading is the middle part
with the serpent and the
woman conversing. Don't
hesitate to inject a bit of
drama into the reading.

Varying tempos are a
great way to note different
voices. Experiment with a
slower speaking voice for
the serpent and a quicker
voice for the woman.

in the middle of the garden that God said,
'You shall not eat it or even touch it, lest
you die.'"
But the serpent said to the woman:
"You certainly will not die!
No, God knows well that the moment you eat
of it
your eyes will be opened and you will be
like gods
who know what is good and what is evil."
The woman saw that the tree was good for
food,
pleasing to the eyes, and desirable for
gaining wisdom.
So she took some of its fruit and ate it;
and she also gave some to her husband,
who was with her,
and he ate it.
Then the eyes of both of them were opened,
and they realized that they were naked;
so they sewed fig leaves together
and made loincloths for themselves.

Responsorial Psalm (Ps 51:3-4, 5-6, 12-13, 17)

R̸. (cf. 3a) Be merciful, O Lord, for we have
sinned.

Have mercy on me, O God, in your goodness;
in the greatness of your compassion wipe
out my offense.
Thoroughly wash me from my guilt
and of my sin cleanse me.

R̸. Be merciful, O Lord, for we have sinned.

For I acknowledge my offense,
and my sin is before me always:
"Against you only have I sinned,
and done what is evil in your sight."

R̸. Be merciful, O Lord, for we have sinned.

A clean heart create for me, O God,
    and a steadfast spirit renew within me.
Cast me not out from your presence,
    and your Holy Spirit take not from me.

R̄. Be merciful, O Lord, for we have sinned.

Give me back the joy of your salvation,
    and a willing spirit sustain in me.
O Lord, open my lips,
    and my mouth shall proclaim your praise.

R̄. Be merciful, O Lord, for we have sinned.

Second Reading (Rom 5:12-19 [or Rom 5:12, 17-19])

A reading from the Letter of Saint Paul to
the Romans

[Brothers and sisters:
Through one man sin entered the world,
    and through sin, death,
        and thus death came to all men, inasmuch
            as all sinned—"
        for up to the time of the law, sin was in the
            world,
        though sin is not accounted when there is
            no law.
But death reigned from Adam to Moses,
    even over those who did not sin
    after the pattern of the trespass of Adam,
    who is the type of the one who was to
        come.

But the gift is not like the transgression.
For if by the transgression of the one, the
        many died,
    how much more did the grace of God
    and the gracious gift of the one man Jesus
        Christ
    overflow for the many.
And the gift is not like the result of the one
        who sinned.

You really need to do your homework on this one! Try to paraphrase the reading in order to understand it. The most clearly written part begins with, "In conclusion . . ."

Always read Paul slowly, paying great attention to punctuation.

For after one sin there was the judgment that
brought condemnation;
but the gift, after many transgressions,
brought acquittal.
[For if, by the transgression of the one,
death came to reign through that one,
how much more will those who receive the
abundance of grace
and of the gift of justification
come to reign in life through the one Jesus
Christ.
In conclusion, just as through one
transgression
condemnation came upon all,
so, through one righteous act,
acquittal and life came to all.
For just as through the disobedience of the
one man
the many were made sinners,
so, through the obedience of the one,
the many will be made righteous.]

Three times Satan tests Jesus after his forty-day fast. Separate the three tests by a nice pause, as well as by the tone of your voice, reflecting the building tension until Jesus says, "Get away, Satan!"

Gospel (Matt 4:1-11; L22A)

A reading from the holy Gospel according
to Matthew

At that time Jesus was led by the Spirit into
the desert
to be tempted by the devil.
He fasted for forty days and forty nights,
and afterwards he was hungry.
The tempter approached and said to him,
"If you are the Son of God,
command that these stones become loaves
of bread."
He said in reply,
"It is written:
One does not live on bread alone,
but on every word that comes forth
from the mouth of God."

Then the devil took him to the holy city,
    and made him stand on the parapet of the
        temple,
    and said to him, "If you are the Son of
        God, throw yourself down.
For it is written:
    He will command his angels concerning you
        and with their hands they will support
            you,
    lest you dash your foot against a stone."
Jesus answered him,
    "Again it is written,
    You shall not put the Lord, your God, to the
        test."
Then the devil took him up to a very high
    mountain,
    and showed him all the kingdoms of the
        world in their magnificence,
    and he said to him, "All these I shall give to
        you,
    if you will prostrate yourself and worship
        me."
At this, Jesus said to him,
    "Get away, Satan!
It is written:
    The Lord, your God, shall you worship
        and him alone shall you serve."

Then the devil left him and, behold,
    angels came and ministered to him.

Preparing to Proclaim
Key words and phrases: "This is my beloved Son . . . listen to him."

To the point: The transfiguration is a mysterious thing; it reveals something about who Jesus is but leaves the disciples (and us) with as many questions as answers. There is both light and shadow in this moment of revelation. We may wish that God would communicate more directly with us; we ask for signs and signals to indicate God's will. Here, though, the disciples who do actually hear God's voice fall to the ground in fear. God does not say anything terribly challenging; the voice in fact affirms that they are doing well in entrusting their lives to Jesus. But there is something about it that overwhelms them. Encountering God in all God's mystery and wildness is not always a reassuring prospect; we are never ready for the ways in which God might call us to change.

Making Connections
Between the readings: Like the disciples in the gospel, Abram receives explicit directions from God. He does not respond in fear but in trust, immediately fulfilling the instructions he receives. His life of love and obedience prepares him to respond when God asks something big of him. The second reading affirms the role of the transfiguration. Along with the entire life of Jesus, the transfiguration makes manifest the grace of God, which has been with us all along.

To experience: We do not often hear the voice of God as explicitly as the disciples do in the gospel. For most of us, God tends to speak in whispers and hints. This does not mean that God is any less present, but it does make God's presence less obvious. Following God's will for our lives is not always as easy as it is for Abram, who receives clear and direct instructions. For us, it is a matter of learning the tools of discernment so that we can hear God's voice—and remain assured of God's loving presence—as we piece together our paths in life.

Prayer

Divine Providence,
you are with all pilgrims who journey to you,
    with you,
a guiding light for sinners who seek you.
[L]et your mercy be on us, as we place our
    trust in you.
Guide us, give to us a glimpse of a future
    with you,
filled with hope, joy, and promise.
Amen.

First Reading (Gen 12:1-4a)

A reading from the Book of Genesis

The LORD said to Abram:
    "Go forth from the land of your kinsfolk
    and from your father's house to a land that
        I will show you.

    "I will make of you a great nation,
        and I will bless you;
    I will make your name great,
        so that you will be a blessing.
    I will bless those who bless you
        and curse those who curse you.
    All the communities of the earth
        shall find blessing in you."

Abram went as the LORD directed him.

Responsorial Psalm (Ps 33:4-5, 18-19, 20, 22)

R℣. (22) Lord, let your mercy be on us, as we
place our trust in you.

Upright is the word of the LORD,
    and all his works are trustworthy.
He loves justice and right;
        of the kindness of the LORD the earth is
            full.

R℣. Lord, let your mercy be on us, as we place
our trust in you.

Pronunciation
Genesis   JEHN-uh-sihs
Abram   AY-br'm

Except for the first line, this is the Lord calling to Abram. It is a glorious calling indeed, for the Lord will:
    1. Give Abram his own land;
    2. make a "great nation" of him;
    3. "make [his] name great";
    4. "bless those who bless [him]";
    5. "curse those who curse [him]."

Give this reading the excitement and energy it deserves!

85

See, the eyes of the LORD are upon those who
    fear him,
    upon those who hope for his kindness,
to deliver them from death
    and preserve them in spite of famine.

R℣. Lord, let your mercy be on us, as we place
our trust in you.

Our soul waits for the LORD,
    who is our help and our shield.
May your kindness, O LORD, be upon us
    who have put our hope in you.

R℣. Lord, let your mercy be on us, as we place
our trust in you.

The first sentence is ex-
plained by the rest of the
reading. Let the opening
line stand on its own.

The second part of the
reading is one sentence.
Rehearse it out loud so
that you know how and
when to pause.

Second Reading (2 Tim 1:8b-10)

A reading from the second Letter of Saint
Paul to Timothy

Beloved:
Bear your share of hardship for the gospel
    with the strength that comes from God.

He saved us and called us to a holy life,
    not according to our works
    but according to his own design
    and the grace bestowed on us in Christ
        Jesus before time began,
    but now made manifest
    through the appearance of our savior
        Christ Jesus,
    who destroyed death and brought life and
        immortality
    to light through the gospel.

Gospel (Matt 17:1-9; L25A)

A reading from the holy Gospel according to Matthew

Jesus took Peter, James, and John his brother,
  and led them up a high mountain by
    themselves.
And he was transfigured before them;
  his face shone like the sun
  and his clothes became white as light.
And behold, Moses and Elijah appeared to
  them,
  conversing with him.
Then Peter said to Jesus in reply,
  "Lord, it is good that we are here.
If you wish, I will make three tents here,
  one for you, one for Moses, and one for
    Elijah."
While he was still speaking, behold,
  a bright cloud cast a shadow over them,
  then from the cloud came a voice that said,
  "This is my beloved Son, with whom I am
    well pleased;
  listen to him."
When the disciples heard this, they fell
    prostrate
  and were very much afraid.
But Jesus came and touched them, saying,
  "Rise, and do not be afraid."
And when the disciples raised their eyes,
  they saw no one else but Jesus alone.

As they were coming down from the
    mountain,
  Jesus charged them,
  "Do not tell the vision to anyone
  until the Son of Man has been raised from
    the dead."

Pronunciation
Elijah   ee-LAI-juh

Jesus is giving a bit of a mind-blowing "behind the scenes" tour to three of his disciples. Peter is responding in an embarrassingly human way when, all of a sudden, a voice from a cloud—the Father—speaks and the three disciples fall prostrate in fear. A dramatic scene? You bet!

You have three voices that speak: Peter, God the Father, and Jesus. What is the energy and tempo behind each voice? And that last line—wow! So keep the energy going all the way to the very end.

87

Preparing to Proclaim
Key words and phrases: "[W]hoever drinks the water I shall give will never thirst."

To the point: In her encounter with Jesus, we see a healing narrative arc for the woman at the well. She begins from a place of defensiveness; she knows what Jews usually think of Samaritans. She continues in a guarded manner, giving only a partial answer when asked about her husband. Deciding that this must be a prophet, she moves to challenge Jesus, asking intelligent questions to probe his wisdom. When he reveals to her his identity as Messiah, she finally arrives in a place of trust—such trust that she leaves her water jar behind and becomes a powerful evangelist, her testimony the cause of many neighbors' belief. Such is the power of encounter with Christ; one who is known to be sinful, who slinks to the well in the heat of the day to avoid the crowds of cooler times, is transformed into one whose testimony is so powerfully true that the same townspeople who would have judged her are transformed, too.

Making Connections
Between the readings: The first reading shares the strong water imagery of the gospel; God provides for us in all ways, including our very human need for water. Our physical thirst reveals the neediness of our human condition; it is never satisfied for long, and we must stay close enough to a source of water to constantly fulfill a need that was satisfied not long ago. The second reading is more oblique, but does speak of the love of God being "poured out" into our hearts—an indication that physical thirst is neither our primary need nor the primary way that God provides.

To experience: Our physical thirst is only an echo of the way in which our hearts are meant to ache for God. Our need for God is infinite, for it takes an infinite God to satisfy the need. That means that our capacity is infinite. We are made for so much more than we realize.

Prayer

Living Water,
you accompany us in all life's trials,
refreshing and enlivening weary souls.
Your voice bids us *"harden not your hearts,"*
lest we never come to drink
from your living spring of eternal life.
Help us receive you and your graces
with a willing, receptive heart.
Amen.

First Reading (Exod 17:3-7)

A reading from the Book of Exodus

In those days, in their thirst for water,
    the people grumbled against Moses,
    saying, "Why did you ever make us leave
        Egypt?
Was it just to have us die here of thirst
    with our children and our livestock?"
So Moses cried out to the LORD,
    "What shall I do with this people?
A little more and they will stone me!"
The LORD answered Moses,
    "Go over there in front of the people,
    along with some of the elders of Israel,
    holding in your hand, as you go,
    the staff with which you struck the river.
I will be standing there in front of you on the
        rock in Horeb.
Strike the rock, and the water will flow from it
    for the people to drink."
This Moses did, in the presence of the elders
    of Israel.
The place was called Massah and Meribah,
    because the Israelites quarreled there
    and tested the LORD, saying,
    "Is the LORD in our midst or not?"

Pronunciation
Horeb   HAWR-ehb
Massah   MAH-suh
Meribah   MEHR-ih-bah

Here is a wonderful, dramatic text of water from a rock! You have three voices in this reading: Moses, the Israelites, and God, along with the narration. What is the emotion behind each voice? Tempo is always a great way to convey emotion.

Responsorial Psalm (Ps 95:1-2, 6-7, 8-9)

R̸. (8) If today you hear his voice, harden not your hearts.

Come, let us sing joyfully to the LORD;
    let us acclaim the Rock of our salvation.
Let us come into his presence with
        thanksgiving;
    let us joyfully sing psalms to him.

R̸. If today you hear his voice, harden not your hearts.

Come, let us bow down in worship;
    let us kneel before the LORD who made us.
For he is our God,
    and we are the people he shepherds, the
        flock he guides.

R̸. If today you hear his voice, harden not your hearts.

Oh, that today you would hear his voice:
    "Harden not your hearts as at Meribah,
    as in the day of Massah in the desert,
where your fathers tempted me;
    they tested me though they had seen my
        works."

R̸. If today you hear his voice, harden not your hearts.

In this reading, Paul is teaching the Christian philosophy of faith, hope, and love.

Read this Scripture passage closely enough so that you feel you really understand it and can convey this understanding to your listeners. Proclaim Paul slowly and with conviction. His writings are

Second Reading (Rom 5:1-2, 5-8)

A reading from the Letter of Saint Paul to the Romans

Brothers and sisters:
Since we have been justified by faith,
    we have peace with God through our Lord
        Jesus Christ,
    through whom we have gained access by
        faith
to this grace in which we stand,
    and we boast in hope of the glory of God.

And hope does not disappoint,
because the love of God has been poured
out into our hearts
through the Holy Spirit who has been given
to us.
For Christ, while we were still helpless,
died at the appointed time for the ungodly.
Indeed, only with difficulty does one die for a
just person,
though perhaps for a good person one
might even find courage to die.
But God proves his love for us
in that while we were still sinners Christ
died for us.

Gospel **(John 4:5-42 [John 4:5-15, 19b-26, 39a, 40-42]; L28A)**

A reading from the holy Gospel according
to John

[Jesus came to a town of Samaria called
Sychar,
near the plot of land that Jacob had given
to his son Joseph.
Jacob's well was there.
Jesus, tired from his journey, sat down there
at the well.
It was about noon.

A woman of Samaria came to draw water.
Jesus said to her,
"Give me a drink."
His disciples had gone into the town to buy food.
The Samaritan woman said to him,
"How can you, a Jew, ask me, a Samaritan
woman, for a drink?"
—For Jews use nothing in common with
Samaritans.—
Jesus answered and said to her,
"If you knew the gift of God
and who is saying to you, 'Give me a drink,'

not simple; therefore, take
time to understand them
and to read them aloud.

Pronunciation
Samaria
suh-MEHR-ih-uh
Sychar   SI-kar
Samaritan
suh-MEHR-ih-tuhn

This is a relatively long
gospel reading with a
number of voices: Jesus,
the Samaritan woman, the
disciples, the Samaritans,
and the narrator.

Jesus's voice is the con-
stant throughout. Other
voices are amazed, ex-
cited, and so on, but Jesus
remains calm, reassuring,
and constant.

91

you would have asked him
and he would have given you living water."
The woman said to him,
  "Sir, you do not even have a bucket and the
    cistern is deep;
  where then can you get this living water?
Are you greater than our father Jacob,
  who gave us this cistern and drank from it
    himself
  with his children and his flocks?"
Jesus answered and said to her,
  "Everyone who drinks this water will be
    thirsty again;
  but whoever drinks the water I shall give
    will never thirst;
  the water I shall give will become in him
  a spring of water welling up to eternal life."
The woman said to him,
  "Sir, give me this water, so that I may not
    be thirsty
  or have to keep coming here to draw water."]

Jesus said to her,
  "Go call your husband and come back."
The woman answered and said to him,
  "I do not have a husband."
Jesus answered her,
  "You are right in saying, 'I do not have a
    husband.'
For you have had five husbands,
  and the one you have now is not your
    husband.
What you have said is true."
The woman said to him,
  "Sir, [I can see that you are a prophet.
Our ancestors worshiped on this mountain;
  but you people say that the place to
    worship is in Jerusalem."
Jesus said to her,
  "Believe me, woman, the hour is coming
  when you will worship the Father

neither on this mountain nor in Jerusalem.
You people worship what you do not
      understand;
   we worship what we understand,
   because salvation is from the Jews.
But the hour is coming, and is now here,
   when true worshipers will worship the
         Father in Spirit and truth;
   and indeed the Father seeks such people to
         worship him.
God is Spirit, and those who worship him
   must worship in Spirit and truth."
The woman said to him,
   "I know that the Messiah is coming, the one
         called the Christ;
   when he comes, he will tell us everything."
Jesus said to her,
   "I am he, the one speaking with you."]

At that moment his disciples returned,
   and were amazed that he was talking with
         a woman,
   but still no one said, "What are you looking
         for?"
   or "Why are you talking with her?"
The woman left her water jar
   and went into the town and said to the
         people,
   "Come see a man who told me everything I
         have done.
Could he possibly be the Christ?"
They went out of the town and came to him.
Meanwhile, the disciples urged him, "Rabbi,
      eat."
But he said to them,
   "I have food to eat of which you do not
         know."
So the disciples said to one another,
   "Could someone have brought him
         something to eat?"

Jesus said to them,
"My food is to do the will of the one who
sent me
and to finish his work.
Do you not say, 'In four months the harvest
will be here'?
I tell you, look up and see the fields ripe for
the harvest.
The reaper is already receiving payment
and gathering crops for eternal life,
so that the sower and reaper can rejoice
together.
For here the saying is verified that 'One sows
and another reaps.'
I sent you to reap what you have not worked
for;
others have done the work,
and you are sharing the fruits of their
work."

[Many of the Samaritans of that town began
to believe in him]
because of the word of the woman who
testified,
"He told me everything I have done."
[When the Samaritans came to him,
they invited him to stay with them;
and he stayed there two days.
Many more began to believe in him because
of his word,
and they said to the woman,
"We no longer believe because of your
word;
for we have heard for ourselves,
and we know that this is truly the savior of
the world.'"]

Preparing to Proclaim

Key words and phrases: "I am the light of the world."

To the point: Like many of our Lenten readings, this gospel plays with themes of light and darkness, seeing and blindness. Here, Jesus makes clear that it is easier for God to heal physical blindness than willful refusal to see God at work. Most of us struggle with some level of spiritual blindness; after all, most of us do not get to witness these clear, decisive miracles of Jesus's time on earth. God does not always operate in ways that are easy for us to perceive. The Pharisees, though, are choosing blindness. Having their eyes opened will challenge a system that keeps them comfortably in power. What God reveals is not always comfortable or easy. We are sometimes called to sacrifice and to use our positions of privilege to advocate for others in unpopular ways. But if we *want* to see, God can heal our spiritual blindness, too.

Making Connections

Between the readings: The first reading contains a much more mundane form of blindness. Jesse merely *overlooks* David, assuming his youngest son cannot be the one chosen by God. But God is clear that his perception is not the same as ours; what God values is not the same as what we value. The second reading continues the themes of light and darkness, exhorting us to choose light over darkness—which is to say, sight over blindness.

To experience: The Pharisees are comfortable with their blindness, unable to recognize how much they don't see. We, too, are often content to remain in ignorance, especially when God's light reveals truth that is uncomfortable. We know God sides with the oppressed, and so we'd rather not know when we've benefited from oppression. This is the work of Lent, though: all the prayer and fasting and almsgiving are meant to illumine places where our lives are keeping us from God, and to aid us in turning away from them, uncomfortable though it may be.

Prayer

Healing Presence,
you anoint all who live in pain and distress,
and guide all to wholeness and boundless, re-
   storative love.
You are *my shepherd; there is nothing I shall
   want.*
Open our eyes, open our hearts,
that all may truly see you, know you, and love
   you in return.
Amen.

Pronunciation
Samuel   SAM-yoo-uhl
Eliab   ee-LAI-ab

What is the most impor-
tant sentence in this reading? I would submit the
following:
"Not as man sees does
God see,
   because man sees the
   appearance
   but the LORD looks into
   the heart."

The final sentence is very
dramatic. The youngest
of the brothers is anointed
with oil in front of his
older siblings.

First Reading (I Sam 16:1b, 6-7, 10-13a)

A reading from the first Book of Samuel
The LORD said to Samuel:
   "Fill your horn with oil, and be on your
      way.
I am sending you to Jesse of Bethlehem,
   for I have chosen my king from among his
      sons."

As Jesse and his sons came to the sacrifice,
   Samuel looked at Eliab and thought,
   "Surely the LORD's anointed is here before
      him."
But the LORD said to Samuel:
   "Do not judge from his appearance or from
      his lofty stature,
   because I have rejected him.
Not as man sees does God see,
   because man sees the appearance
   but the LORD looks into the heart."
In the same way Jesse presented seven sons
      before Samuel,
   but Samuel said to Jesse,
   "The LORD has not chosen any one of
      these."
Then Samuel asked Jesse,
   "Are these all the sons you have?"

Jesse replied,
"There is still the youngest, who is tending
the sheep."
Samuel said to Jesse,
"Send for him;
we will not begin the sacrificial banquet
until he arrives here."
Jesse sent and had the young man brought to
them.
He was ruddy, a youth handsome to behold
and making a splendid appearance.
The LORD said,
"There—anoint him, for this is the one!"
Then Samuel, with the horn of oil in hand,
anointed David in the presence of his
brothers;
and from that day on, the spirit of the LORD
rushed upon David.

Responsorial Psalm (Ps 23:1-3a, 3b-4, 5, 6)

R̞. (1) The Lord is my shepherd; there is
nothing I shall want.

The LORD is my shepherd; I shall not want.
In verdant pastures he gives me repose;
beside restful waters he leads me;
he refreshes my soul.

R̞. The Lord is my shepherd; there is nothing
I shall want.

He guides me in right paths
for his name's sake.
Even though I walk in the dark valley
I fear no evil; for you are at my side
with your rod and your staff
that give me courage.

R̞. The Lord is my shepherd; there is nothing
I shall want.

97

You spread the table before me
in the sight of my foes;
you anoint my head with oil;
my cup overflows.

R℣. The Lord is my shepherd; there is nothing
I shall want.

Only goodness and kindness follow me
all the days of my life;
and I shall dwell in the house of the LORD
for years to come.

R℣. The Lord is my shepherd; there is nothing
I shall want.

Pronunciation
Ephesians
eh-FEE-zhuhnz

Bright can be a quality of sound, as well as describing something visual. Commentators doing recordings often literally smile when they speak in order to sound brighter. Try this technique. Your voice will also sound cleaner.

Of course, there is no reason to not smile while delivering the first part of this reading as well as the very end.

Second Reading (Eph 5:8-14)

A reading from the Letter of Saint Paul to the Ephesians

Brothers and sisters:
You were once darkness,
but now you are light in the Lord.
Live as children of light,
for light produces every kind of goodness
and righteousness and truth.
Try to learn what is pleasing to the Lord.
Take no part in the fruitless works of
darkness;
rather expose them, for it is shameful even
to mention
the things done by them in secret;
but everything exposed by the light
becomes visible,
for everything that becomes visible is light.
Therefore, it says:
"Awake, O sleeper,
and arise from the dead,
and Christ will give you light."

Gospel (John 9:1-41 [John 9:1, 6-9, 13-17, 34-38]; L31A)

A reading from the holy Gospel according to John

[As Jesus passed by he saw a man blind from
    birth.]

His disciples asked him,
    "Rabbi, who sinned, this man or his
        parents,
    that he was born blind?"

Jesus answered,
    "Neither he nor his parents sinned;
    it is so that the works of God might be
        made visible through him.

We have to do the works of the one who sent
    me while it is day.

Night is coming when no one can work.

While I am in the world, I am the light of the
    world."

When he had said this, [he spat on the ground
    and made clay with the saliva,
    and smeared the clay on his eyes, and said
        to him,
    "Go wash in the Pool of Siloam"—which
        means Sent—.

So he went and washed, and came back able
    to see.

His neighbors and those who had seen him
        earlier as a beggar said,
    "Isn't this the one who used to sit and beg?"

Some said, "It is,"
    but others said, "No, he just looks like him."

He said, "I am."]

So they said to him, "How were your eyes
    opened?"

He replied,
    "The man called Jesus made clay and
        anointed my eyes
    and told me, 'Go to Siloam and wash.'

Pronunciation
Siloam   sih-LO-uhm
Pharisees   FEHR-ih-seez

This is a wonderful reading that presents the testimony of the blind man to challenge the Pharisees.

I would do my best to make the passage "This is what is so amazing . . . he would not be able to do anything" (toward the bottom of pg. 101) really stand out.

99

So I went there and washed and was able to
see."
And they said to him, "Where is he?"
He said, "I don't know."

[They brought the one who was once blind to
the Pharisees.
Now Jesus had made clay and opened his eyes
on a sabbath.
So then the Pharisees also asked him how he
was able to see.
He said to them,
"He put clay on my eyes, and I washed, and
now I can see."
So some of the Pharisees said,
"This man is not from God,
because he does not keep the sabbath."
But others said,
"How can a sinful man do such signs?"
And there was a division among them.
So they said to the blind man again,
"What do you have to say about him,
since he opened your eyes?"
He said, "He is a prophet."]

Now the Jews did not believe
that he had been blind and gained his sight
until they summoned the parents of the
one who had gained his sight.
They asked them,
"Is this your son, who you say was born
blind?
How does he now see?"
His parents answered and said,
"We know that this is our son and that he
was born blind.
We do not know how he sees now,
nor do we know who opened his eyes.
Ask him, he is of age;
he can speak for himself."

His parents said this because they were afraid
    of the Jews,
   for the Jews had already agreed
   that if anyone acknowledged him as the
      Christ,
   he would be expelled from the synagogue.
For this reason his parents said,
   "He is of age; question him."

So a second time they called the man who had
    been blind
   and said to him, "Give God the praise!
We know that this man is a sinner."
He replied,
   "If he is a sinner, I do not know.
One thing I do know is that I was blind and
    now I see."
So they said to him,
   "What did he do to you?
   How did he open your eyes?"
He answered them,
   "I told you already and you did not listen.
Why do you want to hear it again?
Do you want to become his disciples, too?"
They ridiculed him and said,
   "You are that man's disciple;
   we are disciples of Moses!
We know that God spoke to Moses,
   but we do not know where this one is
      from."
The man answered and said to them,
   "This is what is so amazing,
   that you do not know where he is from, yet
      he opened my eyes.
We know that God does not listen to sinners,
   but if one is devout and does his will, he
      listens to him.
It is unheard of that anyone ever opened the
    eyes of a person born blind.
If this man were not from God,
   he would not be able to do anything."

[They answered and said to him,
   "You were born totally in sin,
   and are you trying to teach us?"
Then they threw him out.

When Jesus heard that they had thrown him
      out,
   he found him and said, "Do you believe in
      the Son of Man?"
He answered and said,
   "Who is he, sir, that I may believe in him?"
Jesus said to him,
   "You have seen him,
   and the one speaking with you is he."
He said,
   "I do believe, Lord," and he worshiped him.]
Then Jesus said,
   "I came into this world for judgment,
   so that those who do not see might see,
   and those who do see might become blind."

Some of the Pharisees who were with him
      heard this
   and said to him, "Surely we are not also
      blind, are we?"
Jesus said to them,
   "If you were blind, you would have no sin;
   but now you are saying, 'We see,' so your
      sin remains."

Preparing to Proclaim

Key words and phrases: "Yes, Lord. I have come to believe that you are the Christ, the Son of God."

To the point: Mary and Martha reverse roles here. Where Mary once sat at the feet of Jesus, she now sits at home in her grief. Martha, however, the one who was too busy to listen, comes to him as interlocutor, intelligently and faithfully interacting with him. She does not see the whole picture, though, for Jesus is still in the process of revealing all that his life means for the world. Lazarus here becomes a sort of firstfruits, one restored to life before the full restoration occurs. Wonderful as this miracle is, it is a jarring one; this simply does not happen. People who have been dead for four days do not come back to life. And we know nothing of Lazarus's experience here. Whatever his experience was of death, it must have been unsettling to be jolted back to life. Jesus is here to bring life, yes, but he brings it in ways that disrupt the order of things to which we have grown accustomed.

Making Connections

Between the readings: In the first reading, God reveals through Ezekiel that death does not have the final say. Despite death's appearance of permanence, God's power is greater still, and what God wants for us is life. The second reading affirms that while our bodies still die, this is no longer the end it once was. Christ's Spirit living in us allows us to share in his triumph over death.

To experience: When Jesus calls us to fuller life in him, it is not always comfortable or easy. There are often demands and sacrifices we would not have expected and certainly would not have chosen for ourselves. But while Lazarus stood alone as the first called forth from the tomb, we are never left alone with our challenges; it is Christ's own life that we share, and he accompanies us always.

Prayer

God of Promises,
you who raise the dead to new life,
you who cry with us, and set us free:
with you *there is mercy and fullness of
    redemption.*
Fill us with your spirit, know of our trust,
and redeem us, O holy Son of God.
Amen.

Pronunciation
Ezekiel   eh-ZEE-kee-uhl

This is a proclamation by
God though the prophet
Ezekiel. Read it slowly, deliberately, and with total
conviction.

First Reading (Ezek 37:12-14)

A reading from the Book of the Prophet
Ezekiel

Thus says the Lord GOD:
    O my people, I will open your graves
        and have you rise from them,
        and bring you back to the land of Israel.
Then you shall know that I am the LORD,
        when I open your graves and have you rise
            from them,
        O my people!
I will put my spirit in you that you may live,
        and I will settle you upon your land;
            thus you shall know that I am the LORD.
I have promised, and I will do it, says the
        LORD.

Responsorial Psalm (Ps 130:1-2, 3-4, 5-6, 7-8)

R℟. (7) With the Lord there is mercy and
fullness of redemption.

Out of the depths I cry to you, O LORD;
        LORD, hear my voice!
Let your ears be attentive
        to my voice in supplication.

R℟. With the Lord there is mercy and fullness
of redemption.

If you, O LORD, mark iniquities,
   LORD, who can stand?
But with you is forgiveness,
   that you may be revered.

R℣. With the Lord there is mercy and fullness
of redemption.

I trust in the LORD;
   my soul trusts in his word.
More than sentinels wait for the dawn,
   let Israel wait for the LORD.

R℣. With the Lord there is mercy and fullness
of redemption.

For with the LORD is kindness
   and with him is plenteous redemption;
and he will redeem Israel
   from all their iniquities.

R℣. With the Lord there is mercy and fullness
of redemption.

Second Reading (Rom 8:8-11)

A reading from the Letter of Saint Paul to
the Romans

Brothers and sisters:
Those who are in the flesh cannot please God.
But you are not in the flesh;
   on the contrary, you are in the spirit,
   if only the Spirit of God dwells in you.
Whoever does not have the Spirit of Christ
   does not belong to him.
But if Christ is in you,
   although the body is dead because of sin,
   the spirit is alive because of righteousness.
If the Spirit of the One who raised Jesus from
   the dead dwells in you,
   the One who raised Christ from the dead
   will give life to your mortal bodies also,
   through his Spirit dwelling in you.

Here is a relatively short reading that is heavy with meaning—as only St. Paul can write! Separate it into three parts with a generous pause before "But if Christ is in you . . ." and "If the Spirit of the one . . . ," letting what you have read sink in for both the listener and you.

Pay attention to the commas for clarity, as well.

Pronunciation
Lazarus   LAZ-er-uhs
Bethany   BEHTH-uh-nee
Judea   jou-DEE-uh
Didymus   DID-I-mus

This incredible Scripture passage gives us such insight into Jesus's teachings. The reading is full of sadness and family and communal mourning, only to end with a dramatic, joyous final section.

Don't be afraid to give that final section the energy and amazement it deserves.

Gospel (John 11:1-45 [John 11:3-7, 17, 20-27, 33b-45]; L34A)

A reading from the holy Gospel according to John

Now a man was ill, Lazarus from Bethany,
    the village of Mary and her sister Martha.
Mary was the one who had anointed the Lord
        with perfumed oil
    and dried his feet with her hair;
    it was her brother Lazarus who was ill.
So [the sisters* sent word to Jesus saying,
    "Master, the one you love is ill."
When Jesus heard this he said,
    "This illness is not to end in death,
    but is for the glory of God,
    that the Son of God may be glorified
            through it."
Now Jesus loved Martha and her sister and
            Lazarus.
So when he heard that he was ill,
    he remained for two days in the place
            where he was.
Then after this he said to his disciples,
    "Let us go back to Judea."]
The disciples said to him,
    "Rabbi, the Jews were just trying to stone
            you,
    and you want to go back there?"
Jesus answered,
    "Are there not twelve hours in a day?
If one walks during the day, he does not
        stumble,
    because he sees the light of this world.
But if one walks at night, he stumbles,
    because the light is not in him."
He said this, and then told them,
    "Our friend Lazarus is asleep,
    but I am going to awaken him."

*short version: sisters of Lazarus

So the disciples said to him,
 "Master, if he is asleep, he will be saved."
But Jesus was talking about his death,
 while they thought that he meant ordinary
  sleep.
So then Jesus said to them clearly,
 "Lazarus has died.
And I am glad for you that I was not there,
 that you may believe.
Let us go to him."
So Thomas, called Didymus, said to his fellow
 disciples,
 "Let us also go to die with him."

[When Jesus arrived, he found that Lazarus
 had already been in the tomb for four days.]
Now Bethany was near Jerusalem, only about
 two miles away.
And many of the Jews had come to Martha
 and Mary
 to comfort them about their brother.
[When Martha heard that Jesus was coming,
 she went to meet him;
 but Mary sat at home.
Martha said to Jesus,
 "Lord, if you had been here,
 my brother would not have died.
But even now I know that whatever you ask
 of God,
 God will give you."
Jesus said to her,
 "Your brother will rise."
Martha said to him,
 "I know he will rise,
 in the resurrection on the last day."
Jesus told her,
 "I am the resurrection and the life;
 whoever believes in me, even if he dies,
  will live,
 and everyone who lives and believes in me
  will never die.

Do you believe this?"
She said to him, "Yes, Lord.
I have come to believe that you are the Christ,
        the Son of God,
        the one who is coming into the world."]

When she had said this,
        she went and called her sister Mary
                secretly, saying,
        "The teacher is here and is asking for you."
As soon as she heard this,
        she rose quickly and went to him.
For Jesus had not yet come into the village,
        but was still where Martha had met him.
So when the Jews who were with her in the
                house comforting her
        saw Mary get up quickly and go out,
        they followed her,
        presuming that she was going to the tomb
                to weep there.
When Mary came to where Jesus was and saw
        him,
        she fell at his feet and said to him,
        "Lord, if you had been here,
        my brother would not have died."
When Jesus saw her weeping and the Jews
                who had come with her weeping,
        [he became perturbed and deeply troubled,
                and said,
        "Where have you laid him?"
They said to him, "Sir, come and see."
And Jesus wept.
So the Jews said, "See how he loved him."
But some of them said,
        "Could not the one who opened the eyes of
                the blind man
        have done something so that this man
                would not have died?"

So Jesus, perturbed again, came to the tomb.
It was a cave, and a stone lay across it.

Jesus said, "Take away the stone."
Martha, the dead man's sister, said to him,
    "Lord, by now there will be a stench;
    he has been dead for four days."
Jesus said to her,
    "Did I not tell you that if you believe
    you will see the glory of God?"
So they took away the stone.
And Jesus raised his eyes and said,
    "Father, I thank you for hearing me.
I know that you always hear me;
    but because of the crowd here I have said
        this,
    that they may believe that you sent me."
And when he had said this,
    he cried out in a loud voice,
    "Lazarus, come out!"
The dead man came out,
    tied hand and foot with burial bands,
    and his face was wrapped in a cloth.
So Jesus said to them,
    "Untie him and let him go."

Now many of the Jews who had come to Mary
    and seen what he had done began to
        believe in him.]

Preparing to Proclaim

Key words and phrases: "Truly, this was the Son of God!"

To the point: The paired gospels of this Sunday give us the whole narrative arc of Holy Week. The triumph of Jesus's entrance into Jerusalem contrasts painfully with the crowds that turn on him in the passion narrative. One moment, though, brings us back to the truth; the centurion, a most unexpected source, affirms that this man truly was the Son of God. This is not the only time the passion story subverts expectations. The women epitomize bravery, staying near the grisly scene of the cross while the disciples who most staunchly averred their bravery are the first to run away. Religious leaders insist on Jesus's death while the occupying government tries to find ways to release him. Jesus's death does not happen quietly but affects the earth. We do not hear the end of the story here, the resurrection to which we so look forward, but we see very clearly that God is doing something new.

Making Connections

Between the readings: The first reading provides the first moment of stark contrast between the procession's triumphant tones and the gravity of the passion. The glory of Jesus's entrance into Jerusalem was not for its own sake. The beautiful hymn of the second reading captures this paradox in all its fullness: Jesus shares God's being by rights, but by choice humbles himself to death. It is this humility that allows his even greater exaltation and the worship we now bring to the one who gives us life.

To experience: Crucifixes are a common sight for us as Catholics, so common that we can fail to let them call to mind this story in its entirety. On the surface this looks like a gory, tragic story, but we know that it is, more truly, the story of the greatest love the world has ever known. The crucifix also points beyond itself; it is not the end of the story. We know that the resurrection is coming, and we trust in God's ability to make life ever new even as we share in the sorrow of the passion.

Prayer

God of the Lost,
at times it is hard to know your presence,
when life overwhelms and shadows hide your
    face.
In these times, hear our cries:
*My God, my God, why have you abandoned
    me?*
Help us know you are always with us,
abiding in patient support, gentle love, and
    everlasting life.
Amen.

Gospel at the procession with palms (Matt 21:1-11; L37A)

A reading from the holy Gospel according
to Matthew

When Jesus and the disciples drew near
    Jerusalem
    and came to Bethphage on the Mount of
        Olives,
    Jesus sent two disciples, saying to them,
    "Go into the village opposite you,
    and immediately you will find an ass
        tethered,
    and a colt with her.
Untie them and bring them here to me.
And if anyone should say anything to you,
    reply,
    'The master has need of them.'
Then he will send them at once."
This happened so that what had been spoken
    through the prophet
might be fulfilled:
    Say to daughter Zion,
    "Behold, your king comes to you,
        meek and riding on an ass,
        and on a colt, the foal of a beast of
            burden."

Pronunciation
Bethphage
    BEHTH-fuh-jee
Zion   ZAI-uhn

Don't let your listeners
miss the last section of
this reading, particularly
the portion that I
italicized:
"And when he entered
Jerusalem
    the *whole city was
    shaken* and asked,
    'Who is this?'
And the crowds replied,
'This is Jesus the prophet,
from Nazareth in
Galilee.'"

111

The disciples went and did as Jesus had
    ordered them.
They brought the ass and the colt and laid
        their cloaks over them,
    and he sat upon them.
The very large crowd spread their cloaks on
        the road,
    while others cut branches from the trees
    and strewed them on the road.
The crowds preceding him and those
        following
    kept crying out and saying:
        "Hosanna to the Son of David;
            blessed is he who comes in the name
                of the Lord;
        hosanna in the highest."
And when he entered Jerusalem
    the whole city was shaken and asked,
        "Who is this?"
And the crowds replied,
    "This is Jesus the prophet, from Nazareth
        in Galilee."

This reading is strong, passionate, and determined. "I have set my face like *flint*," meaning, like stone. Isaiah the prophet is nothing if not adamant!

Split the reading into three sections, giving a nice pause before "I gave my back . . ." and "The Lord GOD is my help . . ."

First Reading (Isa 50:4-7)

A reading from the Book of the Prophet Isaiah

The Lord GOD has given me
    a well-trained tongue,
that I might know how to speak to the weary
    a word that will rouse them.
Morning after morning
    he opens my ear that I may hear;
and I have not rebelled,
    have not turned back.
I gave my back to those who beat me,
    my cheeks to those who plucked my beard;
my face I did not shield
    from buffets and spitting.

The Lord GOD is my help,
>   therefore I am not disgraced;
I have set my face like flint,
>   knowing that I shall not be put to shame.

Responsorial Psalm (Ps 22:8-9, 17-18, 19-20, 23-24)

R̶/. (2a) My God, my God, why have you abandoned me?

All who see me scoff at me;
>   they mock me with parted lips, they wag
>   their heads:
"He relied on the LORD; let him deliver him,
>   let him rescue him, if he loves him."

R̶/. My God, my God, why have you abandoned me?

Indeed, many dogs surround me,
>   a pack of evildoers closes in upon me;
they have pierced my hands and my feet;
>   I can count all my bones.

R̶/. My God, my God, why have you abandoned me?

They divide my garments among them,
>   and for my vesture they cast lots.
But you, O LORD, be not far from me;
>   O my help, hasten to aid me.

R̶/. My God, my God, why have you abandoned me?

I will proclaim your name to my brethren;
>   in the midst of the assembly I will praise
>   you:
"You who fear the LORD, praise him;
>   all you descendants of Jacob, give glory to
>   him;
>   revere him, all you descendants of Israel!"

R̶/. My God, my God, why have you abandoned me?

PALM SUNDAY OF THE PASSION OF THE LORD

Pronunciation
Philippians
   fih-LIHP-ih-uhnz

This is certainly one of Paul's most notable writings!

Part 1: Jesus, though he was God, did not regard himself as such but rather humbled himself as a human—even to die a terrible death. Part 2: Because of this, God greatly exalted him above all others!

Give a nice pause before the second part, "Because of this . . ." Carry the energy of the second part, which is so positive, all the way through to the very end.

Pronunciation
Iscariot
   ihs-KEHR-ee-uht
Rabbi   RAB-ai
Galilee   GAL-ih-lee
Gethsemane
   gehth-SEHM-uh-ne
Zebedee   ZEH-beh-dee
Caiaphas   KAY-uh-fuhs
Sanhedrin
   san-HEE-drihn
prophesy   PRAA-fuh-sai
Jeremiah
   jehr-eh-MAI-uh
Barabbas
   beh-REH-buhs

Second Reading (Phil 2:6-11)

A reading from the Letter of Saint Paul to the Philippians

Christ Jesus, though he was in the form of God,
   did not regard equality with God
   something to be grasped.
Rather, he emptied himself,
   taking the form of a slave,
   coming in human likeness;
   and found human in appearance,
   he humbled himself,
   becoming obedient to the point of death,
   even death on a cross.
Because of this, God greatly exalted him
   and bestowed on him the name
   which is above every name,
   that at the name of Jesus
   every knee should bend,
   of those in heaven and on earth and under
      the earth,
   and every tongue confess that
   Jesus Christ is Lord,
   to the glory of God the Father.

Gospel at Mass (Matt 26:14–27:66 [or 27:11-54]; L38A)

A reading from the holy Gospel according to Matthew

One of the Twelve, who was called Judas Iscariot,
   went to the chief priests and said,
   "What are you willing to give me
   if I hand him over to you?"
They paid him thirty pieces of silver,
   and from that time on he looked for an
      opportunity to hand him over.

On the first day of the Feast of Unleavened Bread,

114

the disciples approached Jesus and said,
"Where do you want us to prepare
for you to eat the Passover?"
He said,
"Go into the city to a certain man and tell
him,
'The teacher says, "My appointed time
draws near;
in your house I shall celebrate the Passover
with my disciples."'"
The disciples then did as Jesus had ordered,
and prepared the Passover.

When it was evening,
he reclined at table with the Twelve.
And while they were eating, he said,
"Amen, I say to you, one of you will betray
me."
Deeply distressed at this,
they began to say to him one after another,
"Surely it is not I, Lord?"
He said in reply,
"He who has dipped his hand into the dish
with me
is the one who will betray me.
The Son of Man indeed goes, as it is written
of him,
but woe to that man by whom the Son of
Man is betrayed.
It would be better for that man if he had
never been born."
Then Judas, his betrayer, said in reply,
"Surely it is not I, Rabbi?"
He answered,
"You have said so."

While they were eating,
Jesus took bread, said the blessing,
broke it, and giving it to his disciples said,
"Take and eat; this is my body."

Cyrenian
 sai-REE-nih-uhn
Golgotha
 GAHL-guh-thuh
Eloi Eloi Lama
Sabechthani
 AY-lo-ee AY-lo-ee LAH-mah sah-BAHK-tah-nee
Elijah ee-LAI-juh
Magdalene
 MAG-duh-lehn
Arimathea
 ehr-uh-muh-THEE-uh

With such a long reading take time to organize the text in sections, giving yourself a nice pause between each section. (And maybe a sip of water as well!)

A first section might end when Jesus and his disciples depart after the Last Supper to the Mount of Olives. *Pause.* A second section might end at, "Then all the disciples left him and fled." *Pause.*

Continue in that manner.

Then he took a cup, gave thanks, and gave it
    to them, saying,
"Drink from it, all of you,
for this is my blood of the covenant,
which will be shed on behalf of many
for the forgiveness of sins.
I tell you, from now on I shall not drink this
    fruit of the vine
until the day when I drink it with you new
in the kingdom of my Father."
Then, after singing a hymn,
    they went out to the Mount of Olives.

Then Jesus said to them,
"This night all of you will have your faith
    in me shaken,
for it is written:
    I will strike the shepherd,
        and the sheep of the flock will be
            dispersed;
but after I have been raised up,
I shall go before you to Galilee."
Peter said to him in reply,
"Though all may have their faith in you
    shaken,
mine will never be."
Jesus said to him,
"Amen, I say to you,
this very night before the cock crows,
you will deny me three times."
Peter said to him,
"Even though I should have to die with you,
I will not deny you."
And all the disciples spoke likewise.

Then Jesus came with them to a place called
    Gethsemane,
    and he said to his disciples,
"Sit here while I go over there and pray."

He took along Peter and the two sons of
    Zebedee,
  and began to feel sorrow and distress.
Then he said to them,
  "My soul is sorrowful even to death.
Remain here and keep watch with me."
He advanced a little and fell prostrate in
    prayer, saying,
  "My Father, if it is possible,
  let this cup pass from me;
  yet, not as I will, but as you will."
When he returned to his disciples he found
    them asleep.
He said to Peter,
  "So you could not keep watch with me for
    one hour?
Watch and pray that you may not undergo the
  test.
The spirit is willing, but the flesh is weak."
Withdrawing a second time, he prayed again,
  "My Father, if it is not possible that this
    cup pass
  without my drinking it, your will be done!"
Then he returned once more and found them
    asleep,
  for they could not keep their eyes open.
He left them and withdrew again and prayed
    a third time,
  saying the same thing again.
Then he returned to his disciples and said to
    them,
  "Are you still sleeping and taking your rest?
Behold, the hour is at hand
  when the Son of Man is to be handed over
    to sinners.
Get up, let us go.
Look, my betrayer is at hand."

While he was still speaking,
  Judas, one of the Twelve, arrived,

accompanied by a large crowd, with
swords and clubs,
who had come from the chief priests and
the elders of the people.
His betrayer had arranged a sign with them,
saying,
"The man I shall kiss is the one; arrest
him."
Immediately he went over to Jesus and said,
"Hail, Rabbi!"
and he kissed him.
Jesus answered him,
"Friend, do what you have come for."
Then stepping forward they laid hands on
Jesus and arrested him.
And behold, one of those who accompanied
Jesus
put his hand to his sword, drew it,
and struck the high priest's servant,
cutting off his ear.
Then Jesus said to him,
"Put your sword back into its sheath,
for all who take the sword will perish by
the sword.
Do you think that I cannot call upon my
Father
and he will not provide me at this moment
with more than twelve legions of angels?
But then how would the Scriptures be fulfilled
which say that it must come to pass in this
way?"
At that hour Jesus said to the crowds,
"Have you come out as against a robber,
with swords and clubs to seize me?
Day after day I sat teaching in the temple
area,
yet you did not arrest me.
But all this has come to pass

that the writings of the prophets may be
fulfilled."
Then all the disciples left him and fled.

Those who had arrested Jesus led him away
to Caiaphas the high priest,
where the scribes and the elders were
assembled.
Peter was following him at a distance
as far as the high priest's courtyard,
and going inside he sat down with the
servants to see the outcome.
The chief priests and the entire Sanhedrin
kept trying to obtain false testimony
against Jesus
in order to put him to death,
but they found none,
though many false witnesses came
forward.
Finally two came forward who stated,
"This man said, 'I can destroy the temple
of God
and within three days rebuild it.'"
The high priest rose and addressed him,
"Have you no answer?
What are these men testifying against you?"
But Jesus was silent.
Then the high priest said to him,
"I order you to tell us under oath before the
living God
whether you are the Christ, the Son of
God."
Jesus said to him in reply,
"You have said so.
But I tell you:
From now on you will see 'the Son of Man
seated at the right hand of the Power'
and 'coming on the clouds of heaven.'"
Then the high priest tore his robes and said,
"He has blasphemed!
What further need have we of witnesses?

You have now heard the blasphemy;
    what is your opinion?"
They said in reply,
    "He deserves to die!"
Then they spat in his face and struck him,
    while some slapped him, saying,
        "Prophesy for us, Christ: who is it that
            struck you?"

Now Peter was sitting outside in the
        courtyard.
One of the maids came over to him and said,
    "You too were with Jesus the Galilean."
But he denied it in front of everyone, saying,
    "I do not know what you are talking
        about!"
As he went out to the gate, another girl saw
        him
    and said to those who were there,
    "This man was with Jesus the Nazorean."
Again he denied it with an oath,
    "I do not know the man!"
A little later the bystanders came over and
        said to Peter,
    "Surely you too are one of them;
    even your speech gives you away."
At that he began to curse and to swear,
    "I do not know the man."
And immediately a cock crowed.
Then Peter remembered the word that Jesus
        had spoken:
    "Before the cock crows you will deny me
        three times."
He went out and began to weep bitterly.

When it was morning,
    all the chief priests and the elders of the
        people
    took counsel against Jesus to put him to
        death.

They bound him, led him away,
  and handed him over to Pilate, the
    governor.

Then Judas, his betrayer, seeing that Jesus
    had been condemned,
  deeply regretted what he had done.
He returned the thirty pieces of silver
  to the chief priests and elders, saying,
    "I have sinned in betraying innocent
      blood."
They said,
  "What is that to us?
  Look to it yourself."
Flinging the money into the temple,
  he departed and went off and hanged
    himself.
The chief priests gathered up the money, but
    said,
  "It is not lawful to deposit this in the
    temple treasury,
  for it is the price of blood."
After consultation, they used it to buy the
    potter's field
  as a burial place for foreigners.
That is why that field even today is called the
    Field of Blood.
Then was fulfilled what had been said
    through Jeremiah the prophet,
  And they took the thirty pieces of silver,
  the value of a man with a price on his
      head,
  a price set by some of the Israelites,
  and they paid it out for the potter's field
  just as the Lord had commanded me.

Now [Jesus stood before the governor, and he*
    questioned him,
  "Are you the king of the Jews?"
Jesus said,

*shorter version: governor, Pontius Pilate, who

"You say so."
And when he was accused by the chief
    priests and elders,
    he made no answer.
Then Pilate said to him,
    "Do you not hear how many things they
        are testifying against you?"
But he did not answer him one word,
    so that the governor was greatly amazed.

Now on the occasion of the feast
    the governor was accustomed to release to
        the crowd
    one prisoner whom they wished.
And at that time they had a notorious
    prisoner called Barabbas.
So when they had assembled, Pilate said to
    them,
    "Which one do you want me to release to you,
    Barabbas, or Jesus called Christ?"
For he knew that it was out of envy
    that they had handed him over.
While he was still seated on the bench,
    his wife sent him a message,
    "Have nothing to do with that righteous
        man.
I suffered much in a dream today because of
    him."
The chief priests and the elders persuaded
    the crowds
    to ask for Barabbas but to destroy Jesus.
The governor said to them in reply,
    "Which of the two do you want me to
        release to you?"
They answered,
    "Barabbas!"
Pilate said to them,
    "Then what shall I do with Jesus called
        Christ?"

They all said,
    "Let him be crucified!"
But he said,
    "Why? What evil has he done?"
They only shouted the louder,
    "Let him be crucified!"
When Pilate saw that he was not succeeding
       at all,
    but that a riot was breaking out instead,
    he took water and washed his hands in the
        sight of the crowd, saying,
    "I am innocent of this man's blood.
Look to it yourselves."
And the whole people said in reply,
    "His blood be upon us and upon our
        children."
Then he released Barabbas to them,
    but after he had Jesus scourged,
    he handed him over to be crucified.

Then the soldiers of the governor took Jesus
       inside the praetorium
    and gathered the whole cohort around him.
They stripped off his clothes
    and threw a scarlet military cloak about
       him.
Weaving a crown out of thorns, they placed it
       on his head,
    and a reed in his right hand.
And kneeling before him, they mocked him,
       saying,
    "Hail, King of the Jews!"
They spat upon him and took the reed
    and kept striking him on the head.
And when they had mocked him,
    they stripped him of the cloak,
    dressed him in his own clothes,
    and led him off to crucify him.

As they were going out, they met a Cyrenian
       named Simon;

this man they pressed into service
to carry his cross.

And when they came to a place called
Golgotha
—which means Place of the Skull—,
they gave Jesus wine to drink mixed with
gall.
But when he had tasted it, he refused to drink.
After they had crucified him,
they divided his garments by casting lots;
then they sat down and kept watch over
him there.
And they placed over his head the written
charge against him:
This is Jesus, the King of the Jews.
Two revolutionaries were crucified with him,
one on his right and the other on his left.
Those passing by reviled him, shaking their
heads and saying,
"You who would destroy the temple and
rebuild it in three days,
save yourself, if you are the Son of God,
and come down from the cross!"
Likewise the chief priests with the scribes
and elders mocked him and said,
"He saved others; he cannot save himself.
So he is the king of Israel!
Let him come down from the cross now,
and we will believe in him.
He trusted in God;
let him deliver him now if he wants him.
For he said, 'I am the Son of God.'"
The revolutionaries who were crucified with
him
also kept abusing him in the same way.

From noon onward, darkness came over the
whole land
until three in the afternoon.

And about three o'clock Jesus cried out in a
 loud voice,
 "Eli, Eli, lema sabachthani?"
 which means,
 "My God, my God, why have you forsaken
 me?"
Some of the bystanders who heard it said,
 "This one is calling for Elijah."
Immediately one of them ran to get a sponge;
 he soaked it in wine, and putting it on a
 reed,
 gave it to him to drink.
But the rest said,
 "Wait, let us see if Elijah comes to save
 him."
But Jesus cried out again in a loud voice,
 and gave up his spirit.

 Here all kneel and pause for a hort time.

And behold, the veil of the sanctuary
 was torn in two from top to bottom.
The earth quaked, rocks were split, tombs
 were opened,
 and the bodies of many saints who had
 fallen asleep were raised.
And coming forth from their tombs after his
 resurrection,
 they entered the holy city and appeared to
 many.
The centurion and the men with him who
 were keeping watch over Jesus
 feared greatly when they saw the
 earthquake
 and all that was happening, and they said,
 "Truly, this was the Son of God!"]
There were many women there, looking on
 from a distance,
 who had followed Jesus from Galilee,
 ministering to him.

Among them were Mary Magdalene and
    Mary the mother of James and Joseph,
  and the mother of the sons of Zebedee.

When it was evening,
    there came a rich man from Arimathea
        named Joseph,
    who was himself a disciple of Jesus.
He went to Pilate and asked for the body of
    Jesus;
    then Pilate ordered it to be handed over.
Taking the body, Joseph wrapped it in clean
    linen
    and laid it in his new tomb that he had
        hewn in the rock.
Then he rolled a huge stone across the
    entrance to the tomb and departed.
But Mary Magdalene and the other Mary
    remained sitting there, facing the tomb.

The next day, the one following the day of
    preparation,
    the chief priests and the Pharisees
    gathered before Pilate and said,
    "Sir, we remember that this impostor while
        still alive said,
    'After three days I will be raised up.'
Give orders, then, that the grave be secured
    until the third day,
    lest his disciples come and steal him and
        say to the people,
    'He has been raised from the dead.'
This last imposture would be worse than the
    first."
Pilate said to them,
    "The guard is yours;
    go, secure it as best you can."
So they went and secured the tomb
    by fixing a seal to the stone and setting the
        guard.

Preparing to Proclaim

Key words and phrases: "I have given you a model to follow, so that as I have done for you, you should also do."

To the point: On this day when we so wholeheartedly celebrate the institution of the Eucharist, the gospel does not tell that story (although we do hear it in the second reading). It serves as a reminder that our eucharistic lives do not end in the celebration of the Mass; they rather begin there. We are sent out, dismissed to do the work that Jesus models here. Our communion is consummated by acts of service and love.

Making Connections

The Triduum call can be summed up in one word: love. To live in remembrance of Jesus is to love with our whole bodies. The Son of God models the messy movements of love during the Last Supper when he stoops to scrub the feet of his disciples. As we journey through the Triduum, we will see the stakes of Christ's love rise higher and higher. To love in the face of death, to love in the hope of new life—indeed, the love of Christ knows no bounds. Neither should our love. Jesus shows us the way during these most sacred days. Nourished at his table, may we embody Christ's love to the ends of the earth.

Prayer

Servant God,
you show us that to love is to serve,
and that unity with you is sacrifice.
Our blessing-cup is a communion with the
blood of Christ.
As you drank the cup, let us also,
that in your blood we may come to know
your radical self-emptying love.
Amen.

These instructions were given by God so that the families of Israel might escape the wrath of the Lord. How carefully would you read them if you had one chance to understand them in order to protect your family?

This is the seriousness and clarity you need to convey when reading this passage.

First Reading (Exod 12:1-8, 11-14)

A reading from the Book of Exodus

The LORD said to Moses and Aaron in the land
of Egypt,
"This month shall stand at the head of
your calendar;
you shall reckon it the first month of the
year.
Tell the whole community of Israel:
On the tenth of this month every one of
your families
must procure for itself a lamb, one apiece
for each household.
If a family is too small for a whole lamb,
it shall join the nearest household in
procuring one
and shall share in the lamb
in proportion to the number of persons
who partake of it.
The lamb must be a year-old male and
without blemish.
You may take it from either the sheep or the
goats.
You shall keep it until the fourteenth day of
this month,
and then, with the whole assembly of
Israel present,

it shall be slaughtered during the evening
twilight.
They shall take some of its blood
and apply it to the two doorposts and the
lintel
of every house in which they partake of
the lamb.
That same night they shall eat its roasted flesh
with unleavened bread and bitter herbs.

"This is how you are to eat it:
with your loins girt, sandals on your feet
and your staff in hand,
you shall eat like those who are in flight.
It is the Passover of the LORD.
For on this same night I will go through Egypt,
striking down every firstborn of the land,
both man and beast,
and executing judgment on all the gods of
Egypt—I, the LORD!
But the blood will mark the houses where you
are.
Seeing the blood, I will pass over you;
thus, when I strike the land of Egypt,
no destructive blow will come upon you.

"This day shall be a memorial feast for you,
which all your generations shall celebrate
with pilgrimage to the LORD, as a perpetual
institution."

Responsorial Psalm (Ps 116:12-13, 15-16bc, 17-18)

R︲. (cf. 1 Cor 10:16) Our blessing-cup is a
communion with the Blood of Christ.

How shall I make a return to the LORD
for all the good he has done for me?
The cup of salvation I will take up,
and I will call upon the name of the LORD.

R︲. Our blessing-cup is a communion with the
Blood of Christ.

Precious in the eyes of the LORD
is the death of his faithful ones.
I am your servant, the son of your handmaid;
you have loosed my bonds.

R̸. Our blessing-cup is a communion with the Blood of Christ.

To you will I offer sacrifice of thanksgiving,
and I will call upon the name of the LORD.
My vows to the LORD I will pay
in the presence of all his people.

R̸. Our blessing-cup is a communion with the Blood of Christ.

Pronunciation
Corinthians
kawr-IHN-thee-uhnz

Paul writes here what we recall every time we celebrate Mass. What degree of reverence is appropriate for such a reading? Carry this energy all the way through to the last word.

Second Reading (1 Cor 11:23-26)

A reading from the first Letter of Saint Paul to the Corinthians

Brothers and sisters:
I received from the Lord what I also handed
on to you,
that the Lord Jesus, on the night he was
handed over,
took bread, and, after he had given thanks,
broke it and said, "This is my body that is
for you.
Do this in remembrance of me."
In the same way also the cup, after supper,
saying,
"This cup is the new covenant in my blood.
Do this, as often as you drink it, in
remembrance of me."
For as often as you eat this bread and drink
the cup,
you proclaim the death of the Lord until he
comes.

Gospel (John 13:1-15; L39ABC)

A reading from the holy Gospel according to John

Before the feast of Passover, Jesus knew that
    his hour had come
    to pass from this world to the Father.
He loved his own in the world and he loved
    them to the end.
The devil had already induced Judas, son of
    Simon the Iscariot, to hand him over.
So, during supper,
    fully aware that the Father had put
        everything into his power
    and that he had come from God and was
        returning to God,
    he rose from supper and took off his outer
        garments.
He took a towel and tied it around his waist.
Then he poured water into a basin
    and began to wash the disciples' feet
    and dry them with the towel around his
        waist.
He came to Simon Peter, who said to him,
    "Master, are you going to wash my feet?"
Jesus answered and said to him,
    "What I am doing, you do not understand
        now,
    but you will understand later."
Peter said to him, "You will never wash my
    feet."
Jesus answered him,
    "Unless I wash you, you will have no
        inheritance with me."
Simon Peter said to him,
    "Master, then not only my feet, but my
        hands and head as well."
Jesus said to him,
    "Whoever has bathed has no need except
        to have his feet washed,
    for he is clean all over;

Pronunciation
Iscariot
    ihs-KEHR-ee-uht

Daring to state the obvious, the last two sentences are arguably the most important in this reading.

Make sure your energy leads up to: "Do you realize what I have done for you?" and then really deliver the lines that follow.

131

so you are clean, but not all."
For he knew who would betray him;
> for this reason, he said, "Not all of you are
> > clean."

So when he had washed their feet
> and put his garments back on and reclined
> > at table again,
> he said to them, "Do you realize what I
> > have done for you?
You call me 'teacher' and 'master,' and rightly
> so, for indeed I am.
If I, therefore, the master and teacher, have
> washed your feet,
> you ought to wash one another's feet.
I have given you a model to follow,
> so that as I have done for you, you should
> > also do."

Preparing to Proclaim
Key words and phrases: "It is finished."

To the point: John's version of the passion is replete with promises fulfilled; he likes to remind us that Jesus's death is a realization of Scripture. He also portrays Jesus as more divine than human; here, Jesus is calm and in control, responding with enviable tranquility to the chaos around him. While the story is not yet over—we have yet to see the resurrection and ascension—he is already acting as the king Pilate will name him as, sovereign over the world even as evil rages in very close proximity to him.

Making Connections
The Son of God suffers. On this Good Friday, the church slows down to be present to the incredible gift Jesus gives the world: his very self. Today the Word made flesh, the all-powerful one born of the Father before all ages, gets whipped. He gets spat at and mocked. He gets nailed to the cross. Today we listen as our Savior cries out in agony. We kneel in reverence as he breathes his last breath. Soon, our Savior will rise again. But for today, we carry the grief of death. We lament the sin and evil that brought Christ to this place. We mourn the countless people who face similar fates in our world today.

Prayer

God, Silenced for Us,
your passion and death teach us
that our words mean nothing if not lived,
and that our lives must take as example
your sacrifice, your everlasting covenant.
May then our only words today be these:
into your hands I commend my spirit.
Bring us into greater union with you.
Amen.

Here the prophet Isaiah is foretelling the death of Jesus! Yes, indeed Isaiah was a true prophet.

A strong but solemn voice is appropriate for this reading. Carry the energy through to the end of every line. Take a decent pause between sections.

First Reading (Isa 52:13–53:12)

A reading from the Book of the Prophet Isaiah

See, my servant shall prosper,
    he shall be raised high and greatly exalted.
Even as many were amazed at him—
    so marred was his look beyond human
        semblance
    and his appearance beyond that of the
        sons of man—
so shall he startle many nations,
    because of him kings shall stand
        speechless;
for those who have not been told shall see,
    those who have not heard shall ponder it.

Who would believe what we have heard?
    To whom has the arm of the LORD been
        revealed?
He grew up like a sapling before him,
    like a shoot from the parched earth;
there was in him no stately bearing to make
        us look at him,
    nor appearance that would attract us to
        him.
He was spurned and avoided by people,
    a man of suffering, accustomed to
        infirmity,

one of those from whom people hide their
    faces,
      spurned, and we held him in no esteem.

Yet it was our infirmities that he bore,
    our sufferings that he endured,
while we thought of him as stricken,
    as one smitten by God and afflicted.
But he was pierced for our offenses,
    crushed for our sins;
upon him was the chastisement that makes us
    whole,
    by his stripes we were healed.
We had all gone astray like sheep,
    each following his own way;
but the LORD laid upon him
    the guilt of us all.

Though he was harshly treated, he submitted
    and opened not his mouth;
like a lamb led to the slaughter
    or a sheep before the shearers,
    he was silent and opened not his mouth.
Oppressed and condemned, he was taken
    away,
    and who would have thought any more of
    his destiny?
When he was cut off from the land of the
    living,
    and smitten for the sin of his people,
a grave was assigned him among the wicked
    and a burial place with evildoers,
though he had done no wrong
    nor spoken any falsehood.
But the LORD was pleased
    to crush him in infirmity.

If he gives his life as an offering for sin,
    he shall see his descendants in a long life,
    and the will of the LORD shall be
    accomplished through him.

Because of his affliction
 he shall see the light in fullness of days;
through his suffering, my servant shall justify
  many,
 and their guilt he shall bear.
Therefore I will give him his portion among
  the great,
 and he shall divide the spoils with the
  mighty,
because he surrendered himself to death
 and was counted among the wicked;
and he shall take away the sins of many,
 and win pardon for their offenses.

Responsorial Psalm (Ps 31:2, 6, 12-13, 15-16, 17, 25)

R̸. (Luke 23:46) Father, into your hands I commend my spirit.

In you, O Lord, I take refuge;
 let me never be put to shame.
In your justice rescue me.
Into your hands I commend my spirit;
 you will redeem me, O Lord, O faithful God.

R̸. Father, into your hands I commend my spirit.

For all my foes I am an object of reproach,
 a laughingstock to my neighbors, and a
  dread to my friends;
 they who see me abroad flee from me.
I am forgotten like the unremembered dead;
 I am like a dish that is broken.

R̸. Father, into your hands I commend my spirit.

But my trust is in you, O Lord;
 I say, "You are my God.
In your hands is my destiny; rescue me
 from the clutches of my enemies and my
  persecutors."

R⁊. Father, into your hands I commend my spirit.

Let your face shine upon your servant;
    save me in your kindness.
Take courage and be stouthearted,
    all you who hope in the LORD.

R⁊. Father, into your hands I commend my spirit.

Second Reading (Heb 4:14-16; 5:7-9)

A reading from the Letter to the Hebrews

Brothers and sisters:
Since we have a great high priest who has
      passed through the heavens,
    Jesus, the Son of God,
    let us hold fast to our confession.
For we do not have a high priest
    who is unable to sympathize with our
      weaknesses,
    but one who has similarly been tested in
      every way,
    yet without sin.
So let us confidently approach the throne of
      grace
    to receive mercy and to find grace for
      timely help.

In the days when Christ was in the flesh,
    he offered prayers and supplications with
      loud cries and tears
    to the one who was able to save him from
      death,
    and he was heard because of his reverence.
Son though he was, he learned obedience
    from what he suffered;
    and when he was made perfect,
    he became the source of eternal salvation
      for all who obey him.

Part 1: Jesus, our Lord, knows our human condition for he was once human himself. For that reason, don't be afraid to ask for his help and mercy. *Pause.*

Part 2: Jesus, when he was human, was obedient to his Father. Because of this, he was made perfect.

The bottom line: Do your best to be like Christ and you will live forever.

Pronunciation
Kidron   KIHD-ruhn
Pharisees   FEHR-ih-seez
Nazorean   NAZ-awr-een
Malchus   MAL-kuhz
Annas   AN-uhs
Caiaphas   KAY-uh-fuhs
praetorium
   pray-TAWR-ih-uhm
Barabbas
   beh-REH-buhs
Caesar   SEE-zer
Gabbatha   GAB-uh-thuh
Golgotha
   GAHL-guh-thuh
Clopas   KLO-pas
Magdala   MAG-duh-luh
Hyssop   HIH-suhp
Arimathea
   ehr-uh-muh-THEE-uh
Nicodemus
   nih-ko-DEE-muhs

As with the lengthy reading on Palm Sunday, make sure you have a glass of water near you, if possible, during your delivery.

Break the reading into parts or episodes, taking a decent pause between each to catch your breath and let the listeners prepare to hear the next portion of the reading.

Gospel   (John 18:1–19:42; L40ABC)

A reading from the holy Gospel according to John

Jesus went out with his disciples across the Kidron valley
   to where there was a garden,
   into which he and his disciples entered.
Judas his betrayer also knew the place,
   because Jesus had often met there with his disciples.
So Judas got a band of soldiers and guards
   from the chief priests and the Pharisees
   and went there with lanterns, torches, and weapons.
Jesus, knowing everything that was going to happen to him,
   went out and said to them, "Whom are you looking for?"
They answered him, "Jesus the Nazorean."
He said to them, "I AM."
Judas his betrayer was also with them.
When he said to them, "I AM,"
   they turned away and fell to the ground.
So he again asked them,
   "Whom are you looking for?"
They said, "Jesus the Nazorean."
Jesus answered,
   "I told you that I AM.
So if you are looking for me, let these men go."
This was to fulfill what he had said,
   "I have not lost any of those you gave me."
Then Simon Peter, who had a sword, drew it,
   struck the high priest's slave, and cut off his right ear.
The slave's name was Malchus.
Jesus said to Peter,
   "Put your sword into its scabbard.

Shall I not drink the cup that the Father gave
  me?"

So the band of soldiers, the tribune, and the
    Jewish guards seized Jesus,
  bound him, and brought him to Annas first.
He was the father-in-law of Caiaphas,
  who was high priest that year.
It was Caiaphas who had counseled the Jews
    that it was better that one man should die
      rather than the people.

Simon Peter and another disciple followed Jesus.
Now the other disciple was known to the high
    priest,
  and he entered the courtyard of the high
      priest with Jesus.
But Peter stood at the gate outside.
So the other disciple, the acquaintance of the
    high priest,
  went out and spoke to the gatekeeper and
      brought Peter in.
Then the maid who was the gatekeeper said
    to Peter,
  "You are not one of this man's disciples, are
      you?"
He said, "I am not."
Now the slaves and the guards were standing
    around a charcoal fire
  that they had made, because it was cold,
  and were warming themselves.
Peter was also standing there keeping warm.

The high priest questioned Jesus
  about his disciples and about his doctrine.
Jesus answered him,
  "I have spoken publicly to the world.
I have always taught in a synagogue
  or in the temple area where all the Jews
      gather,
  and in secret I have said nothing. Why ask
      me?

Ask those who heard me what I said to them.
They know what I said."
When he had said this,
  one of the temple guards standing there
      struck Jesus and said,
  "Is this the way you answer the high
      priest?"
Jesus answered him,
  "If I have spoken wrongly, testify to the
      wrong;
  but if I have spoken rightly, why do you
      strike me?"
Then Annas sent him bound to Caiaphas the
    high priest.

Now Simon Peter was standing there keeping
    warm.
And they said to him,
  "You are not one of his disciples, are you?"
He denied it and said,
  "I am not."
One of the slaves of the high priest,
  a relative of the one whose ear Peter had
      cut off, said,
  "Didn't I see you in the garden with him?"
Again Peter denied it.
And immediately the cock crowed.

Then they brought Jesus from Caiaphas to the
    praetorium.
It was morning.
And they themselves did not enter the
    praetorium,
  in order not to be defiled so that they could
      eat the Passover.
So Pilate came out to them and said,
  "What charge do you bring against this
      man?"
They answered and said to him,
  "If he were not a criminal,

we would not have handed him over to you."
At this, Pilate said to them,
"Take him yourselves, and judge him
according to your law."
The Jews answered him,
"We do not have the right to execute
anyone,"
in order that the word of Jesus might be
fulfilled
that he said indicating the kind of death he
would die.
So Pilate went back into the praetorium
and summoned Jesus and said to him,
"Are you the King of the Jews?"
Jesus answered,
"Do you say this on your own
or have others told you about me?"
Pilate answered,
"I am not a Jew, am I?
Your own nation and the chief priests handed
you over to me.
What have you done?"
Jesus answered,
"My kingdom does not belong to this
world.
If my kingdom did belong to this world,
my attendants would be fighting
to keep me from being handed over to the
Jews.
But as it is, my kingdom is not here."
So Pilate said to him,
"Then you are a king?"
Jesus answered,
"You say I am a king.
For this I was born and for this I came into
the world,
to testify to the truth.
Everyone who belongs to the truth listens to
my voice."
Pilate said to him, "What is truth?"

When he had said this,
he again went out to the Jews and said to
them,
"I find no guilt in him.
But you have a custom that I release one
prisoner to you at Passover.
Do you want me to release to you the King of
the Jews?"
They cried out again,
"Not this one but Barabbas!"
Now Barabbas was a revolutionary.

Then Pilate took Jesus and had him scourged.
And the soldiers wove a crown out of thorns
and placed it on his head,
and clothed him in a purple cloak,
and they came to him and said,
"Hail, King of the Jews!"
And they struck him repeatedly.
Once more Pilate went out and said to them,
"Look, I am bringing him out to you,
so that you may know that I find no guilt in
him."
So Jesus came out,
wearing the crown of thorns and the
purple cloak.
And he said to them, "Behold, the man!"
When the chief priests and the guards saw
him they cried out,
"Crucify him, crucify him!"
Pilate said to them,
"Take him yourselves and crucify him.
I find no guilt in him."
The Jews answered,
"We have a law, and according to that law
he ought to die,
because he made himself the Son of God."
Now when Pilate heard this statement,
he became even more afraid,

and went back into the praetorium and
said to Jesus,
"Where are you from?"
Jesus did not answer him.
So Pilate said to him,
"Do you not speak to me?
Do you not know that I have power to release
you
and I have power to crucify you?"
Jesus answered him,
"You would have no power over me
if it had not been given to you from above.
For this reason the one who handed me over
to you
has the greater sin."
Consequently, Pilate tried to release him; but
the Jews cried out,
"If you release him, you are not a Friend of
Caesar.
Everyone who makes himself a king opposes
Caesar."

When Pilate heard these words he brought
Jesus out
and seated him on the judge's bench
in the place called Stone Pavement, in
Hebrew, Gabbatha.
It was preparation day for Passover, and it
was about noon.
And he said to the Jews,
"Behold, your king!"
They cried out,
"Take him away, take him away! Crucify
him!"
Pilate said to them,
"Shall I crucify your king?"
The chief priests answered,
"We have no king but Caesar."
Then he handed him over to them to be
crucified.

So they took Jesus, and, carrying the cross himself,
> he went out to what is called the Place of the Skull,
> in Hebrew, Golgotha.
There they crucified him, and with him two others,
> one on either side, with Jesus in the middle.
Pilate also had an inscription written and put on the cross.
It read,
> "Jesus the Nazorean, the King of the Jews."
Now many of the Jews read this inscription,
> because the place where Jesus was crucified was near the city;
> and it was written in Hebrew, Latin, and Greek.
So the chief priests of the Jews said to Pilate,
> "Do not write 'The King of the Jews,'
> but that he said, 'I am the King of the Jews.'"
Pilate answered,
> "What I have written, I have written."

When the soldiers had crucified Jesus,
> they took his clothes and divided them into four shares,
> a share for each soldier.
They also took his tunic, but the tunic was seamless,
> woven in one piece from the top down.
So they said to one another,
> "Let's not tear it, but cast lots for it to see whose it will be,"
> in order that the passage of Scripture might be fulfilled that says:
> > *They divided my garments among them,*
> > *and for my vesture they cast lots.*
This is what the soldiers did.

Standing by the cross of Jesus were his mother
and his mother's sister, Mary the wife of
Clopas,
and Mary of Magdala.
When Jesus saw his mother and the disciple
there whom he loved
he said to his mother, "Woman, behold,
your son."
Then he said to the disciple,
"Behold, your mother."
And from that hour the disciple took her into
his home.

After this, aware that everything was now
finished,
in order that the Scripture might be
fulfilled,
Jesus said, "I thirst."
There was a vessel filled with common wine.
So they put a sponge soaked in wine on a
sprig of hyssop
and put it up to his mouth.
When Jesus had taken the wine, he said,
"It is finished."
And bowing his head, he handed over the
spirit.

Here all kneel and pause for a short time.

Now since it was preparation day,
in order that the bodies might not remain
on the cross on the sabbath,
for the sabbath day of that week was a
solemn one,
the Jews asked Pilate that their legs be
broken
and that they be taken down.
So the soldiers came and broke the legs of the
first
and then of the other one who was
crucified with Jesus.

But when they came to Jesus and saw that he
was already dead,
they did not break his legs,
but one soldier thrust his lance into his side,
and immediately blood and water flowed out.
An eyewitness has testified, and his testimony
is true;
he knows that he is speaking the truth,
so that you also may come to believe.
For this happened so that the Scripture
passage might be fulfilled:
Not a bone of it will be broken.
And again another passage says:
*They will look upon him whom they have
pierced.*

After this, Joseph of Arimathea,
secretly a disciple of Jesus for fear of the
Jews,
asked Pilate if he could remove the body of
Jesus.
And Pilate permitted it.
So he came and took his body.
Nicodemus, the one who had first come to him
at night,
also came bringing a mixture of myrrh and
aloes
weighing about one hundred pounds.
They took the body of Jesus
and bound it with burial cloths along with
the spices,
according to the Jewish burial custom.
Now in the place where he had been crucified
there was a garden,
and in the garden a new tomb, in which no
one had yet been buried.
So they laid Jesus there because of the Jewish
preparation day;
for the tomb was close by.

Preparing to Proclaim

Key words and phrases: "[He] has been raised from the dead."

To the point: This empty tomb narrative has more drama than any of the others. Rather than quietly finding the stone already rolled away, the women feel an earthquake and actually witness an angel descend to move it aside. They also get to see Jesus as they leave the tomb, another departure from the other Synoptics that leave Jesus's appearance for later. The women leave the tomb feeling both fear and joy; there is room for both of these in a response to the resurrection. This drama is appropriate in this great narrative that changes the whole world.

Making Connections

This is the night! In Matthew's resurrection account, Jesus meets Mary Magdalene and the other Mary on the road. The two women are on their way to share news of Jesus's resurrection to the disciples. Women—who have been marginalized and discounted since the beginning—are the first people entrusted with preaching the good news. Generations of women and others followed Mary Magdalene and the other Mary's lead. As we rejoice in tonight's great feast of victory, let us be thankful for the witnesses of these first evangelizers. Let us also be emboldened to share the good news in our own communities.

Pronunciation
Genesis   JEHN-uh-sihs

Is there a better-known Scripture passage? Yes, you must read it as though it was written yesterday with all the joy and awe you can muster.

Relish the transition of each day: "Thus evening came, and morning followed—the ____ day." This is not just a simple, boring accounting of the days but a miraculous happening with incredible anticipation for the *next* wonderful day.

Prayer

Living, Risen Lord,
death is defeated, the grave is conquered!
There is no greater good news than this!
May our gratitude know no bounds,
and with zeal and sacred fervor may we al-
    ways proclaim:
Alleluia! Give thanks to the Lord for he is good!
Love is living, now and forever!
Amen.

First Reading (Gen 1:1–2:2 [or 1:1, 26-31a])

A reading from the Book of Genesis

[In the beginning, when God created the
    heavens and the earth,]
    the earth was a formless wasteland, and
        darkness covered the abyss,
    while a mighty wind swept over the waters.

Then God said,
    "Let there be light," and there was light.
God saw how good the light was.
God then separated the light from the
    darkness.
God called the light "day," and the darkness
    he called "night."
Thus evening came, and morning followed—
    the first day.

Then God said,
    "Let there be a dome in the middle of the
        waters,
    to separate one body of water from the
        other."
And so it happened:
    God made the dome,
    and it separated the water above the dome
        from the water below it.
God called the dome "the sky."

Evening came, and morning followed—the
    second day.

Then God said,
    "Let the water under the sky be gathered
        into a single basin,
    so that the dry land may appear."
And so it happened:
    the water under the sky was gathered into
        its basin,
    and the dry land appeared.
God called the dry land "the earth,"
    and the basin of the water he called "the
        sea."
God saw how good it was.
Then God said,
    "Let the earth bring forth vegetation:
    every kind of plant that bears seed
    and every kind of fruit tree on earth
    that bears fruit with its seed in it."
And so it happened:
    the earth brought forth every kind of plant
        that bears seed
    and every kind of fruit tree on earth
    that bears fruit with its seed in it.
God saw how good it was.
Evening came, and morning followed—the
    third day.

Then God said:
    "Let there be lights in the dome of the sky,
    to separate day from night.
Let them mark the fixed times, the days and
        the years,
    and serve as luminaries in the dome of the
        sky,
    to shed light upon the earth."
And so it happened:
    God made the two great lights,
    the greater one to govern the day,
    and the lesser one to govern the night;

and he made the stars.
God set them in the dome of the sky,
    to shed light upon the earth,
    to govern the day and the night,
    and to separate the light from the darkness.
God saw how good it was.
Evening came, and morning followed—the
    fourth day.

Then God said,
    "Let the water teem with an abundance of
        living creatures,
    and on the earth let birds fly beneath the
        dome of the sky."
And so it happened:
    God created the great sea monsters
    and all kinds of swimming creatures with
        which the water teems,
    and all kinds of winged birds.
God saw how good it was, and God blessed
    them, saying,
    "Be fertile, multiply, and fill the water of
        the seas;
    and let the birds multiply on the earth."
Evening came, and morning followed—the
    fifth day.

Then God said,
    "Let the earth bring forth all kinds of
        living creatures:
    cattle, creeping things, and wild animals of
        all kinds."
And so it happened:
    God made all kinds of wild animals, all
        kinds of cattle,
    and all kinds of creeping things of the
        earth.
God saw how good it was.
Then [God said:

"Let us make man in our image, after our
likeness.
Let them have dominion over the fish of the
sea,
the birds of the air, and the cattle,
and over all the wild animals
and all the creatures that crawl on the
ground."
God created man in his image;
in the image of God he created him;
male and female he created them.
God blessed them, saying:
"Be fertile and multiply;
fill the earth and subdue it.
Have dominion over the fish of the sea, the
birds of the air,
and all the living things that move on the
earth."
God also said:
"See, I give you every seed-bearing plant
all over the earth
and every tree that has seed-bearing fruit
on it to be your food;
and to all the animals of the land, all the
birds of the air,
and all the living creatures that crawl on
the ground,
I give all the green plants for food."
And so it happened.
God looked at everything he had made, and
he found it very good.]
Evening came, and morning followed—the
sixth day.

Thus the heavens and the earth and all their
array were completed.
Since on the seventh day God was finished
with the work he had been doing,
he rested on the seventh day from all the
work he had undertaken.

Responsorial Psalm (Ps 104:1-2, 5-6, 10, 12, 13-14, 24, 35)

R̸. (30) Lord, send out your Spirit, and renew the face of the earth.

Bless the LORD, O my soul!
    O LORD, my God, you are great indeed!
You are clothed with majesty and glory,
    robed in light as with a cloak.

R̸. Lord, send out your Spirit, and renew the face of the earth.

You fixed the earth upon its foundation,
    not to be moved forever;
with the ocean, as with a garment, you
        covered it;
    above the mountains the waters stood.

R̸. Lord, send out your Spirit, and renew the face of the earth.

You send forth springs into the watercourses
    that wind among the mountains.
Beside them the birds of heaven dwell;
    from among the branches they send forth
        their song.

R̸. Lord, send out your Spirit, and renew the face of the earth.

You water the mountains from your palace;
    the earth is replete with the fruit of your
        works.
You raise grass for the cattle,
    and vegetation for man's use,
producing bread from the earth.

R̸. Lord, send out your Spirit, and renew the face of the earth.

How manifold are your works, O LORD!
    In wisdom you have wrought them all—
the earth is full of your creatures.
    Bless the LORD, O my soul!

Ry. Lord, send out your Spirit, and renew the face of the earth.

or

Ps 33:4-5, 6-7, 12-13, 20 and 22

Ry. (5b) The earth is full of the goodness of the Lord.

Upright is the word of the LORD,
   and all his works are trustworthy.
He loves justice and right;
   of the kindness of the LORD the earth is full.

Ry. The earth is full of the goodness of the Lord.

By the word of the LORD the heavens were
      made;
   by the breath of his mouth all their host.
He gathers the waters of the sea as in a flask;
   in cellars he confines the deep.

Ry. The earth is full of the goodness of the Lord.

Blessed the nation whose God is the LORD,
   the people he has chosen for his own
         inheritance.
From heaven the LORD looks down;
   he sees all mankind.

Ry. The earth is full of the goodness of the Lord.

Our soul waits for the LORD,
   who is our help and our shield.
May your kindness, O LORD, be upon us
   who have put our hope in you.

Ry. The earth is full of the goodness of the Lord.

Second Reading (Gen 22:1-18 [or 22:1-2, 9a, 10-13, 15-18] [or 1 Cor 5:6b-8])

A reading from the Book of Genesis

God put Abraham to the test.
He called to him, "Abraham!"
"Here I am," he replied.
Then God said:

Pronunciation
Genesis   JEHN-uh-sihs
Moriah   maw-RAI-uh
Yahweh-yireh
   YAH-weh-yer-AY

This reading easily lends
itself to be read by four

people. God might be read by an elderly person with a rich voice. Abraham and Isaac can be a father and son, which leaves the voice of the narrator and the angel.

Do not hold back on the emotion of this reading! Imagine what is happening here and let it energize your execution.

"Take your son Isaac, your only one, whom you love,
and go to the land of Moriah.
There you shall offer him up as a holocaust
on a height that I will point out to you."]
Early the next morning Abraham saddled his donkey,
took with him his son Isaac and two of his servants as well,
and with the wood that he had cut for the holocaust,
set out for the place of which God had told him.

On the third day Abraham got sight of the place from afar.
Then he said to his servants:
"Both of you stay here with the donkey,
while the boy and I go on over yonder.
We will worship and then come back to you."
Thereupon Abraham took the wood for the holocaust
and laid it on his son Isaac's shoulders,
while he himself carried the fire and the knife.
As the two walked on together, Isaac spoke to his father Abraham:
"Father!" Isaac said.
"Yes, son," he replied.
Isaac continued, "Here are the fire and the wood,
but where is the sheep for the holocaust?"
"Son," Abraham answered,
"God himself will provide the sheep for the holocaust."
Then the two continued going forward.

[When they came to the place of which God had told him,
Abraham built an altar there and arranged the wood on it.]

Next he tied up his son Isaac,
    and put him on top of the wood on the
        altar.
[Then he reached out and took the knife to
    slaughter his son.
But the LORD's messenger called to him from
    heaven,
    "Abraham, Abraham!"
"Here I am," he answered.
"Do not lay your hand on the boy," said the
    messenger.
"Do not do the least thing to him.
I know now how devoted you are to God,
    since you did not withhold from me your
        own beloved son."
As Abraham looked about,
    he spied a ram caught by its horns in the
        thicket.
So he went and took the ram
    and offered it up as a holocaust in place of
        his son.]
Abraham named the site Yahweh-yireh;
    hence people now say, "On the mountain
        the LORD will see."

[Again the LORD's messenger called to
    Abraham from heaven and said:
    "I swear by myself, declares the LORD,
    that because you acted as you did
    in not withholding from me your beloved
        son,
  I will bless you abundantly
    and make your descendants as countless
    as the stars of the sky and the sands of the
        seashore;
    your descendants shall take possession
    of the gates of their enemies,
    and in your descendants all the nations of
        the earth
      shall find blessing—
    all this because you obeyed my command."]

Responsorial Psalm (Ps 16:5, 8, 9-10, 11)

℟. (1) You are my inheritance, O Lord.

O LORD, my allotted portion and my cup,
  you it is who hold fast my lot.
I set the LORD ever before me;
    with him at my right hand I shall not be
      disturbed.

℟. You are my inheritance, O Lord.

Therefore my heart is glad and my soul
    rejoices,
  my body, too, abides in confidence;
because you will not abandon my soul to the
    netherworld,
    nor will you suffer your faithful one to
      undergo corruption.

℟. You are my inheritance, O Lord.

You will show me the path to life,
  fullness of joys in your presence,
    the delights at your right hand forever.

℟. You are my inheritance, O Lord.

Pronunciation
Pharaoh   FEHR-o

If you don't find this to be
a thrilling reading, then
you have missed its
drama completely.
  1. The Israelites are
  trapped against the sea
  and Pharaoh's army is
  in pursuit.
  2. Moses parts the sea.
  (Seriously? Yes, really!)
  The Israelites walk to
  freedom.
  3. Pharaoh's army fol-
  lows them. What

Third Reading (Exod 14:15–15:1)

A reading from the Book of Exodus

The LORD said to Moses, "Why are you crying
    out to me?
Tell the Israelites to go forward.
And you, lift up your staff and, with hand
    outstretched over the sea,
  split the sea in two,
    that the Israelites may pass through it on
      dry land.
But I will make the Egyptians so obstinate
    that they will go in after them.
Then I will receive glory through Pharaoh
    and all his army,
  his chariots and charioteers.

The Egyptians shall know that I am the LORD,
  when I receive glory through Pharaoh
  and his chariots and charioteers."

The angel of God, who had been leading
    Israel's camp,
  now moved and went around behind them.
The column of cloud also, leaving the front,
  took up its place behind them,
    so that it came between the camp of the
      Egyptians
  and that of Israel.
But the cloud now became dark, and thus the
    night passed
  without the rival camps coming any closer
    together all night long.
Then Moses stretched out his hand over the
    sea,
  and the LORD swept the sea
  with a strong east wind throughout the
    night
  and so turned it into dry land.
When the water was thus divided,
  the Israelites marched into the midst of the
    sea on dry land,
  with the water like a wall to their right and
    to their left.

The Egyptians followed in pursuit;
  all Pharaoh's horses and chariots and
    charioteers went after them
  right into the midst of the sea.
In the night watch just before dawn
  the LORD cast through the column of the
    fiery cloud
  upon the Egyptian force a glance that
    threw it into a panic;
  and he so clogged their chariot wheels
  that they could hardly drive.

happens? The sea flows back, completely destroying the entirety of Pharaoh's army.

Rehearse this out loud and increase the excitement as you get further into the story. Note: Pharaoh's "chariots" and "charioteers" is repeated five times. Why do you suppose that is? The writer wants the listener to know that *all* of Pharaoh's army was involved and destroyed.

157

With that the Egyptians sounded the retreat
before Israel,
because the LORD was fighting for them
against the Egyptians.

Then the LORD told Moses, "Stretch out your
hand over the sea,
that the water may flow back upon the
Egyptians,
upon their chariots and their charioteers."
So Moses stretched out his hand over the sea,
and at dawn the sea flowed back to its
normal depth.
The Egyptians were fleeing head on toward
the sea,
when the LORD hurled them into its midst.
As the water flowed back,
it covered the chariots and the charioteers
of Pharaoh's whole army
which had followed the Israelites into the
sea.
Not a single one of them escaped.
But the Israelites had marched on dry land
through the midst of the sea,
with the water like a wall to their right and
to their left.
Thus the LORD saved Israel on that day
from the power of the Egyptians.
When Israel saw the Egyptians lying dead on
the seashore
and beheld the great power that the LORD
had shown against the Egyptians,
they feared the LORD and believed in him
and in his servant Moses.

Then Moses and the Israelites sang this song
to the LORD:
I will sing to the LORD, for he is gloriously
triumphant;
horse and chariot he has cast into the sea.

Responsorial Psalm (Exod 15:1-2, 3-4, 5-6, 17-18)

R̝. (1b) Let us sing to the Lord; he has covered himself in glory.

I will sing to the LORD, for he is gloriously
    triumphant;
  horse and chariot he has cast into the sea.
My strength and my courage is the LORD,
  and he has been my savior.
He is my God, I praise him;
  the God of my father, I extol him.

R̝. Let us sing to the Lord; he has covered himself in glory.

The LORD is a warrior,
  LORD is his name!
Pharaoh's chariots and army he hurled into
    the sea;
  the elite of his officers were submerged in
    the Red Sea.

R̝. Let us sing to the Lord; he has covered himself in glory.

The flood waters covered them,
  they sank into the depths like a stone.
Your right hand, O LORD, magnificent in power,
  your right hand, O LORD, has shattered the
    enemy.

R̝. Let us sing to the Lord; he has covered himself in glory.

You brought in the people you redeemed
  and planted them on the mountain of your
    inheritance—
the place where you made your seat, O LORD,
  the sanctuary, LORD, which your hands
    established.
The LORD shall reign forever and ever.

R̝. Let us sing to the Lord; he has covered himself in glory.

Pronunciation
carnelians
    kahr-NEEL-yuhnz

Take a nice pause before, "For a brief moment . . ." Then, with a sorrowful delivery, read, "For a brief moment I abandoned you . . ." Then shift to a joyful delivery: "but with great tenderness I will take you back." Do the same with the next sentence.

Deliver the last part with great joy!

Fourth Reading (Isa 54:5-14)

A reading from the Book of the Prophet Isaiah

The One who has become your husband is
    your Maker;
    his name is the LORD of hosts;
your redeemer is the Holy One of Israel,
    called God of all the earth.
The LORD calls you back,
    like a wife forsaken and grieved in spirit,
    a wife married in youth and then cast off,
    says your God.
For a brief moment I abandoned you,
    but with great tenderness I will take you back.
In an outburst of wrath, for a moment
    I hid my face from you;
but with enduring love I take pity on you,
    says the LORD, your redeemer.
This is for me like the days of Noah,
    when I swore that the waters of Noah
    should never again deluge the earth;
so I have sworn not to be angry with you,
    or to rebuke you.
Though the mountains leave their place
    and the hills be shaken,
my love shall never leave you
    nor my covenant of peace be shaken,
    says the LORD, who has mercy on you.
O afflicted one, storm-battered and unconsoled,
    I lay your pavements in carnelians,
    and your foundations in sapphires;
I will make your battlements of rubies,
    your gates of carbuncles,
    and all your walls of precious stones.
All your children shall be taught by the LORD,
    and great shall be the peace of your children.
In justice shall you be established,
    far from the fear of oppression,
    where destruction cannot come near you.

Responsorial Psalm (Ps 30:2, 4, 5-6, 11-12, 13)

R̸. (2a) I will praise you, Lord, for you have rescued me.

I will extol you, O LORD, for you drew me clear
and did not let my enemies rejoice over me.
O LORD, you brought me up from the
netherworld;
you preserved me from among those going
down into the pit.

R̸. I will praise you, Lord, for you have rescued me.

Sing praise to the LORD, you his faithful ones,
and give thanks to his holy name.
For his anger lasts but a moment;
a lifetime, his good will.
At nightfall, weeping enters in,
but with the dawn, rejoicing.

R̸. I will praise you, Lord, for you have rescued me.

Hear, O LORD, and have pity on me;
O LORD, be my helper.
You changed my mourning into dancing;
O LORD, my God, forever will I give you
thanks.

R̸. I will praise you, Lord, for you have rescued me.

Fifth Reading (Isa 55:1-11)

A reading from the Book of the Prophet Isaiah

Thus says the LORD:
All you who are thirsty,
come to the water!
You who have no money,
come, receive grain and eat;
come, without paying and without cost,
drink wine and milk!
Why spend your money for what is not bread,

This reading has such *great* news!

In the very first part imagine the joy felt by those who have nothing being told that they have access to *everything.* And this is everything that is important and everlasting. This is the spirit in which

you should deliver this
reading.

your wages for what fails to satisfy?
Heed me, and you shall eat well,
    you shall delight in rich fare.
Come to me heedfully,
    listen, that you may have life.
I will renew with you the everlasting
        covenant,
    the benefits assured to David.
As I made him a witness to the peoples,
    a leader and commander of nations,
so shall you summon a nation you knew not,
    and nations that knew you not shall run to
        you,
because of the LORD, your God,
    the Holy One of Israel, who has glorified you.

Seek the LORD while he may be found,
    call him while he is near.
Let the scoundrel forsake his way,
    and the wicked man his thoughts;
let him turn to the LORD for mercy;
    to our God, who is generous in forgiving.
For my thoughts are not your thoughts,
    nor are your ways my ways, says the LORD.
As high as the heavens are above the earth,
    so high are my ways above your ways
    and my thoughts above your thoughts.

For just as from the heavens
    the rain and snow come down
and do not return there
    till they have watered the earth,
    making it fertile and fruitful,
giving seed to the one who sows
    and bread to the one who eats,
so shall my word be
    that goes forth from my mouth;
my word shall not return to me void,
    but shall do my will,
    achieving the end for which I sent it.

Responsorial Psalm (Isa 12:2-3, 4, 5-6)

R℣. (3) You will draw water joyfully from the springs of salvation.

God indeed is my savior;
  I am confident and unafraid.
My strength and my courage is the LORD,
  and he has been my savior.
With joy you will draw water
  at the fountain of salvation.

R℣. You will draw water joyfully from the springs of salvation.

Give thanks to the LORD, acclaim his name;
  among the nations make known his deeds,
  proclaim how exalted is his name.

R℣. You will draw water joyfully from the springs of salvation.

Sing praise to the LORD for his glorious
    achievement;
  let this be known throughout all the earth.
Shout with exultation, O city of Zion,
  for great in your midst
  is the Holy One of Israel!

R℣. You will draw water joyfully from the springs of salvation.

Sixth Reading (Bar 3:9-15, 32–4:4)

A reading from the Book of the Prophet Baruch

Hear, O Israel, the commandments of life:
  listen, and know prudence!
How is it, Israel,
  that you are in the land of your foes,
  grown old in a foreign land,
defiled with the dead,
  accounted with those destined for the
      netherworld?
You have forsaken the fountain of wisdom!

Pronunciation
Baruch   BEHR-ook

It is Israel's own fault that it has grown old in the land of its foes because "[y]ou have forsaken the fountain of wisdom!"— basically meaning, "Israel, wise up!" This line provides the shift of emotion.

The reading begins in a scolding voice and by the

163

close transitions to a pleading tone asking Jacob to turn and receive her: "walk by her light toward splendor."

Had you walked in the way of God,
　　you would have dwelt in enduring peace.
Learn where prudence is,
　　where strength, where understanding;
that you may know also
　　where are length of days, and life,
　　where light of the eyes, and peace.
Who has found the place of wisdom,
　　who has entered into her treasuries?

The One who knows all things knows her;
　　he has probed her by his knowledge—
the One who established the earth for all time,
　　and filled it with four-footed beasts;
　　he who dismisses the light, and it departs,
　　calls it, and it obeys him trembling;
before whom the stars at their posts
　　shine and rejoice;
when he calls them, they answer, "Here we
　　are!"
　　shining with joy for their Maker.
Such is our God;
　　no other is to be compared to him:
he has traced out the whole way of
　　　understanding,
　　and has given her to Jacob, his servant,
　　to Israel, his beloved son.

Since then she has appeared on earth,
　　and moved among people.
She is the book of the precepts of God,
　　the law that endures forever;
all who cling to her will live,
　　but those will die who forsake her.
Turn, O Jacob, and receive her:
　　walk by her light toward splendor.
Give not your glory to another,
　　your privileges to an alien race.
Blessed are we, O Israel;
　　for what pleases God is known to us!

Responsorial Psalm (Ps 19:8, 9, 10, 11)

℟. (John 6:68c) Lord, you have the words of everlasting life.

The law of the LORD is perfect,
   refreshing the soul;
the decree of the LORD is trustworthy,
   giving wisdom to the simple.

℟. Lord, you have the words of everlasting life.

The precepts of the LORD are right,
   rejoicing the heart;
the command of the LORD is clear,
   enlightening the eye.

℟. Lord, you have the words of everlasting life.

The fear of the LORD is pure,
   enduring forever;
the ordinances of the LORD are true,
   all of them just.

℟. Lord, you have the words of everlasting life.

They are more precious than gold,
   than a heap of purest gold;
sweeter also than syrup
   or honey from the comb.

℟. Lord, you have the words of everlasting life.

Seventh Reading (Ezek 36:16-17a, 18-28)

A reading from the Book of the Prophet Ezekiel

The word of the LORD came to me, saying:
   Son of man, when the house of Israel lived
      in their land,
   they defiled it by their conduct and deeds.
Therefore I poured out my fury upon them
   because of the blood that they poured out
      on the ground,
   and because they defiled it with idols.

Pronunciation
Ezekiel   eh-ZEE-kee-uhl

The repetition of "profaned" is purposeful and very serious. With each repetition it should be more profoundly pronounced.

The reading begins with a very dark voice but ends happily in great joy. Make sure you convey that shift in your voice.

I scattered them among the nations,
    dispersing them over foreign lands;
    according to their conduct and deeds I
        judged them.
But when they came among the nations
    wherever they came,
    they served to profane my holy name,
    because it was said of them: "These are the
        people of the LORD,
    yet they had to leave their land."
So I have relented because of my holy name
    which the house of Israel profaned
    among the nations where they came.
Therefore say to the house of Israel: Thus
        says the Lord GOD:
    Not for your sakes do I act, house of Israel,
    but for the sake of my holy name,
    which you profaned among the nations to
        which you came.
I will prove the holiness of my great name,
    profaned among the nations,
    in whose midst you have profaned it.
Thus the nations shall know that I am the
    LORD, says the Lord GOD,
    when in their sight I prove my holiness
        through you.
For I will take you away from among the nations,
    gather you from all the foreign lands,
    and bring you back to your own land.
I will sprinkle clean water upon you
    to cleanse you from all your impurities,
    and from all your idols I will cleanse you.
I will give you a new heart and place a new
        spirit within you,
    taking from your bodies your stony hearts
    and giving you natural hearts.
I will put my spirit within you and make you
        live by my statutes,
    careful to observe my decrees.

You shall live in the land I gave your fathers;
    you shall be my people, and I will be your
        God.

Responsorial Psalm (Ps 42:3, 5; 43:3, 4)

R̸. (42:2) Like a deer that longs for running
streams, my soul longs for you, my God.

Athirst is my soul for God, the living God.
    When shall I go and behold the face of
        God?

R̸. Like a deer that longs for running streams,
my soul longs for you, my God.

I went with the throng
    and led them in procession to the house of
        God,
amid loud cries of joy and thanksgiving,
    with the multitude keeping festival.

R̸. Like a deer that longs for running streams,
my soul longs for you, my God.

Send forth your light and your fidelity;
    they shall lead me on
and bring me to your holy mountain,
    to your dwelling-place.

R̸. Like a deer that longs for running streams,
my soul longs for you, my God.

Then will I go in to the altar of God,
    the God of my gladness and joy;
then will I give you thanks upon the harp,
    O God, my God!

R̸. Like a deer that longs for running streams,
my soul longs for you, my God.

or

Isa 12:2-3, 4bcd, 5-6

R₣. (3) You will draw water joyfully from the springs of salvation.

God indeed is my savior;
    I am confident and unafraid.
My strength and my courage is the Lord,
    and he has been my savior.
With joy you will draw water
    at the fountain of salvation.

R₣. You will draw water joyfully from the springs of salvation.

Give thanks to the Lord, acclaim his name;
    among the nations make known his deeds,
    proclaim how exalted is his name.

R₣. You will draw water joyfully from the springs of salvation.

Sing praise to the Lord for his glorious
    achievement;
    let this be known throughout all the earth.
Shout with exultation, O city of Zion,
    for great in your midst
    is the Holy One of Israel!

R₣. You will draw water joyfully from the springs of salvation.

or

Ps 51:12-13, 14-15, 18-19

R₣. (12a) Create a clean heart in me, O God.

A clean heart create for me, O God,
    and a steadfast spirit renew within me.
Cast me not out from your presence,
    and your Holy Spirit take not from me.

R₣. Create a clean heart in me, O God.

Give me back the joy of your salvation,
and a willing spirit sustain in me.
I will teach transgressors your ways,
and sinners shall return to you.

R̷. Create a clean heart in me, O God.

For you are not pleased with sacrifices;
should I offer a holocaust, you would not
accept it.
My sacrifice, O God, is a contrite spirit;
a heart contrite and humbled, O God, you
will not spurn.

R̷. Create a clean heart in me, O God.

Epistle (Rom 6:3-11)

A reading from the Letter of Saint Paul to
the Romans

Brothers and sisters:
Are you unaware that we who were baptized
into Christ Jesus
were baptized into his death?
We were indeed buried with him through
baptism into death,
so that, just as Christ was raised from the
dead
by the glory of the Father,
we too might live in newness of life.

For if we have grown into union with him
through a death like his,
we shall also be united with him in the
resurrection.
We know that our old self was crucified with
him,
so that our sinful body might be done away
with,
that we might no longer be in slavery to
sin.
For a dead person has been absolved from sin.

Take time to make sure
you understand what Paul
is saying so you can read
this passage with confi-
dence. This is great news!

Pause nicely between the
two sections, and after
"we shall also live with
him." Rehearse the places
where there are commas
and periods, and treat
them appropriately.

If, then, we have died with Christ,
>we believe that we shall also live with him.
We know that Christ, raised from the dead,
>>dies no more;
>death no longer has power over him.
As to his death, he died to sin once and for all;
>as to his life, he lives for God.
Consequently, you too must think of
>>yourselves as being dead to sin
>and living for God in Christ Jesus.

Responsorial Psalm (Ps 118:1-2, 16-17, 22-23)

R̦. Alleluia, alleluia, alleluia.

Give thanks to the LORD, for he is good,
>for his mercy endures forever.
Let the house of Israel say,
>"His mercy endures forever."

R̦. Alleluia, alleluia, alleluia.

The right hand of the LORD has struck with
>>power;
>the right hand of the LORD is exalted.
I shall not die, but live,
>and declare the works of the LORD.

R̦. Alleluia, alleluia, alleluia.

The stone which the builders rejected
>has become the cornerstone.
By the LORD has this been done;
>it is wonderful in our eyes.

R̦. Alleluia, alleluia, alleluia.

Gospel   (Matt 28:1-10; L41ABC)

A reading from the holy Gospel according
to Matthew

After the sabbath, as the first day of the week
was dawning,
Mary Magdalene and the other Mary came
to see the tomb.
And behold, there was a great earthquake;
for an angel of the Lord descended from
heaven,
approached, rolled back the stone, and sat
upon it.
His appearance was like lightning
and his clothing was white as snow.
The guards were shaken with fear of him
and became like dead men.
Then the angel said to the women in reply,
"Do not be afraid!
I know that you are seeking Jesus the
crucified.
He is not here, for he has been raised just as
he said.
Come and see the place where he lay.
Then go quickly and tell his disciples,
'He has been raised from the dead,
and he is going before you to Galilee;
there you will see him.'
Behold, I have told you."
Then they went away quickly from the tomb,
fearful yet overjoyed,
and ran to announce this to his disciples.
And behold, Jesus met them on their way and
greeted them.
They approached, embraced his feet, and did
him homage.
Then Jesus said to them, "Do not be afraid.
Go tell my brothers to go to Galilee,
and there they will see me."

Pronunciation
Magdalene
   MAG-duh-lehn
Galilee   GAL-ih-lee

Easter morning: how glorious! Certainly one of my favorite sentences in this gospel is:
"Then they went away
quickly from the tomb,
   fearful yet overjoyed,
   and ran to announce
   this to his disciples."

Perhaps this passage best describes the energy with which this reading might be delivered.

Realize that the women actually don't see Jesus until the last part. How might you read this gospel, as everything leading up to the last part is rather dramatic? What is the tempo and energy of the last part?

Preparing to Proclaim
Key words and phrases: "They have taken the Lord from the tomb."

To the point: John's empty tomb narrative is mysterious. We do not see Jesus here, and not even the angel of the Synoptics reassures these witnesses about what is happening. There are only oblique signs: a moved stone, burial cloths, and no body. The gospel ends without understanding and there is still a journey ahead of coming to understand what God has done here. Our Easter joy is not always immediate; we cannot start it on demand. But God remains with us in the journey of coming to share in this joy more fully.

Making Connections
In company with the psalmist, let us pray once more: "This is the day the Lord has made; let us rejoice and be glad!" Our call for the next fifty days of Easter is to spread Christ's joy to all we meet. This does not mean we need to be happy every second of every day. It does not mean we ignore the real suffering plaguing our world. Easter joy is strong enough to carry the wounds of the world together with the deep conviction that hope always wins. Death does not have the final say. Through Christ, the Easter victory is ours for eternity.

Prayer

Cornerstone of Life,
risen from the dead, marvelous to behold:
This is the day the Lord has made; let us re-
     joice and be glad.
You are hope incarnate, reigning forever;
you are redemption, you are healing,
you are forgiveness.
Help us build upon you a life of holiness and
     love.
Alleluia!
Amen.

First Reading (Acts 10:34a, 37-43)

A reading from the Acts of the Apostles

Peter proceeded to speak and said:
     "You know what has happened all over Judea,
     beginning in Galilee after the baptism
     that John preached,
          how God anointed Jesus of Nazareth
          with the Holy Spirit and power.
He went about doing good
     and healing all those oppressed by the devil,
     for God was with him.
We are witnesses of all that he did
     both in the country of the Jews and in
          Jerusalem.
They put him to death by hanging him on a
     tree.
This man God raised on the third day and
     granted that he be visible,
     not to all the people, but to us,
     the witnesses chosen by God in advance,
     who ate and drank with him after he rose
          from the dead.
He commissioned us to preach to the people
     and testify that he is the one appointed by
          God
     as judge of the living and the dead.
To him all the prophets bear witness,

Pronunciation
Judea   jou-DEE-uh
Galilee   GAL-ih-lee

Take a nice pause before
"We are witnesses of all
that he did . . ." and "He
commissioned us to
preach . . ."

The section beginning
with "We are witnesses"
tells of how the disciples
saw Jesus and even ate
with him after his resur-
rection; therefore, all are
to believe in the risen
Christ. Don't underesti-
mate the importance of
this section.

that everyone who believes in him
will receive forgiveness of sins through his
name."

Responsorial Psalm (Ps 118:1-2, 16-17, 22-23)

R̂. (24) This is the day the Lord has made; let
us rejoice and be glad. *or:* R̂. Alleluia.

Give thanks to the LORD, for he is good,
for his mercy endures forever.
Let the house of Israel say,
"His mercy endures forever."

R̂. This is the day the Lord has made; let us
rejoice and be glad. *or:* R̂. Alleluia.

"The right hand of the LORD has struck with
power;
the right hand of the LORD is exalted.
I shall not die, but live,
and declare the works of the LORD."

R̂. This is the day the Lord has made; let us
rejoice and be glad. *or:* R̂. Alleluia.

The stone which the builders rejected
has become the cornerstone.
By the LORD has this been done;
it is wonderful in our eyes.

R̂. This is the day the Lord has made; let us
rejoice and be glad. *or:* R̂. Alleluia.

Second Reading (Col 3:1-4 [or 1 Cor 5:6b-8])

A reading from the Letter of Saint Paul to
the Colossians

Brothers and sisters:
If then you were raised with Christ, seek what
is above,
where Christ is seated at the right hand of
God.
Think of what is above, not of what is on earth.

Pronunciation
Colossians
kuh-LAA-shnz

Make sure you know what
yeast has to do with baking bread and what unleavened bread is.

This analogy would have
made great sense to Paul's

For you have died, and your life is hidden
    with Christ in God.
When Christ your life appears,
    then you too will appear with him in glory.

Gospel (John 20:1-9; L42ABC)

or Gospel (Matt 28:1-10; L41A)

*or at an afternoon or evening Mass
Gospel (Luke 24:13-35; L46)*

A reading from the holy Gospel according
to John

On the first day of the week,
    Mary of Magdala came to the tomb early
        in the morning,
    while it was still dark,
    and saw the stone removed from the tomb.
So she ran and went to Simon Peter
    and to the other disciple whom Jesus loved,
        and told them,
    "They have taken the Lord from the tomb,
    and we don't know where they put him."
So Peter and the other disciple went out and
        came to the tomb.
They both ran, but the other disciple ran
        faster than Peter
    and arrived at the tomb first;
    he bent down and saw the burial cloths
        there, but did not go in.
When Simon Peter arrived after him,
    he went into the tomb and saw the burial
        cloths there,
    and the cloth that had covered his head,
    not with the burial cloths but rolled up in a
        separate place.
Then the other disciple also went in,
    the one who had arrived at the tomb first,
    and he saw and believed.
For they did not yet understand the Scripture
    that he had to rise from the dead.

listeners as baking was
known and practiced by
nearly everyone at that
time.

Pronunciation
Magdala   MAG-duh-luh

This is such an interesting
reading. The two disciples
run to the tomb, but at
least the one disciple who
arrives first is hesitant
about entering by himself.

Is he afraid? I would be!
How might that element
of fear energize this
reading?

Preparing to Proclaim

Key words and phrases: "We have seen the Lord."

To the point: Poor Thomas here gets such a bad reputation, known mockingly as "Doubting Thomas" when in reality he demonstrates great faith. His need for proof is only human; the other disciples were shown Jesus's hands and side before they came to believe, too! In fact, Thomas's questioning demonstrates an intelligent and responsible engagement with his faith. He ponders the truth of what he hears and brings his questions to the table, not shutting down when something does not immediately make sense to him. At the same time, he does not blindly accept what he has been told, even though it is something he deeply hopes is true. And when he does encounter Jesus, his response is immediate: "My Lord and my God!" He gives over his heart and life to the one who has risen from the dead.

Making Connections

Between the readings: The gospel tells the story of one of the first encounters with the risen Christ; the first reading tells us about a community living in the wake of such an encounter. They respond to the gospel with awe and generosity, with prayer and communal living. The second reading is written to a community slightly more removed from immediately witnessing the resurrection; while they (and we) need to rely on the testimony of others, it affirms that joy and hope are at the heart of their response.

To experience: Most of us do not get to experience the risen Christ as tangibly and viscerally as Thomas does. Our encounters will more likely be encounters of the heart, more subtle and less subject to the proof that he asks for. Our firsthand encounters usually need to be contextualized by the tradition we have inherited; we are dependent on the testimony of those who came before us.

Prayer

Ever-living God,
your son conquered death
that he might be mercy for a thousand
    generations.
Be our help when we fail, our strength in our
    weakness,
and a loving presence in our doubts.
*[G]ive thanks to the Lord for he is good, his
    love is everlasting.*
Help our unbelief, hold us close.
Amen.

First Reading (Acts 2:42-47)

A reading from the Acts of the Apostles

They devoted themselves
    to the teaching of the apostles and to the
        communal life,
    to the breaking of bread and to the prayers.
Awe came upon everyone,
    and many wonders and signs were done
        through the apostles.
All who believed were together and had all
    things in common;
    they would sell their property and
        possessions
    and divide them among all according to
        each one's need.
Every day they devoted themselves
    to meeting together in the temple area
    and to breaking bread in their homes.
They ate their meals with exultation and
    sincerity of heart,
    praising God and enjoying favor with all
        the people.
And every day the Lord added to their
    number those who were being saved.

Here we have the early Christian community in action! There are three themes in each of the first three parts:
1. All followed the teachings of the apostles.
2. Signs and wonders were done through the apostles.
3. All took care of the needs of others so that no one went without.

Are we as a Christian community doing as well today? What sort of energy might you use to deliver this reading with that in mind?

177

SECOND SUNDAY OF EASTER
(OR OF DIVINE MERCY)

Responsorial Psalm (Ps 118:2-4, 13-15, 22-24)

℟. (1) Give thanks to the Lord for he is good, his love is everlasting. *or:* ℟. Alleluia.

Let the house of Israel say,
 "His mercy endures forever."
Let the house of Aaron say,
 "His mercy endures forever."
Let those who fear the LORD say,
 "His mercy endures forever."

℟. Give thanks to the Lord for he is good, his love is everlasting. *or:* ℟. Alleluia.

I was hard pressed and was falling,
 but the LORD helped me.
My strength and my courage is the LORD,
 and he has been my savior.
The joyful shout of victory
 in the tents of the just.

℟. Give thanks to the Lord for he is good, his love is everlasting. *or:* ℟. Alleluia.

The stone which the builders rejected
 has become the cornerstone.
By the LORD has this been done;
 it is wonderful in our eyes.
This is the day the LORD has made;
 let us be glad and rejoice in it.

℟. Give thanks to the Lord for he is good, his love is everlasting. *or:* ℟. Alleluia.

Second Reading (1 Pet 1:3-9)

Each of the three parts in this reading is a single sentence. Read this aloud a number of times so that you really understand the punctuation. Otherwise, what you think is a period

A reading from the first Letter of Saint Peter

Blessed be the God and Father of our Lord
 Jesus Christ,
 who in his great mercy gave us a new birth
 to a living hope

through the resurrection of Jesus Christ
from the dead,
to an inheritance that is imperishable,
undefiled, and unfading,
kept in heaven for you
who by the power of God are safeguarded
through faith,
to a salvation that is ready to be revealed in
the final time.
In this you rejoice, although now for a little
while
you may have to suffer through various
trials,
so that the genuineness of your faith,
more precious than gold that is perishable
even though tested by fire,
may prove to be for praise, glory, and
honor
at the revelation of Jesus Christ.
Although you have not seen him you love
him;
even though you do not see him now yet
believe in him,
you rejoice with an indescribable and
glorious joy,
as you attain the goal of your faith, the
salvation of your souls.

Gospel (John 20:19-31; L43A)

A reading from the holy Gospel according
to John

On the evening of that first day of the week,
when the doors were locked, where the
disciples were,
for fear of the Jews,
Jesus came and stood in their midst
and said to them, "Peace be with you."
When he had said this, he showed them his
hands and his side.

might actually be a
comma!

Pronunciation
Didymus   DID-I-mus

Of course, we have read
and heard this reading
many times, and the reference to doubting Thomas
maybe even more. Maybe
the challenge, then, is to
read it with new eyes.
Mind-blowing? I guess!

179

SECOND SUNDAY OF EASTER
(OR OF DIVINE MERCY)

Don't worry about delivering Thomas's line too dramatically. Jesus's follow up to Thomas's line: "Blessed are those who have not seen and have believed" is equally dramatic and memorable.

The disciples rejoiced when they saw the
  Lord.
Jesus said to them again, "Peace be with you.
As the Father has sent me, so I send you."
And when he had said this, he breathed on
      them and said to them,
    "Receive the Holy Spirit.
Whose sins you forgive are forgiven them,
    and whose sins you retain are retained."

Thomas, called Didymus, one of the Twelve,
    was not with them when Jesus came.
So the other disciples said to him, "We have
    seen the Lord."
But he said to them,
    "Unless I see the mark of the nails in his
      hands
    and put my finger into the nailmarks
    and put my hand into his side, I will not
      believe."

Now a week later his disciples were again
      inside
  and Thomas was with them.
Jesus came, although the doors were locked,
    and stood in their midst and said, "Peace
      be with you."
Then he said to Thomas, "Put your finger
      here and see my hands,
    and bring your hand and put it into my
      side,
    and do not be unbelieving, but believe."
Thomas answered and said to him, "My Lord
    and my God!"
Jesus said to him, "Have you come to believe
    because you have seen me?
Blessed are those who have not seen and have
    believed."

Now Jesus did many other signs in the
    presence of his disciples
  that are not written in this book.
But these are written that you may come to
    believe
  that Jesus is the Christ, the Son of God,
  and that through this belief you may have
    life in his name.

Preparing to Proclaim

Key words and phrases: "Were not our hearts burning within us while he spoke to us on the way . . . ?"

To the point: This Easter encounter is a beloved story, and with good reason. It transitions us from the disciples' encounters with the risen Christ to our ongoing encounters with Christ in the Mass. Their hearts burn within them as he speaks to them about Scripture, a forerunner to our Liturgy of the Word, when we hear Scripture opened for us and meet Jesus alive and speaking to us there. Then they recognized him in the breaking of the bread, which is how he will remain with them—and us—long beyond his ascension into heaven. For us, too, Mass serves as a point of encounter in the midst of our lifelong journey. Jesus chooses to be with us and walk with us, and while we might not always recognize him, we are never left alone.

Making Connections

Between the readings: The first reading shows Peter in his redemption arc—after his cowardly denial of Jesus in the passion narrative, he here stands up and proclaims the truth of Jesus's life, death, and resurrection. He is ready to take a risk because his encounter with the risen Jesus has transformed him; this courage comes from God. The second reading continues his preaching and reminds us of the source of his courage, a courage that would enable him to follow Jesus to a death by crucifixion: this is not human courage, but courage that only comes when our "faith and hope are in God."

To experience: We may be tempted to think of the disciples as extremely privileged to have encountered the Risen Christ so immediately. They certainly are, but so are we, who continue to encounter Jesus at every Mass as he humbly comes to be with us, fully and completely, in the Scriptures and Eucharist we receive at every Mass.

Prayer

Divine Revelation,
you journey with us always,
making known your presence and sustaining us
with your word and with the gift of yourself.
When we are discouraged, disheartened,
whenever we need your help,
Lord, you will show us the path of life.
Make our hearts burn with your love.
Amen.

First Reading (Acts 2:14, 22-33)

A reading from the Acts of the Apostles

Then Peter stood up with the Eleven,
    raised his voice, and proclaimed:
    "You who are Jews, indeed all of you
        staying in Jerusalem.
Let this be known to you, and listen to my
    words.
You who are Israelites, hear these words.
Jesus the Nazorean was a man commended to
    you by God
    with mighty deeds, wonders, and signs,
    which God worked through him in your
        midst, as you yourselves know.
This man, delivered up by the set plan and
    foreknowledge of God,
    you killed, using lawless men to crucify
        him.
But God raised him up, releasing him from
    the throes of death,
    because it was impossible for him to be
        held by it.
For David says of him:
    I saw the Lord ever before me,
        with him at my right hand I shall not be
            disturbed.
    Therefore my heart has been glad and my
        tongue has exulted;
    my flesh, too, will dwell in hope,

Pronunciation
Nazorean   NAZ-awr-een

Obviously, Peter, along
with the eleven other disciples, had gathered a
great crowd here. He is
making a major proclama-
tion without a public ad-
dress system! He is
speaking slowly and de-
liberately so that the
people do not miss one
word.

How might you deliver
this reading in a similar
way? You probably have a
sound system but that
does not replace a slow,
deliberate delivery of the
reading, making sure that
every word is heard
clearly.

because you will not abandon my soul to the netherworld,
nor will you suffer your holy one to see corruption.
You have made known to me the paths of life;
you will fill me with joy in your presence.

"My brothers, one can confidently say to you
about the patriarch David that he died and
was buried,
and his tomb is in our midst to this day.
But since he was a prophet and knew that
God had sworn an oath to him
that he would set one of his descendants
upon his throne,
he foresaw and spoke of the resurrection
of the Christ,
that neither was he abandoned to the
netherworld
nor did his flesh see corruption.
God raised this Jesus;
of this we are all witnesses.
Exalted at the right hand of God,
he received the promise of the Holy Spirit
from the Father
and poured him forth, as you see and hear."

Responsorial Psalm (Ps 16:1-2, 5, 7-8, 9-10, 11)

℟. (11a) Lord, you will show us the path of
life. *or:* ℟. Alleluia.

Keep me, O God, for in you I take refuge;
    I say to the LORD, "My Lord are you."
O LORD, my allotted portion and my cup,
    you it is who hold fast my lot.

℟. Lord, you will show us the path of life. *or:*
℟. Alleluia.

I bless the LORD who counsels me;
    even in the night my heart exhorts me.
I set the LORD ever before me;
    with him at my right hand I shall not be
        disturbed.

R̸. Lord, you will show us the path of life. *or:*
R̸. Alleluia.

Therefore my heart is glad and my soul
        rejoices,
    my body, too, abides in confidence;
because you will not abandon my soul to the
        netherworld,
    nor will you suffer your faithful one to
        undergo corruption.

R̸. Lord, you will show us the path of life. *or:*
R̸. Alleluia.

You will show me the path to life,
    abounding joy in your presence,
    the delights at your right hand forever.

R̸. Lord, you will show us the path of life. *or:*
R̸. Alleluia.

Second Reading (1 Pet 1:17-21)

A reading from the first Letter of Saint Peter
Beloved:
If you invoke as Father him who judges
        impartially
    according to each one's works,
    conduct yourselves with reverence during
        the time of your sojourning,
    realizing that you were ransomed from
        your futile conduct,
    handed on by your ancestors,
    not with perishable things like silver or
        gold
    but with the precious blood of Christ
    as of a spotless unblemished lamb.

The second part of this reading is not easy to read or understand right away. Read it a number of times to make sure you understand it. If you don't know what you are saying, those listening to you will have a difficult time as well.

He was known before the foundation of the
world
but revealed in the final time for you,
who through him believe in God
who raised him from the dead and gave
him glory,
so that your faith and hope are in God.

Gospel   (Luke 24:13-35; L46A)

A reading from the holy Gospel according
to Luke

That very day, the first day of the week,
two of Jesus' disciples were going
to a village seven miles from Jerusalem
called Emmaus,
and they were conversing about all the
things that had occurred.
And it happened that while they were
conversing and debating,
Jesus himself drew near and walked with
them,
but their eyes were prevented from
recognizing him.
He asked them,
"What are you discussing as you walk
along?"
They stopped, looking downcast.
One of them, named Cleopas, said to him in
reply,
"Are you the only visitor to Jerusalem
who does not know of the things
that have taken place there in these days?"
And he replied to them, "What sort of
things?"
They said to him,
"The things that happened to Jesus the
Nazarene,
who was a prophet mighty in deed and word

Pronunciation
Emmaus   eh-MAY-uhs
Cleopas   KLEE-o-pas
Nazarene   NAZ-awr-een

This is a long reading but
one that is not without
some wonderful drama. It
seems the two men have
part of the story, but
Jesus finishes it for them
in a most astounding way!

The climax is in the
breaking of the bread,
when "their eyes were
opened and they recog-
nized him." Make sure to
give this moment in the
reading its due.

before God and all the people,
how our chief priests and rulers both
handed him over
to a sentence of death and crucified him.
But we were hoping that he would be the one
to redeem Israel;
and besides all this,
it is now the third day since this took place.
Some women from our group, however, have
astounded us:
they were at the tomb early in the morning
and did not find his body;
they came back and reported
that they had indeed seen a vision of
angels
who announced that he was alive.
Then some of those with us went to the tomb
and found things just as the women had
described,
but him they did not see."
And he said to them, "Oh, how foolish you
are!
How slow of heart to believe all that the
prophets spoke!
Was it not necessary that the Christ should
suffer these things
and enter into his glory?"
Then beginning with Moses and all the
prophets,
he interpreted to them what referred to him
in all the Scriptures.
As they approached the village to which they
were going,
he gave the impression that he was going
on farther.
But they urged him, "Stay with us,
for it is nearly evening and the day is
almost over."
So he went in to stay with them.

And it happened that, while he was with them
    at table,
  he took bread, said the blessing,
  broke it, and gave it to them.
With that their eyes were opened and they
    recognized him,
  but he vanished from their sight.
Then they said to each other,
  "Were not our hearts burning within us
  while he spoke to us on the way and
    opened the Scriptures to us?"
So they set out at once and returned to
    Jerusalem
  where they found gathered together
  the eleven and those with them who were
    saying,
  "The Lord has truly been raised and has
    appeared to Simon!"
Then the two recounted
  what had taken place on the way
  and how he was made known to them in
    the breaking of bread.

Preparing to Proclaim

Key words and phrases: "I came so that
they might have life and have it more
abundantly."

To the point: In this gospel for Good Shepherd Sunday, Jesus mixes his metaphors a bit.
We usually think of him as the Good Shepherd, and he is that; he is the one who contrasts with the thief sneaking in to steal and
slaughter. He is the one who calls us by name
and whose voice we know. He is the one who
provides our sustenance and protection. But
in this parable, he also identifies himself as
the gate into the sheepfold. This is an even humbler image than that of
shepherd, for in this metaphor, he is not even human. He is our way, our
path to all that is good and real. It is through him that we enter safety
and rest. And it is he who serves as our protection, because he has conquered those evil forces in the world that would wish us harm.

Making Connections

Between the readings: The second reading explicitly repeats the
sheep and shepherd image of the gospel; sheep sometimes go astray, but
returning to their shepherd keeps them safe. Peter's preaching of baptism in the first reading is an important connection to the sheepfold gate
of the gospel. Baptism is how we share in Christ's death and thus his life.
It is our entry point to the safety of Christ's flock.

To experience: For many of us, baptism was long ago. We take for
granted that we are part of God's flock of sheep and do not remember
what it was like to ever be outside it. This is an important season to listen to the witness of those more newly initiated into the church; their
stories of coming in from the outside are often very powerful and can remind us of what we're about. If you are a newer convert, consider ways
you might share your story with those around you.

Prayer

Sacred Gate of Life,

through you is heaven, and union with the
divine.

You guard our coming and going,

keeping us safe, granting abundant life to
each human soul.

Each human heart knows you,

each voice lifts their thanks and praise:

You are *my shepherd; there is nothing I shall
want.*

Amen.

Whoa! The whole house of Israel is being notified by Peter that they have crucified the Son of God. This terrifying news "cut [them] to the heart." Then, of course, Peter goes on to tell the people what they are to do in order to be saved.

Pause after the first part, which delivers such horrific news. How successful was Peter in announcing this news? Well, about three thousand were baptized that day.

First Reading (Acts 2:14a, 36-41)

A reading from the Acts of the Apostles

Then Peter stood up with the Eleven,
    raised his voice, and proclaimed:
"Let the whole house of Israel know for
        certain
    that God has made both Lord and Christ,
    this Jesus whom you crucified."

Now when they heard this, they were cut to
        the heart,
    and they asked Peter and the other
            apostles,
    "What are we to do, my brothers?"
Peter said to them,
    "Repent and be baptized, every one of you,
    in the name of Jesus Christ for the
            forgiveness of your sins;
    and you will receive the gift of the Holy
            Spirit.
For the promise is made to you and to your
        children
    and to all those far off,
    whomever the Lord our God will call."
He testified with many other arguments, and
        was exhorting them,

"Save yourselves from this corrupt
    generation."
Those who accepted his message were
    baptized,
    and about three thousand persons were
        added that day.

Responsorial Psalm (Ps 23:1-3a, 3b-4, 5, 6)

℟. (1) The Lord is my shepherd; there is
nothing I shall want. *or:* ℟. Alleluia.

The LORD is my shepherd; I shall not want.
    In verdant pastures he gives me repose;
beside restful waters he leads me;
    he refreshes my soul.

℟. The Lord is my shepherd; there is nothing
I shall want. *or:* ℟. Alleluia.

He guides me in right paths
    for his name's sake.
Even though I walk in the dark valley
    I fear no evil; for you are at my side
with your rod and your staff
    that give me courage.

℟. The Lord is my shepherd; there is nothing
I shall want. *or:* ℟. Alleluia.

You spread the table before me
    in the sight of my foes;
you anoint my head with oil;
    my cup overflows.

℟. The Lord is my shepherd; there is nothing
I shall want. *or:* ℟. Alleluia.

Only goodness and kindness follow me
    all the days of my life;
and I shall dwell in the house of the LORD
    for years to come.

℟. The Lord is my shepherd; there is nothing
I shall want. *or:* ℟. Alleluia.

Take your time with this reading; slow and deliberate is a good way to go. It is short, and therefore, can be missed at least in part by the listeners. A nice pause after "Beloved" can remedy this.

Make sure you don't drop the end of the sentence beginning with "When he was insulted . . ." The "one who judges justly" is God.

Second Reading (1 Pet 2:20b-25)

A reading from the first Letter of Saint Peter

Beloved:
If you are patient when you suffer for doing
    what is good,
    this is a grace before God.
For to this you have been called,
    because Christ also suffered for you,
    leaving you an example that you should
        follow in his footsteps.
*He committed no sin, and no deceit was found
    in his mouth.*

When he was insulted, he returned no insult;
    when he suffered, he did not threaten;
    instead, he handed himself over to the one
        who judges justly.
He himself bore our sins in his body upon the
    cross,
    so that, free from sin, we might live for
        righteousness.
By his wounds you have been healed.
For you had gone astray like sheep,
    but you have now returned to the shepherd
        and guardian of your souls.

Pronunciation
Pharisees   FEHR-ih-seez

The Pharisees are not the brightest people here, are they? Jesus seems to take a moment when he realizes they are not understanding him. Likewise, take a nice pause after the first part, enough time to echo what Jesus may have been thinking: OK, how can I make this easier for these people?

Gospel   (John 10:1-10; L49A)

A reading from the holy Gospel according to John

Jesus said:
    "Amen, amen, I say to you,
    whoever does not enter a sheepfold
        through the gate
    but climbs over elsewhere is a thief and a
        robber.
But whoever enters through the gate is the
    shepherd of the sheep.
The gatekeeper opens it for him, and the
    sheep hear his voice,

as the shepherd calls his own sheep by
    name and leads them out.
When he has driven out all his own,
    he walks ahead of them, and the sheep
        follow him,
    because they recognize his voice.
But they will not follow a stranger;
    they will run away from him,
    because they do not recognize the voice of
        strangers."
Although Jesus used this figure of speech,
· the Pharisees did not realize what he was
        trying to tell them.

So Jesus said again, "Amen, amen, I say to
        you,
    I am the gate for the sheep.
All who came before me are thieves and
        robbers,
    but the sheep did not listen to them.
I am the gate.
Whoever enters through me will be saved,
    and will come in and go out and find
        pasture.
A thief comes only to steal and slaughter and
        destroy;
    I came so that they might have life and
        have it more abundantly."

Much greater intensity or energy could be easily used in the second part in order to drive home Jesus's point.

Preparing to Proclaim

Key words and phrases: "I am the way and the truth and the life."

To the point: We are past the midpoint of the Easter season, and the readings start to turn from the immediate aftermath of the resurrection and toward the ongoing work the church will face after Jesus's bodily presence departs earth. We see that while the work of Easter is complete in one sense—Jesus has conquered death once and for all—it will be an ongoing project to bring it to its fullness. Jesus has gone ahead of us in death and has conquered it for us so that we might participate in his life. In this gospel, Jesus tells us that he will go ahead of us to heaven, as well, but it is not to leave us alone. He goes ahead to open the way for us and to prepare our place there. Jesus also affirms his unity with his Father here; he already dwells in the Father and the Father in him, and we are called to follow him into such intimacy with God, which is truly heaven.

Making Connections

Between the readings: Like the gospel, the second reading calls us to follow in Christ's footsteps. Here, we are to follow him in becoming "living stones" that might be built into a "spiritual house." This house is akin to the temple, a place for offering sacrifice. But it can also serve as shelter for others. The first reading reminds us that part of the work of the church is to distribute goods in a just way. This is so important that a new group is established: deacons are initiated to oversee the social work of the church.

To experience: Some of the metaphors in these readings can seem obscure and unreachable. We are to wait for Jesus to prepare a place for us in his Father's house; we are in the meantime to become living stones built into another house. Reflecting on themes of home and hospitality might help these readings take on a more robust meaning.

Prayer

Way, Truth, and Life,
guiding beacon and gracious consoler:
you are the one true path and one true
destination.
At times we stray from you, human weakness
prevails.
*Lord, let your mercy be on us, as we place our
trust in you.*
Show us divine love, and we shall be saved.
Amen.

First Reading (Acts 6:1-7)

A reading from the Acts of the Apostles

As the number of disciples continued to grow,
the Hellenists complained against the
Hebrews
because their widows
were being neglected in the daily
distribution.
So the Twelve called together the community
of the disciples and said,
"It is not right for us to neglect the word of
God to serve at table.
Brothers, select from among you seven
reputable men,
filled with the Spirit and wisdom,
whom we shall appoint to this task,
whereas we shall devote ourselves to prayer
and to the ministry of the word."
The proposal was acceptable to the whole
community,
so they chose Stephen, a man filled with
faith and the Holy Spirit,
also Philip, Prochorus, Nicanor, Timon,
Parmenas,
and Nicholas of Antioch, a convert to
Judaism.
They presented these men to the apostles
who prayed and laid hands on them.

Pronunciation
Hellenists HEH-leh-nists
Prochorus
   PRAH-kaw-ruhs
Nicanor Nai-KAY-nawr
Timon TAI-muhn
Parmenas
   PAHR-mee-nas
Antioch AN-tih-ahk

Make sure you are comfortable with the above names so that the meaning—seven being chosen or ordained by the Twelve—is not lost by stumbling on the names!

195

The word of God continued to spread,
and the number of the disciples in
Jerusalem increased greatly;
even a large group of priests were
becoming obedient to the faith.

Responsorial Psalm (Ps 33:1-2, 4-5, 18-19)

R℣. (22) Lord, let your mercy be on us, as we
place our trust in you. *or:* R℣. Alleluia.

Exult, you just, in the Lord;
praise from the upright is fitting.
Give thanks to the LORD on the harp;
with the ten-stringed lyre chant his praises.

R℣. Lord, let your mercy be on us, as we place
our trust in you. *or:* R℣. Alleluia.

Upright is the word of the LORD,
and all his works are trustworthy.
He loves justice and right;
of the kindness of the LORD the earth is full.

R℣. Lord, let your mercy be on us, as we place
our trust in you. *or:* R℣. Alleluia.

See, the eyes of the LORD are upon those who
fear him,
upon those who hope for his kindness,
to deliver them from death
and preserve them in spite of famine.

R℣. Lord, let your mercy be on us, as we place
our trust in you. *or:* R℣. Alleluia.

A colon (:) often precedes
an explanation, a list, or
the introduction to a
quoted sentence. There-
fore, after the two times a
colon precedes the itali-
cized Scripture quotes,
take a nice pause. The
voice reciting the itali-

Second Reading (1 Pet 2:4-9)

A reading from the first Letter of Saint Peter

Beloved:
Come to him, a living stone, rejected by
human beings
but chosen and precious in the sight of God,
and, like living stones,
let yourselves be built into a spiritual house

to be a holy priesthood to offer spiritual
sacrifices
acceptable to God through Jesus Christ.
For it says in Scripture:
Behold, I am laying a stone in Zion,
a cornerstone, chosen and precious,
and whoever believes in it shall not be put
to shame.
Therefore, its value is for you who have faith,
but for those without faith:
The stone that the builders rejected
has become the cornerstone,
and
A stone that will make people stumble,
and a rock that will make them fall.
They stumble by disobeying the word, as is
their destiny.

You are "a chosen race, a royal priesthood,
a holy nation, a people of his own,
so that you may announce the praises" of
him
who called you out of darkness into his
wonderful light.

Gospel (John 14:1-12; L52A)

A reading from the holy Gospel according
to John

Jesus said to his disciples:
"Do not let your hearts be troubled.
You have faith in God; have faith also in me.
In my Father's house there are many dwelling
places.
If there were not,
would I have told you that I am going to
prepare a place for you?
And if I go and prepare a place for you,
I will come back again and take you to
myself,
so that where I am you also may be.

cized passage can be a bit more declarative than the preceding line.

At all times, take your time. Pause appropriately at commas and, of course, for the white space after the larger part of the reading.

In this poetic Scripture passage Jesus is really making an effort to calm his disciples! Philip is exposing his less-than-brilliant mind, giving those listeners an opportunity to understand, in a simpler way, who Jesus is.

For this reason, even though you may know this passage almost by heart, take your time delivering it in the same way that Jesus had to "slow it down" for Philip.

Where I am going you know the way."
Thomas said to him,
    "Master, we do not know where you are
        going;
    how can we know the way?"
Jesus said to him, "I am the way and the truth
    and the life.
No one comes to the Father except through
    me.
If you know me, then you will also know my
    Father.
From now on you do know him and have seen
    him."
Philip said to him,
    "Master, show us the Father, and that will
        be enough for us."
Jesus said to him, "Have I been with you for
    so long a time
    and you still do not know me, Philip?
Whoever has seen me has seen the Father.
How can you say, 'Show us the Father'?
Do you not believe that I am in the Father and
    the Father is in me?
The words that I speak to you I do not speak
    on my own.
The Father who dwells in me is doing his
    works.
Believe me that I am in the Father and the
    Father is in me,
    or else, believe because of the works
        themselves.
Amen, amen, I say to you,
    whoever believes in me will do the works
        that I do,
    and will do greater ones than these,
    because I am going to the Father."

Preparing to Proclaim
Key words and phrases: "I will not leave you orphans."

To the point: This gospel echoes the themes of last week as Jesus is preparing his disciples to live without him for a time, or at least without the bodily presence they have come to know and which will depart earth at the ascension. This week adds a foreshadowing of the upcoming Pentecost feast; Jesus's presence will remain in the Holy Spirit, who will accompany the disciples and the church beyond their lifetime in their remaining work on earth. For us, too, the Holy Spirit is a promised companion, providing continuity with these earliest of Jesus's followers. Like the disciples, we are not left alone in the struggle.

Making Connections
Between the readings: In the first reading, we see an affirmation of the gospel's idea of the Holy Spirit as an ongoing presence with us beyond Christ's bodily presence on earth. This is depicted in a forerunner of what we now know as the sacrament of confirmation. Those who have been baptized in Samaria have their baptisms completed in a sense when the apostles lay hands on them and the Holy Spirit descends.

To experience: There have always been and will always be struggles that accompany a life of faith, and we might wonder why Jesus does not make his presence more visible and obvious to us and to those who would criticize us. But God is not about "winning" in the way we would sometimes choose; the "win" here is not that we will never struggle or suffer but that we will never be left alone in our struggles.

Prayer

Mighty Healer, Eternal Love,
your Spirit is among us, within us,
restoring those in need of wholeness,
uplifting those who have fallen.
Let all the earth cry out to God with joy.
You never abandon us, your adopted children,
but always show us your love,
a revelation of life and truth.
Amen.

Pronunciation
Samaria
   suh-MEHR-ih-uh

Here is a wonderful reading describing the early church flourishing under the direction of the apostles. There are two different themes here:

1. The first part has Philip working miracles in addition to proclaiming the Christ.

2. The second has Peter and John arriving and praying that the Holy Spirit descend upon the apostles.

These are similar but different happenings, with the second part going deeper in faith with the people. How might you read the two sections differently (separated by a nice pause), given the above understanding?

First Reading (Acts 8:5-8, 14-17)

A reading from the Acts of the Apostles

Philip went down to the city of Samaria
   and proclaimed the Christ to them.
With one accord, the crowds paid attention to
    what was said by Philip
   when they heard it and saw the signs he
     was doing.
For unclean spirits, crying out in a loud voice,
   came out of many possessed people,
   and many paralyzed or crippled people
    were cured.
There was great joy in that city.

Now when the apostles in Jerusalem
   heard that Samaria had accepted the word
    of God,
   they sent them Peter and John,
   who went down and prayed for them,
   that they might receive the Holy Spirit,
   for it had not yet fallen upon any of them;
   they had only been baptized in the name of
    the Lord Jesus.
Then they laid hands on them
   and they received the Holy Spirit.

Responsorial Psalm (Ps 66:1-3, 4-5, 6-7, 16, 20)

℟. (1) Let all the earth cry out to God with joy.
or: ℟. Alleluia.

Shout joyfully to God, all the earth,
 sing praise to the glory of his name;
 proclaim his glorious praise.
Say to God, "How tremendous are your
  deeds!"

℟. Let all the earth cry out to God with joy. *or:*
℟. Alleluia.

"Let all on earth worship and sing praise to
  you,
 sing praise to your name!"
Come and see the works of God,
 his tremendous deeds among the children
  of Adam.

℟. Let all the earth cry out to God with joy. *or:*
℟. Alleluia.

He has changed the sea into dry land;
 through the river they passed on foot;
 therefore let us rejoice in him.
He rules by his might forever.

℟. Let all the earth cry out to God with joy. *or:*
℟. Alleluia.

Hear now, all you who fear God, while I
  declare
 what he has done for me.
Blessed be God who refused me not
 my prayer or his kindness!

℟. Let all the earth cry out to God with joy. *or:*
℟. Alleluia.

SIXTH SUNDAY OF EASTER

There is that colon once again, so take a nice pause after "Beloved." The next line, "Sanctify Christ as Lord in your hearts," can and should totally stand by itself, so pause after it as well.

Then Peter goes on to tell or explain what he means by making that statement. Take another nice pause after "evil," as Peter then presents the summary.

John's reassuring words that Jesus will not leave us orphans are a balm to the soul.

Pause before "I will not leave you orphans . . ." and "Whoever has my commandments . . ." I would recommend that this whole reading be de-livered more slowly than most in order to prevent confusion by the listeners.

Second Reading (1 Pet 3:15-18)

A reading from the first Letter of Saint Peter

Beloved:
Sanctify Christ as Lord in your hearts.
Always be ready to give an explanation
    to anyone who asks you for a reason for
        your hope,
    but do it with gentleness and reverence,
    keeping your conscience clear,
    so that, when you are maligned,
    those who defame your good conduct in
        Christ
    may themselves be put to shame.
For it is better to suffer for doing good,
    if that be the will of God, than for doing
        evil.

For Christ also suffered for sins once,
    the righteous for the sake of the
        unrighteous,
    that he might lead you to God.
Put to death in the flesh,
    he was brought to life in the Spirit.

Gospel (John 14:15-21; L55A)

A reading from the holy Gospel according to John

Jesus said to his disciples:
    "If you love me, you will keep my
        commandments.
And I will ask the Father,
    and he will give you another Advocate to
        be with you always,
    the Spirit of truth, whom the world cannot
        accept,
    because it neither sees nor knows him.
But you know him, because he remains with
    you,
    and will be in you.

I will not leave you orphans; I will come to
you.
In a little while the world will no longer see
me,
but you will see me, because I live and you
will live.
On that day you will realize that I am in my
Father
and you are in me and I in you.
Whoever has my commandments and
observes them
is the one who loves me.
And whoever loves me will be loved by my
Father,
and I will love him and reveal myself to
him."

Preparing to Proclaim

Key words and phrases: "And behold, I am with you always, until the end of the age."

To the point: Finally comes the moment for which the last weeks have prepared us. Jesus is going away, at least in one sense: the disciples will not have his bodily presence to which they have become accustomed. He gives them their mission for while he is away: to make disciples, to baptize, to teach all that Jesus has taught. This will be the ongoing work of the church, work that continues even today. And Jesus does not leave the disciples—or us—alone in this work. Many of our Easter season readings have prepared us for this moment. He remains present in the breaking of the bread; he has promised the Holy Spirit as guide and companion. He is with us always, never leaving us alone, even when the life of faith is a struggle.

Making Connections

Between the readings: The second reading affirms the power of Christ and that the church, his body, continues his work on earth beyond the ascension. While the gospel has another moment of Jesus's preparing the disciples for his departure, the first reading contains the actual ascension narrative. Here, too, he leaves them with a mission—they are to be his witnesses all through the world. And here, too, there is a promise to return. This is still not the end of the story.

To experience: Each of us is called to share in the evangelizing work that Christ entrusts to the disciples here. For laypersons, it is not always apparent how we are making disciples or teaching the faith or leading others to baptism. But opportunities abound and every relationship is a chance to make Christ more present to someone, baptized or not, who might not know him well.

Prayer

All-powerful God,
amidst *shouts of joy* and *a blare of trumpets*
you were lifted into the sky by a cloud,
promising one day to return.
As we who remain set about the mission you
gave us,
grant us zeal, persistence, and patience.
Through us, may the whole world
come to know your good news.
Amen.

First Reading (Acts 1:1-11)

A reading from the Acts of the Apostles

In the first book, Theophilus,
   I dealt with all that Jesus did and taught
   until the day he was taken up,
   after giving instructions through the Holy
      Spirit
   to the apostles whom he had chosen.
He presented himself alive to them
   by many proofs after he had suffered,
   appearing to them during forty days
   and speaking about the kingdom of God.
While meeting with them,
   he enjoined them not to depart from
      Jerusalem,
   but to wait for "the promise of the Father
   about which you have heard me speak;
   for John baptized with water,
   but in a few days you will be baptized with
      the Holy Spirit."

When they had gathered together they asked
   him,
   "Lord, are you at this time going to restore
      the kingdom to Israel?"
He answered them, "It is not for you to know
   the times or seasons

Pronunciation
Theophilus
   thee-AH-fih-luhs
Judea   jou-DEE-uh
Samaria
   suh-MEHR-ih-uh
Galilee   GAL-ih-lee

This reading begins with a gentle recounting of Jesus's life after his resurrection. Before you know it, we are witnessing his ascension!

Take your time with this reading, separating it into sections with nice pauses. When you arrive at the line beginning with "When he had said this," then your voice needs to begin to communicate the incredible thing that is happening! This is the climax of the reading. The two men (angels) simply reassure the apostles about what they have just witnessed.

that the Father has established by his own
authority.

But you will receive power when the Holy
Spirit comes upon you,
and you will be my witnesses in Jerusalem,
throughout Judea and Samaria,
and to the ends of the earth."

When he had said this, as they were looking on,
he was lifted up, and a cloud took him from
their sight.

While they were looking intently at the sky as
he was going,
suddenly two men dressed in white
garments stood beside them.

They said, "Men of Galilee,
why are you standing there looking at the
sky?

This Jesus who has been taken up from you
into heaven
will return in the same way as you have
seen him going into heaven."

Responsorial Psalm (Ps 47:2-3, 6-7, 8-9)

R̸. (6) God mounts his throne to shouts of joy:
a blare of trumpets for the Lord. *or:*
R̸. Alleluia.

All you peoples, clap your hands,
shout to God with cries of gladness,
for the Lord, the Most High, the awesome,
is the great king over all the earth.

R̸. God mounts his throne to shouts of joy: a
blare of trumpets for the Lord. *or:* R̸. Alleluia.

God mounts his throne amid shouts of joy;
the Lord, amid trumpet blasts.
Sing praise to God, sing praise;
sing praise to our king, sing praise.

R̸. God mounts his throne to shouts of joy: a
blare of trumpets for the Lord. *or:* R̸. Alleluia.

For king of all the earth is God;
    sing hymns of praise.
God reigns over the nations,
    God sits upon his holy throne.

℞. God mounts his throne to shouts of joy: a blare of trumpets for the Lord. *or:* ℞. Alleluia.

Second Reading (Eph 1:17-23)

A reading from the Letter of Saint Paul to the Ephesians

Brothers and sisters:
May the God of our Lord Jesus Christ, the
    Father of glory,
    give you a Spirit of wisdom and revelation
    resulting in knowledge of him.
May the eyes of your hearts be enlightened,
    that you may know what is the hope that
        belongs to his call,
    what are the riches of glory
    in his inheritance among the holy ones,
    and what is the surpassing greatness of
        his power
    for us who believe,
    in accord with the exercise of his great might,
    which he worked in Christ,
    raising him from the dead
    and seating him at his right hand in the
        heavens,
    far above every principality, authority,
        power, and dominion,
    and every name that is named
    not only in this age but also in the one to
        come.
And he put all things beneath his feet
    and gave him as head over all things to the
        church,
    which is his body,
    the fullness of the one who fills all things
        in every way.

Pronunciation
Ephesians
    eh-FEE-zhuhnz

Paul is blessing the reader and listener here, which he often does at the very beginning. Your delivery should therefore sound just like a sincere blessing.

Pronunciation
Galilee   GAL-ih-lee

Matthew is short and to
the point here!

In the beginning the dis-
ciples "doubted." They are
then given the simplest
but most profound for-
mula to move forward. At
the end Jesus says he will
never leave them.

What could be more
important?

Gospel (Matt 28:16-20; L58A)

A reading from the holy Gospel according
to Matthew

The eleven disciples went to Galilee,
    to the mountain to which Jesus had ordered
        them.
When they saw him, they worshiped, but they
    doubted.
Then Jesus approached and said to them,
    "All power in heaven and on earth has been
        given to me.
Go, therefore, and make disciples of all
    nations,
    baptizing them in the name of the Father,
    and of the Son, and of the Holy Spirit,
    teaching them to observe all that I have
        commanded you.
And behold, I am with you always, until the
    end of the age."

Preparing to Proclaim

Key words and phrases: "Give glory to
your son . . . so that your son may give eternal life to all you gave him."

To the point: John's Gospel tends to give us
the most sophisticated trinitarian theology of
the four, and this gospel with its dizzying
array of prepositions shows how the early
church was coming to understand the relationship between Jesus and his Father. There
is shared glory here—glory that Jesus had
"before the world began" but to which he now
needs to be returned after he has humbled himself to share in the human
condition even up to death. There is a reciprocity; what glorifies the son
also glorifies the father. And there is unity—all who belong to the son
belong also to the father, and they will remain on earth to continue
Jesus's work while he returns to the fullness of his glory in heaven.

Making Connections

Between the readings: The first reading shows the disciples in the
state Jesus describes in the gospel—remaining faithfully in the world
after he has returned to heaven. The Holy Spirit has not yet descended,
and they have not yet taken up their missions of preaching and service
to the poor. Before these things, they devote themselves to prayer, main-
taining a relationship with God that will become the basis of their mission in a very short time.

To experience: The promise of eternal life can sometimes sound too
big for us, and as with Jesus's words in the gospel it can be hard to even
wrap our minds around it. This is an astonishingly huge thing that we've
been promised, and it can seem sometimes that we don't have the capacity for it. But the truth of the matter is that we do. God made us with an
infinite capacity for God, with a space in our hearts that can only be
filled by the infinitude of God.

Prayer

God of Sacred Mysteries,
your Son, Jesus, has no hands,
no feet on Earth now but ours.
Fill us with your Spirit, that by our lives
each person you created in love may
*see the good things of the Lord in the land of
the living.*
Help us glorify your name.
Amen.

Pronunciation
Olivet   AH-lih-veht
Bartholomew
    bar-THAHL-uh-myoo
Alphaeus   AL-fee-uhs
Zealot   ZEE-laht

The naming of the
apostles is very important
to the Christian commu-
nity. Take your time pro-
nouncing their names.

First Reading (Acts 1:12-14)

A reading from the Acts of the Apostles

After Jesus had been taken up to heaven the
    apostles
        returned to Jerusalem
        from the mount called Olivet, which is near
            Jerusalem,
        a sabbath day's journey away.

When they entered the city
        they went to the upper room where they
            were staying,
        Peter and John and James and Andrew,
        Philip and Thomas, Bartholomew and
            Matthew,
        James son of Alphaeus, Simon the Zealot,
        and Judas son of James.
All these devoted themselves with one accord
        to prayer,
        together with some women,
        and Mary the mother of Jesus, and his
            brothers.

Responsorial Psalm (Ps 27:1, 4, 7-8)

℞. (13) I believe that I shall see the good things of the Lord in the land of the living.
or: ℞. Alleluia.

The LORD is my light and my salvation;
    whom should I fear?
The LORD is my life's refuge;
    of whom should I be afraid?

℞. I believe that I shall see the good things of the Lord in the land of the living. *or:*
℞. Alleluia.

One thing I ask of the LORD;
    this I seek:
To dwell in the house of the LORD
    all the days of my life,
that I may gaze on the loveliness of the LORD
    and contemplate his temple.

℞. I believe that I shall see the good things of the Lord in the land of the living. *or:*
℞. Alleluia.

Hear, O LORD, the sound of my call;
    have pity on me, and answer me.
Of you my heart speaks; you my glance
        seeks.

℞. I believe that I shall see the good things of the Lord in the land of the living. *or:*
℞. Alleluia.

Second Reading (1 Pet 4:13-16)

A reading from the first Letter of Saint Peter

Beloved:
Rejoice to the extent that you share in the
        sufferings of Christ,
    so that when his glory is revealed
    you may also rejoice exultantly.
If you are insulted for the name of Christ,
    blessed are you,

Take two nice pauses here, one right after "Beloved," and the other after "God rests upon you."

Peter makes himself very clear that to suffer for Christ is *not* the same thing as suffering for a murderer, a thief, or an evildoer.

for the Spirit of glory and of God rests
upon you.
But let no one among you be made to suffer
as a murderer, a thief, an evildoer, or as an
intriguer.
But whoever is made to suffer as a Christian
should not be ashamed
but glorify God because of the name.

Gospel   (John 17:1-11a; L59A)

A reading from the holy Gospel according
to John

Jesus raised his eyes to heaven and said,
"Father, the hour has come.
Give glory to your son, so that your
son may glorify you,
just as you gave him authority over all
people,
so that your son may give eternal life to all
you gave him.
Now this is eternal life,
that they should know you, the only true
God,
and the one whom you sent, Jesus Christ.
I glorified you on earth
by accomplishing the work that you gave
me to do.
Now glorify me, Father, with you,
with the glory that I had with you before
the world began.

"I revealed your name to those whom you
gave me out of the world.
They belonged to you, and you gave them to
me,
and they have kept your word.
Now they know that everything you gave me
is from you,
because the words you gave to me I have
given to them,

John's writing here reminds me of the soliloquy technique that Shakespeare employs in his plays, in that we are hearing what sounds like Jesus's thoughts spoken aloud.

There are also lots of "I" statements:
"I glorified you . . ."
"I revealed your name . . ."
"I pray for them. . . ."

Obviously, this is a very thoughtful and revealing reading. How might you use the tone of your voice to communicate that?

and they accepted them and truly
understood that I came from you,
and they have believed that you sent me.
I pray for them.
I do not pray for the world but for the ones
you have given me,
because they are yours, and everything of
mine is yours
and everything of yours is mine,
and I have been glorified in them.
And now I will no longer be in the world,
but they are in the world, while I am
coming to you."

Preparing to Proclaim
Key words and phrases: "Receive the Holy Spirit."

To the point: It can come as a surprise, even for those of us who are attentive to the cycle of readings, that the Pentecost narrative is not today's gospel. Instead, we have a preliminary passing on of the Holy Spirit at another Easter encounter story. In this one, Jesus's breath is the means of transmission, a gentler image than the driving wind and tongues of fire we associate with this day. The Pentecost story we might expect here occurs only in Acts, and thus remains in the position of first reading. This reminds us that Pentecost is removed enough from the life of Jesus that it does not appear in the gospels. This story is about what the church will do now that Jesus's bodily presence has left earth. And what it does is run out and preach, unable to contain the good news of Jesus.

Making Connections
Between the readings: The gospel narrates a small, contained passing of the Holy Spirit. Jesus appears behind locked doors only to those who knew him. He offers them something of a commission, but the story ends the way it started: in a small room in a contained community, behind locked doors. The first reading begins in a similar way but ends with a massively inclusive image: the disciples are preaching not only to those who share their language and culture but to those outside these bounds.

To experience: All of us are part of some culture or another. "Culture" does not just mean racial or ethnic background but includes things like our age, our social location, and even the micro-cultures of each of our families. The Holy Spirit can and does work through all of these, but the Pentecost story makes clear that we are also called to a unity that transcends them.

Prayer

Triune God,
the fullness of your presence
is made manifest in the activity of your Holy
 Spirit,
enlivening, refreshing, propelling, and
 quickening.
Creator God, Redeeming Son:
*send out your Spirit, and renew the face of
 the earth.*
Set us ablaze with your love, gift us with your
 holy presence.
Amen.

First Reading (Acts 2:1-11)

A reading from the Acts of the Apostles

When the time for Pentecost was fulfilled,
 they were all in one place together.
And suddenly there came from the sky
 a noise like a strong driving wind,
 and it filled the entire house in which they
 were.
Then there appeared to them tongues as of
 fire,
 which parted and came to rest on each one
 of them.
And they were all filled with the Holy Spirit
 and began to speak in different tongues,
 as the Spirit enabled them to proclaim.

Now there were devout Jews from every
 nation under heaven
 staying in Jerusalem.
At this sound, they gathered in a large crowd,
 but they were confused
 because each one heard them speaking in
 his own language.
They were astounded, and in amazement they
 asked,

Pronunciation
Parthians
 PAHR-thee-uhnz
Elamites   EE-luh-maitz
Judea   jou-DEE-uh
Cappadocia
 kap-ih-DO-shee-uh
Phrygia   FRIH-jih-uh
Pamphylia
 pam-FIHL-ih-uh
Cyrene   sai-REE-nee

First of all, make sure
that you rehearse out loud
the names that have been
phonetically written out
for you, helping to elimi-
nate any struggling with
pronunciation that can
distract from the meaning
of the passage.

Write in pencil anything
that you think will help
you with pronunciation.
Finally, slow down! Give
yourself time to pro-
nounce these curious
names correctly.

215

"Are not all these people who are speaking
Galileans?
Then how does each of us hear them in his
native language?
We are Parthians, Medes, and Elamites,
inhabitants of Mesopotamia, Judea and
Cappadocia,
Pontus and Asia, Phrygia and Pamphylia,
Egypt and the districts of Libya near
Cyrene,
as well as travelers from Rome,
both Jews and converts to Judaism, Cretans
and Arabs,
yet we hear them speaking in our own
tongues
of the mighty acts of God."

Responsorial Psalm (Ps 104:1, 24, 29-30, 31, 34)

℟. (cf. 30) Lord, send out your Spirit, and
renew the face of the earth. *or:* ℟. Alleluia.

Bless the LORD, O my soul!
O LORD, my God, you are great indeed!
How manifold are your works, O LORD!
The earth is full of your creatures.

℟. Lord, send out your Spirit, and renew the
face of the earth. *or:* ℟. Alleluia.

If you take away their breath, they perish
and return to their dust.
When you send forth your spirit, they are
created,
and you renew the face of the earth.

℟. Lord, send out your Spirit, and renew the
face of the earth. *or:* ℟. Alleluia.

May the glory of the Lord endure forever;
  may the Lord be glad in his works!
Pleasing to him be my theme;
  I will be glad in the Lord.

R⎋. Lord, send out your Spirit, and renew the face of the earth. *or:* R⎋. Alleluia.

Second Reading (1 Cor 12:3b-7, 12-13)

A reading from the first Letter of Saint Paul to the Corinthians

Brothers and sisters:
No one can say, "Jesus is Lord," except by the
  Holy Spirit.

There are different kinds of spiritual gifts but
  the same Spirit;
  there are different forms of service but the
    same Lord;
  there are different workings but the same
    God
who produces all of them in everyone.
To each individual the manifestation of the
  Spirit
is given for some benefit.

As a body is one though it has many parts,
  and all the parts of the body, though many,
    are one body,
  so also Christ.
For in one Spirit we were all baptized into one
  body,
  whether Jews or Greeks, slaves or free
    persons,
  and we were all given to drink of one
    Spirit.

Pronunciation
Corinthians
  kawr-IHN-thee-uhnz

Paul repeats the same phrases throughout this passage to make a point, such as different kinds, different forms, different workings, etc. Don't be afraid to really emphasize the repeated words or phrases. And of course, since this is Paul, take a nice pause after each period.

This is such a short gospel, especially after the first and second readings. For that very reason be careful, and make sure you engage the listeners from the very beginning.

Gospel (John 20:19-23; L63A)

A reading from the holy Gospel according to John

On the evening of that first day of the week,
    when the doors were locked, where the
        disciples were,
    for fear of the Jews,
    Jesus came and stood in their midst
    and said to them, "Peace be with you."
When he had said this, he showed them his
    hands and his side.
The disciples rejoiced when they saw the
    Lord.
Jesus said to them again, "Peace be with you.
As the Father has sent me, so I send you."
And when he had said this, he breathed on
    them and said to them,
    "Receive the Holy Spirit.
Whose sins you forgive are forgiven them,
    and whose sins you retain are retained."

Preparing to Proclaim
Key words and phrases: "God so loved
the world that he gave his only Son."

To the point: At first glance, this gospel
may seem an odd choice for the Sunday we
celebrate the tripartite personhood of God.
The Father and Son are mentioned, but the
Holy Spirit is nowhere to be seen. But despite
the lack of explicit mention, this gospel is rich
in the Spirit. It is through the Spirit overshad-
owing Mary that Jesus comes to be in the
world, and the Spirit accompanies Jesus
throughout his ministry and mission on earth.
The silence here is often part of how the Spirit works, in subtleties and
whispers rather than in obvious or understandable ways. We might pre-
fer the Spirit's work—like all of God's work—to be more evident to us,
but the wisdom of God differs from ours and so our work is training our
eyes to see the quiet hints of God's hand in the world.

Making Connections
Between the readings: The second reading finally names all three
members of the Trinity explicitly on this Trinity Sunday. St. Paul uses
their names as a greeting, one we still use at Mass today. This is a
powerful greeting. We begin everything we do in the names of these
three persons in one God. The familiarity of this triad—Father, Son, and
Spirit—can make us forget that there is a beautiful mystery at play here.
God's very essence is relationship, is love, to the point that God needs to
be three persons so that the love has someplace to go.

To experience: We live out the mystery of the Trinity in the ongoing
dance of all our human relationships. As the ancient hymn "Ubi Caritas"
reminds us, wherever love is, God is present. God is the source and sustenance of all the different ways we experience love in our human
relationships.

Prayer

God,

you are a holy community, lover, beloved, and
loving.

Formed in your image, we too are called
to be with one another in a holy community
of love.

Your love saves us, brings us peace and
justice,

and leads us to eternal life.

Glory and praise forever!

Amen.

Pronunciation

Sinai   SAI-nai

Whoa! This is an incredibly intense scene. The
first part is calm enough.
The second part is terrifying, as the Lord actually
appeared to Moses and
"cried out" to him. Then
Moses somehow had the
courage to speak to the
Lord, asking pardon for
"a stiff-necked people"!

Of course, pause between
the sections as the longer
the pause, the more drama
you will create.

The one word I would use
to describe this passage is
"incredulous." Remember
that description when you
deliver this reading.

First Reading (Exod 34:4b-6, 8-9)

A reading from the Book of Exodus

Early in the morning Moses went up Mount
Sinai
as the LORD had commanded him,
taking along the two stone tablets.

Having come down in a cloud, the LORD stood
with Moses there
and proclaimed his name, "LORD."
Thus the LORD passed before him and cried
out,
"The LORD, the LORD, a merciful and
gracious God,
slow to anger and rich in kindness and
fidelity."
Moses at once bowed down to the ground in
worship.
Then he said, "If I find favor with you,
O LORD,
do come along in our company.
This is indeed a stiff-necked people; yet
pardon our wickedness and sins,
and receive us as your own."

Responsorial Psalm (Dan 3:52, 53, 54, 55)

℟. (52b) Glory and praise forever!

Blessed are you, O Lord, the God of our fathers,
    praiseworthy and exalted above all forever;
and blessed is your holy and glorious name,
    praiseworthy and exalted above all for all
        ages.

℟. Glory and praise forever!

Blessed are you in the temple of your holy
        glory,
    praiseworthy and glorious above all forever.

℟. Glory and praise forever!

Blessed are you on the throne of your
        kingdom,
    praiseworthy and exalted above all forever.

℟. Glory and praise forever!

Blessed are you who look into the depths
    from your throne upon the cherubim,
    praiseworthy and exalted above all forever.

℟. Glory and praise forever!

Second Reading (2 Cor 13:11-13)

A reading from the second Letter of Saint
Paul to the Corinthians

Brothers and sisters, rejoice. Mend your ways,
        encourage one another,
    agree with one another, live in peace,
        and the God of love and peace will be with
            you.
Greet one another with a holy kiss.
All the holy ones greet you.

The grace of the Lord Jesus Christ
    and the love of God
    and the fellowship of the Holy Spirit be
        with all of you.

Pronunciation
Corinthians
    kawr-IHN-thee-uhnz

Paul is sending us a wonderful valentine! We need it today no less than in his time. Each phrase in the second sentence can stand on its own, so slow down the delivery of those phrases with a nice pause at every comma.

Finally, take a nice pause before Paul blesses the community.

221

This is such a well-known piece by John. And there lies the possible trap: Oh, we've heard this before.

Slow this reading way down to make the congregation listen more carefully. If you emphasize the verbs, it will enhance the reading further.

Gospel (John 3:16-18; L164A)

A reading from the holy Gospel according to John

God so loved the world that he gave his only Son,
> so that everyone who believes in him might not perish
> but might have eternal life.

For God did not send his Son into the world to condemn the world,
> but that the world might be saved through him.

Whoever believes in him will not be condemned,
> but whoever does not believe has already been condemned,
> because he has not believed in the name of the only Son of God.

Preparing to Proclaim

Key words and phrases: "Whoever eats my flesh and drinks my blood remains in me and I in him."

To the point: The latter part of the Easter season is all about the Holy Spirit; Jesus promises to send an advocate who will not leave us orphaned. Now, two Sundays after Pentecost, we celebrate another astonishing way that Jesus remains with us after the ascension. Through the power of that Spirit, he becomes fully present at every Mass; his body and blood are really there. While we might envy the disciples who got to walk alongside Jesus in his lifetime, we are given the extraordinary gift of being united with him—deeply and really—at every eucharistic celebration. Eating is one of the few acts that bypasses the barriers of the human body; the closeness is such that even on a molecular level, Jesus becomes part of us. The humility of God joining us in our human condition was an inconceivable gift; the humility of giving his flesh and blood as food and drink continues the mind-bending generosity of our God.

Making Connections

Between the readings: The first reading shows that God has a long history of providing food and drink for God's people. The Eucharist carries on this long tradition, but in an entirely new way that gives life previously unimaginable. The second reading reminds us that the Eucharist is a way of participating in the life of Jesus himself. We become his Body by participating. We are also bound together, becoming united in a reality that transcends all the human divisions we continue to enforce.

To experience: The Second Vatican Council calls the Eucharist the "source and summit" of our faith, but its repeatability can make it feel less special or exciting than some of the other sacraments. But Jesus reminds us of the reason for this repeatability; this sacrament is food, and like the food we eat to nourish our physical selves, this meal needs to be repeated for spiritual health and vigor.

Prayer

Sustaining Presence,
you created us to be your people,
to be your holy city, Jerusalem, now and
always.
Preserve us with your body and teach us with
your word.
Let us *[p]raise the Lord*, we who call ourselves Christians,
and forever lift up our hearts to his holy name.
Amen.

First Reading (Deut 8:2-3, 14b-16a)

A reading from the Book of Deuteronomy

Moses said to the people:
"Remember how for forty years now the
LORD, your God,
has directed all your journeying in the desert,
so as to test you by affliction
and find out whether or not it was your
intention
to keep his commandments.
He therefore let you be afflicted with hunger,
and then fed you with manna,
a food unknown to you and your fathers,
in order to show you that not by bread
alone does one live,
but by every word that comes forth from
the mouth of the LORD.

"Do not forget the LORD, your God,
who brought you out of the land of Egypt,
that place of slavery;
who guided you through the vast and
terrible desert
with its saraph serpents and scorpions,
its parched and waterless ground;
who brought forth water for you from the
flinty rock

Pronunciation
Deuteronomy
dyoo-ter-AH-num-mee
Saraph   SAY-raf

Here are three wonderful decrees by Moses. You want to deliver these decrees with confidence and strength. Note that each is filled with verbs. To give more energy to the readings try emphasizing the verbs.

Of course, give a good pause between each of the three main parts, the first ending with "keep his commandments," the second with "mouth of the LORD."

and fed you in the desert with manna,
a food unknown to your fathers."

Responsorial Psalm (Ps 147:12-13, 14-15, 19-20)

R℟. (12) Praise the Lord, Jerusalem. *or:*
R℟. Alleluia.

Glorify the LORD, O Jerusalem;
    praise your God, O Zion.
For he has strengthened the bars of your gates;
    he has blessed your children within you.

R℟. Praise the Lord, Jerusalem. *or:* R℟. Alleluia.

He has granted peace in your borders;
    with the best of wheat he fills you.
He sends forth his command to the earth;
    swiftly runs his word!

R℟. Praise the Lord, Jerusalem. *or:* R℟. Alleluia.

He has proclaimed his word to Jacob,
    his statutes and his ordinances to Israel.
He has not done thus for any other nation;
    his ordinances he has not made known to
        them. Alleluia.

R℟. Praise the Lord, Jerusalem. *or:* R℟. Alleluia.

Second Reading (1 Cor 10:16-17)

A reading from the first Letter of Saint Paul to the Corinthians

Brothers and sisters:
The cup of blessing that we bless,
    is it not a participation in the blood of Christ?
The bread that we break,
    is it not a participation in the body of Christ?
Because the loaf of bread is one,
    we, though many, are one body,
    for we all partake of the one loaf.

Pronunciation
Corinthians
    kawr-IHN-thee-uhnz

Paul was an amazing theologian! In just a very few words he is giving us the meaning of the sacrament of the Eucharist. Brothers and sisters: Paul is addressing this to *everyone.*

That being said, slow down. These words could

225

be called sacred simply because of their profound subject matter. Again, a nice pause after "Brothers and sisters," and then after "participation in the body of Christ."

The Jews might seem a bit less than intelligent in this reading, but let us not forget that we would have probably made the same comment at the time. The balance of this reading explains how Jesus is indeed the flesh and blood of eternal life.

To me, this is one of John's greatest accounts of Jesus's teaching, so take it slowly as it is carefully written (translated). You don't want the listeners to miss one word of the reading.

Gospel (John 6:51-58; L167A)

A reading from the holy Gospel according to John

Jesus said to the Jewish crowds:
"I am the living bread that came down
from heaven;
whoever eats this bread will live forever;
and the bread that I will give
is my flesh for the life of the world."

The Jews quarreled among themselves, saying,
"How can this man give us his flesh to eat?"
Jesus said to them,
"Amen, amen, I say to you,
unless you eat the flesh of the Son of Man
and drink his blood,
you do not have life within you.
Whoever eats my flesh and drinks my blood
has eternal life,
and I will raise him on the last day.
For my flesh is true food,
and my blood is true drink.
Whoever eats my flesh and drinks my blood
remains in me and I in him.
Just as the living Father sent me
and I have life because of the Father,
so also the one who feeds on me
will have life because of me.
This is the bread that came down from heaven.
Unlike your ancestors who ate and still died,
whoever eats this bread will live forever."

Preparing to Proclaim

Key words and phrases: "[H]e summoned his twelve disciples and gave them authority over unclean spirits . . . and to cure every disease and every illness."

To the point: This gospel reveals Jesus's human nature in a number of ways. First, he is moved with pity; he has an emotional response to seeing people in need. Next, he seems to realize that he cannot do this work alone; there are too many needs to meet. Even Jesus, the second person of the Trinity, needs to ask for help. This is not a weakness of the human condition, not an effect of sin, but rather a normal part of our healthy functioning. And finally, he gives instructions that we know will be incomplete: at this point he sends his disciples only "to the lost sheep of the house of Israel." Jesus allows himself to be limited by the human constraints of time and resources and personnel. The fullness of his mission, where all nations are joined in praise of the one God, will develop over time.

Making Connections

Between the readings: The first reading affirms Jesus's understanding of Israel as God's particularly beloved people. They are to be "a kingdom of priests," tasked with acting as something of a liaison between God and the rest of the world. In the gospel, the disciples take part in this priesthood in a new way, sent out to bring God back to Israel and Israel back to God. Ultimately, they will be further commissioned to go to all nations; the Holy Spirit at Pentecost will enable them to speak beyond the boundaries of their own language and culture.

To experience: This gospel shows Jesus getting organized. While his personal touch is irreplaceable, his ministry will be more effective with delegation and teamwork. There is a model of servant leadership here; good leaders are both willing to do the work themselves and willing to step aside when the situation calls for it.

Prayer

God of Peace, God of Rest,
your son is for us a loving shepherd,
safety and security through the night.
We are his people: the sheep of his flock.
We praise you for your kindness and
faithfulness.
Grant us always your reconciliation and
salvation.
Amen.

Pronunciation
Sinai   SAI-nai

Well, you shouldn't try to
impersonate God, but you
should deliver God's
words to Moses with
great conviction and
clarity. Speak slowly and
deliberately. Emphasizing
the verbs is a good tech-
nique to bring life to a
reading.

First Reading (Exod 19:2-6a)

A reading from the Book of Exodus

In those days, the Israelites came to the desert
of Sinai and pitched camp.
While Israel was encamped here in front of
the mountain,
Moses went up the mountain to God.
Then the LORD called to him and said,
"Thus shall you say to the house of Jacob;
tell the Israelites:
You have seen for yourselves how I treated
the Egyptians
and how I bore you up on eagle wings
and brought you here to myself.
Therefore, if you hearken to my voice and
keep my covenant,
you shall be my special possession,
dearer to me than all other people,
though all the earth is mine.
You shall be to me a kingdom of priests, a
holy nation."

Responsorial Psalm (Ps 100:1-2, 3, 5)

℟. (3c) We are his people: the sheep of his flock.

Sing joyfully to the LORD, all you lands;
   serve the LORD with gladness;
   come before him with joyful song.

℟. We are his people: the sheep of his flock.

Know that the LORD is God;
   he made us, his we are;
   his people, the flock he tends.

℟. We are his people: the sheep of his flock.

The LORD is good:
   his kindness endures forever,
   and his faithfulness to all generations.

℟. We are his people: the sheep of his flock.

Second Reading (Rom 5:6-11)

A reading from the Letter of Saint Paul to the Romans

Brothers and sisters:
Christ, while we were still helpless,
   yet died at the appointed time for the
      ungodly.
Indeed, only with difficulty does one die for a
      just person,
   though perhaps for a good person
   one might even find courage to die.
But God proves his love for us
   in that while we were still sinners Christ
      died for us.
How much more then, since we are now
      justified by his blood,
   will we be saved through him from the
      wrath.

Here is Paul again with his complex sentences. Pay attention to the punctuation and rehearse the reading aloud, making sure you place the right emphasis on the correct words and phrases.

Don't forget to take a nice pause after the line ending "will we be saved through him from the wrath" as you get ready for six commas in the next sentence.

Indeed, if, while we were enemies,
we were reconciled to God through the
death of his Son,
how much more, once reconciled,
will we be saved by his life.
Not only that,
but we also boast of God through our Lord
Jesus Christ,
through whom we have now received
reconciliation.

Pronunciation
Zebedee   ZEH-beh-dee
Bartholomew
   bar-THAHL-uh-myoo
Alphaeus   AL-fee-uhs
Thaddeus
   THAD-dee-uhs
Cana   KAY-nuh
Iscariot   ihs-KEHR-ee-uht

How might you deliver the names of the twelve apostles if they were seated in your congregation and stood up when you announced them? This is just a trick to give each one a little different emphasis because, after all, these were real people, most of whom became saints.

Gospel   (Matt 9:36–10:8; L91A)

A reading from the holy Gospel according to Matthew

At the sight of the crowds, Jesus' heart was
moved with pity for them
because they were troubled and abandoned,
like sheep without a shepherd.
Then he said to his disciples,
"The harvest is abundant but the laborers
are few;
so ask the master of the harvest
to send out laborers for his harvest."

Then he summoned his twelve disciples
and gave them authority over unclean
spirits
to drive them out and to cure every disease
and every illness.
The names of the twelve apostles are these:
first, Simon called Peter, and his brother
Andrew;
James, the son of Zebedee, and his brother
John;
Philip and Bartholomew, Thomas and
Matthew the tax collector;
James, the son of Alphaeus, and Thaddeus;
Simon from Cana, and Judas Iscariot who
betrayed him.

Jesus sent out these twelve after instructing
    them thus,
    "Do not go into pagan territory or enter a
        Samaritan town.
Go rather to the lost sheep of the house of
    ·Israel.
As you go, make this proclamation: 'The
    kingdom of heaven is at hand.'
Cure the sick, raise the dead, cleanse lepers,
    drive out demons.
Without cost you have received; without cost
    you are to give."

Preparing to Proclaim

Key words and phrases: "Even all the hairs of your head are counted."

To the point: In this gospel, Jesus is reassuring the disciples, for he has just revealed that their mission of preaching and healing will also lead them into the path of persecutions and hatred. In this passage, he reminds them at least three times not to be afraid. Their mission is true and trustworthy and worth the pain it will bring. More importantly, they do not go alone; they are accompanied always by a God who knows all and sees all and loves them intimately. The image of God seeing and noting the deaths of even sparrows is a charming one; sparrows are referred to by birders as "little brown jobs," interesting in their own way but nondescript, good at camouflage, and hard to tell apart. We know now of their ecological importance, but on the surface they are not the most interesting bird there is to see. But God sees and notices each of them individually, and God's care for us is many orders of magnitude more.

Making Connections

Between the readings: Jeremiah here acknowledges the same fear the disciples experience in the gospel. Being a messenger for God can make us unpopular; encountering God often calls people to change in ways for which they are not ready, and their resulting scorn is sometimes directed at those who bring the message. But again, strength is found in God's companionship and protection. Courage is called for, and it is justified, because the one who goes with us can do all things.

To experience: In the contemporary Western world, Christians often do not face the sort of persecutions encountered by the disciples. For us, courageous faith is still needed but occurs in much more subtle ways: in standing up for truth in a conversation with a loved one, in treating those with love whose choices might make us uncomfortable. Wherever and whenever we need courage, God goes with us, seeing our fears and accompanying us through them.

Prayer

God of the Prophets,
at times, speaking your truth and living your
    love
brings only insults and loneliness,
and seems a failure in the world's eyes.
Hear my call, hear my cry: *in your great love,
    answer me.*
The life of a Christian is difficult, but full of
    hope:
give us joy in your presence.
Amen.

First Reading (Jer 20:10-13)

A reading from the Book of the Prophet
Jeremiah

Jeremiah said:
"I hear the whisperings of many:
    'Terror on every side!
    Denounce! Let us denounce him!'
All those who were my friends
    are on the watch for any misstep of mine.
'Perhaps he will be trapped; then we can
        prevail,
    and take our vengeance on him.'
But the LORD is with me, like a mighty
        champion:
    my persecutors will stumble, they will
        not triumph.
In their failure they will be put to utter shame,
    to lasting, unforgettable confusion.
O LORD of hosts, you who test the just,
    who probe mind and heart,
let me witness the vengeance you take on
        them,
    for to you I have entrusted my cause.
Sing to the LORD,
    praise the LORD,
for he has rescued the life of the poor
    from the power of the wicked!"

Pronunciation
Jeremiah
    jehr-eh-MAI-uh

This is a rather dramatic
reading from Jeremiah! He
is terrified, as he says his
enemies really are out to
destroy him.

Make sure that your lis-
teners hear "Jeremiah
said" at the very begin-
ning so they know who is
speaking. Once who is
speaking is established,
then the first part will be
understood.

Take a nice pause after
"vengeance on him," "un-
forgettable confusion,"
and "entrusted my cause"
to emphasize the different
tone of these sections.

Responsorial Psalm (Ps 69:8-10, 14, 17, 33-35)

R︒. (14c) Lord, in your great love, answer me.

For your sake I bear insult,
    and shame covers my face.
I have become an outcast to my brothers,
    a stranger to my children,
because zeal for your house consumes me,
    and the insults of those who blaspheme
        you fall upon me.

R︒. Lord, in your great love, answer me.

I pray to you, O LORD,
    for the time of your favor, O God!
In your great kindness answer me
    with your constant help.
Answer me, O LORD, for bounteous is your
        kindness;
    in your great mercy turn toward me.

R︒. Lord, in your great love, answer me.

"See, you lowly ones, and be glad;
    you who seek God, may your hearts revive!
For the LORD hears the poor,
    and his own who are in bonds he spurns
        not.
Let the heavens and the earth praise him,
    the seas and whatever moves in them!"

R︒. Lord, in your great love, answer me.

Second Reading (Rom 5:12-15)

A reading from the Letter of Saint Paul to the Romans

Brothers and sisters:
Through one man sin entered the world,
 and through sin, death,
  and thus death came to all men, inasmuch
   as all sinned—
  for up to the time of the law, sin was in the
   world,
  though sin is not accounted when there is
   no law.
But death reigned from Adam to Moses,
 even over those who did not sin
 after the pattern of the trespass of Adam,
 who is the type of the one who was to come.

But the gift is not like the transgression.
For if by the transgression of the one the
  many died,
 how much more did the grace of God
 and the gracious gift of the one man Jesus
  Christ
 overflow for the many.

Of course, Paul is referring to Adam in the first sentence. As is usual with Paul rehearse this reading out loud a number of times so that it becomes obvious where and when and how to pause.

The pause after each sentence is as important as always.

Gospel (Matt 10:26-33; L94A)

A reading from the holy Gospel according to Matthew

Jesus said to the Twelve:
 "Fear no one.
Nothing is concealed that will not be revealed,
 nor secret that will not be known.
What I say to you in the darkness, speak in
  the light;
 what you hear whispered, proclaim on the
   housetops.
And do not be afraid of those who kill the
  body but cannot kill the soul;
 rather, be afraid of the one who can destroy
 both soul and body in Gehenna.

Pronunciation
Gehenna   geh-HEHN-uh

The opening three-word sentence is rather amazing: "Fear no one." That is quite an opening directive at any time. Allow that sentence to stand on its own for a moment to let it sink in for the listeners.

235

Are not two sparrows sold for a small coin?
Yet not one of them falls to the ground
without your Father's knowledge.
Even all the hairs of your head are counted.
So do not be afraid; you are worth more than
many sparrows.
Everyone who acknowledges me before others
I will acknowledge before my heavenly
Father.
But whoever denies me before others,
I will deny before my heavenly Father."

Preparing to Proclaim

Key words and phrases: "Whoever finds his life will lose it, and whoever loses his life for my sake will find it."

To the point: This gospel calls us to hospitality; it is about receiving others and thereby receiving Christ. But this hospitality goes beyond what we usually mean by the word. It is not about throwing parties or offering a bed when it will make us look good or give us fodder for our social media feeds. It's not a hospitality of convenience. This is rather a hospitality of the heart; it is about being willing to move around our very selves in order to make space for others. That's why Jesus's words about receiving others and offering cups of cold water are paired with those about taking up our crosses and losing our lives. This hospitality is about giving of ourselves, which is sometimes uncomfortable. But Jesus is calling us to something deeper here. We do not give up our lives for no reason, but because in doing so we imitate the self-giving love of God. By making this space for others, we find our truest selves.

Making Connections

Between the readings: The first reading shows a practice of radical hospitality, the same kind to which we are called by the gospel. The Shunammite woman and her husband do not just provide for Elisha's needs as is convenient for them. They rearrange their very lives and home to make space for him. In the end, this is what hospitality is all about—making space for others, in our homes, in our lives, and in our hearts.

To experience: Many of us are adept at surface-level hospitality; we know how to greet someone new, to make conversation, to be friendly. Many of us know how to open our homes to others, to create a pleasant experience and tend to the immediate needs of those who eat or sleep under our roofs. But Jesus asks us for something more; hospitality of the heart requires deeper vulnerability, radical generosity, and profound trust in God.

Prayer

Good and Gracious God,
you fulfill your promises to your people,
giving new life to those who live your
    covenant.
Forever let us *sing the goodness of the Lord.*
You are holy, our strength, our deliverer.
Bring us to more deeply live your truth
and to follow in your ways.
Amen.

Pronunciation
Elisha   ee-LAI-shuh
Shunem   SHOO-nehm
Gehazi   gee-HAY-zai

Make sure that you are
well rehearsed with the
above names so that you
won't hesitate over them
distracting from the
meaning of the reading.
If you'd like, write down
the pronunciation of these
names on a piece of paper
and place it in the Lection-
ary to refer to as you read.

First Reading (2 Kgs 4:8-11, 14-16a)

A reading from the second Book of Kings

One day Elisha came to Shunem,
    where there was a woman of influence,
        who urged him to dine with her.
Afterward, whenever he passed by, he used to
    stop there to dine.
So she said to her husband, "I know that
    Elisha is a holy man of God.
Since he visits us often, let us arrange a little
    room on the roof
    and furnish it for him with a bed, table,
        chair, and lamp,
    so that when he comes to us he can stay
        there."
Sometime later Elisha arrived and stayed in
    the room overnight.

Later Elisha asked, "Can something be done
    for her?"
His servant Gehazi answered, "Yes!
    She has no son, and her husband is getting
        on in years."
Elisha said, "Call her."
When the woman had been called and stood
    at the door,
    Elisha promised, "This time next year
    you will be fondling a baby son."

Responsorial Psalm (Ps 89:2-3, 16-17, 18-19)

R︰. (2a) Forever I will sing the goodness of the Lord.

The promises of the LORD I will sing forever,
    through all generations my mouth shall
        proclaim your faithfulness.
For you have said, "My kindness is
    established forever";
    in heaven you have confirmed your
        faithfulness.

R︰. Forever I will sing the goodness of the Lord.

Blessed the people who know the joyful shout;
    in the light of your countenance, O LORD,
        they walk.
At your name they rejoice all the day,
    and through your justice they are exalted.

R︰. Forever I will sing the goodness of the Lord.

You are the splendor of their strength,
    and by your favor our horn is exalted.
For to the LORD belongs our shield,
    and to the Holy One of Israel, our king.

R︰. Forever I will sing the goodness of the Lord.

Second Reading (Rom 6:3-4, 8-11)

A reading from the Letter of Saint Paul to the Romans

Brothers and sisters:
Are you unaware that we who were baptized
    into Christ Jesus
    were baptized into his death?
We were indeed buried with him through
    baptism into death,
    so that, just as Christ was raised from the
        dead
    by the glory of the Father,
    we too might live in newness of life.

So, as usual with Paul's writings rehearse this reading out loud, paying close attention to punctuation. Take your time and never rush through Paul's writings, as you are almost always sure to stumble if you do.

Paraphrase the reading so that you can be assured that you are communicating Paul's point.

239

THIRTEENTH SUNDAY
IN ORDINARY TIME

If, then, we have died with Christ,
    we believe that we shall also live with him.
We know that Christ, raised from the dead,
        dies no more;
    death no longer has power over him.
As to his death, he died to sin once and for all;
    as to his life, he lives for God.
Consequently, you too must think of
        yourselves as dead to sin
    and living for God in Christ Jesus.

Gospel (Matt 10:37-42; L97A)

A reading from the holy Gospel according
to Matthew

Jesus said to his apostles:
    "Whoever loves father or mother more than
            me is not worthy of me,
    and whoever loves son or daughter more
            than me is not worthy of me;
    and whoever does not take up his cross
    and follow after me is not worthy of me.
"Whoever finds his life will lose it,
    and whoever loses his life for my sake will
        find it.
Whoever receives you receives me,
    and whoever receives me receives the one
        who sent me.
Whoever receives a prophet because he is a
        prophet
    will receive a prophet's reward,
    and whoever receives a righteous man
    because he is a righteous man
    will receive a righteous man's reward.
And whoever gives only a cup of cold water
    to one of these little ones to drink
    because the little one is a disciple—
    amen, I say to you, he will surely not lose
        his reward."

Each one of Matthew's phrases in this reading can stand on its own. I would advise that taking time to do just that is not a bad idea. These are not throwaway lines; give the listeners time to let them sink in.

Preparing to Proclaim

Key words and phrases: "[M]y yoke is easy, and my burden light."

To the point: After several weeks of affirming the challenges of following him, Jesus offers here a word of consolation. "My yoke is easy, and my burden light" does not sound like it aligns well with all we have been hearing about persecution and suffering. But Jesus is reminding us that even though suffering might be part of the life of his followers, it is not of God and is not God's will for us—it is a side effect of living in a world where sin still has a hold. Following Jesus is in fact a joyful thing; this is the God who loves us desperately and wants nothing but our good. Jesus wants peace for us; he *promises* peace for us. This peace comes at many different levels: between nations, between individuals, and within our own hearts.

Making Connections

Between the readings: The first reading also speaks a word of consolation: God comes to save us, and our response is to rejoice. God is not a God of war who will deal harsh justice to our enemies. Rather, he comes meekly, in a way we would not expect. He banishes not Israel's enemies but the very tools of war. Once again, God subverts our expectations. He does not engage in the futile means humans have for fighting each other but rather bypasses the fight altogether.

To experience: There is an invitation in these readings to rest, an invitation our productivity-driven culture doesn't often let us hear clearly. The life of faith often calls us to hard work—to self-gift, to mission, to tireless preaching of the gospel. But God does not expect us to do this all the time. Our creator made us to need rhythms that include times of repose. He even *commands* us to rest in the Old Testament, carving out one of every seven days as a time to set aside our work.

Prayer

Savior and Solace,
with you is justice and peace, rest and respite.
We shall *praise your name forever*
for you call us to child-like faith,
to abandon riches, power, and influence.
Rather, your reign is one of dependence on you,
revealed in your son, Jesus Christ,
who is Lord for ever and ever.
Amen.

Pronunciation
Zechariah
   zeh-kuh-RAI-uh
Zion   ZAI-uhn
Ephraim   EE-fray-ihm

This is good news! Proclaim it joyously with a smile on your face. Take a nice pause between sentences. There is even greater news as "he shall proclaim peace to the nations"!

First Reading (Zech 9:9-10)

A reading from the Book of the Prophet Zechariah

Thus says the LORD:
Rejoice heartily, O daughter Zion,
   shout for joy, O daughter Jerusalem!
See, your king shall come to you;
   a just savior is he,
meek, and riding on an ass,
   on a colt, the foal of an ass.
He shall banish the chariot from Ephraim,
   and the horse from Jerusalem;
the warrior's bow shall be banished,
   and he shall proclaim peace to the nations.
His dominion shall be from sea to sea,
   and from the River to the ends of the earth.

Responsorial Psalm (Ps 145:1-2, 8-9, 10-11, 13-14)

R̊. (cf. 1) I will praise your name forever, my king and my God. *or:* R̊. Alleluia.

I will extol you, O my God and King,
   and I will bless your name forever and ever.
Every day will I bless you,
   and I will praise your name forever and ever.

R̊. I will praise your name forever, my king and my God. *or:* R̊. Alleluia.

The Lord is gracious and merciful,
  slow to anger and of great kindness.
The Lᴏʀᴅ is good to all
  and compassionate toward all his works.

R̸. I will praise your name forever, my king
and my God. *or:* R̸. Alleluia.

Let all your works give you thanks, O Lᴏʀᴅ,
  and let your faithful ones bless you.
Let them discourse of the glory of your
    kingdom
  and speak of your might.

R̸. I will praise your name forever, my king
and my God. *or:* R̸. Alleluia.

The Lᴏʀᴅ is faithful in all his words
  and holy in all his works.
The Lᴏʀᴅ lifts up all who are falling
  and raises up all who are bowed down.

R̸. I will praise your name forever, my king
and my God. *or:* R̸. Alleluia.

Second Reading (Rom 8:9, 11-13)

A reading from the Letter of Saint Paul to
the Romans

Brothers and sisters:
You are not in the flesh;
  on the contrary, you are in the spirit,
  if only the Spirit of God dwells in you.
Whoever does not have the Spirit of Christ
    does not belong to him.
If the Spirit of the one who raised Jesus from
    the dead dwells in you,
  the one who raised Christ from the dead
  will give life to your mortal bodies also,
  through his Spirit that dwells in you.
Consequently, brothers and sisters,
  we are not debtors to the flesh,
  to live according to the flesh.

Typically, when listeners hear "You are not in the flesh," they think, Well, yes, I am!

So pause a bit after "You are not in the flesh"; then you really have the attention of the congregation when you follow with the next line, "on the contrary, you are in the spirit."

Then emphasize the word "only" in the next line, and the remainder of the reading will be much more easily understood.

243

FOURTEENTH SUNDAY IN ORDINARY TIME

For if you live according to the flesh, you will die,
>   but if by the Spirit you put to death the deeds of the body,
>   you will live.

Take your time with this wonderful reading!

Take pauses after "such has been your gracious will" and "the Son wishes to reveal him." The final part is, of course, highlighted in Handel's *Messiah*. Do not underestimate the soothing relief it can provide for the human soul.

Gospel (Matt 11:25-30; L100A)

A reading from the holy Gospel according to Matthew

At that time Jesus exclaimed:
"I give praise to you, Father, Lord of heaven and earth,
for although you have hidden these things from the wise and the learned
you have revealed them to little ones.
Yes, Father, such has been your gracious will.
All things have been handed over to me by my Father.
No one knows the Son except the Father,
and no one knows the Father except the Son
and anyone to whom the Son wishes to reveal him.

"Come to me, all you who labor and are burdened,
and I will give you rest.
Take my yoke upon you and learn from me,
for I am meek and humble of heart;
and you will find rest for yourselves.
For my yoke is easy, and my burden light."

Preparing to Proclaim

Key words and phrases: "[S]ome seed fell on rich soil, and produced fruit."

To the point: Midsummer is a powerful time to hear this parable for the earth has warmed and is starting to produce. If you visit a local farmer's market you will start to see a rich and wide variety of produce from now until the fall. And the work of growing plants— whether in pots on an apartment balcony or on large-scale agricultural operations—is rich with imagery that can be meaningful for the life of faith. Plants start as seeds, which are not living things on their own. But they carry potential for far more than seems possible at first glance. Given the right conditions, they grow to many times their size, eventually bearing fruit (whose botanical job, by the way, is to produce and spread more seeds!). We, too, need the right conditions and care to grow and bear good fruit; God offers us all this so that we might bear life abundantly.

Making Connections

Between the readings: The first reading and psalm echo the farming imagery of the gospel. God's word is likened to the rain that comes forth from heaven to nourish the earth and to feed us. The second reading pairs our seed and fruit imagery with another of nature's great wonders—that of childbirth. Labor pains are another reflection of God's cyclical work, for great pain and groaning bring new life and abundant joy. The pain of labor, like the suffering of Christ, is lifegiving. It is not pain without purpose.

To experience: If you hear the longer version of this gospel, Jesus makes clear what each seed is a metaphor for. Lack of understanding, lack of rootedness, and worldly anxiety can all prevent us from bearing fruit for Christ. If we are not deeply rooted, challenges can easily topple us. It takes constant weeding away of distractions and unimportant things to maintain space in our lives and hearts for God's word.

Prayer

Creator God,
you call us into the mission field,
to plant, tend, and reap.
The seed that falls on good ground
will yield a fruitful harvest.
Help us find open ears and willing hearts,
that all may come to know and help create
your reign of wholeness and love.
Amen.

Rehearse this reading out loud a number of times as it is all one sentence with five commas and one semicolon.

Don't give up on the energy at the end because the last three lines are very important.

First Reading (Isa 55:10-11)

A reading from the Book of the Prophet Isaiah

Thus says the LORD:
Just as from the heavens
    the rain and snow come down
and do not return there
    till they have watered the earth,
    making it fertile and fruitful,
giving seed to the one who sows
    and bread to the one who eats,
so shall my word be
    that goes forth from my mouth;
my word shall not return to me void,
    but shall do my will,
    achieving the end for which I sent it.

Responsorial Psalm (Ps 65:10, 11, 12-13, 14)

R⁊. (Luke 8:8) The seed that falls on good ground will yield a fruitful harvest.

You have visited the land and watered it;
    greatly have you enriched it.
God's watercourses are filled;
    you have prepared the grain.

R⁊. The seed that falls on good ground will yield a fruitful harvest.

Thus have you prepared the land: drenching
  its furrows,
 breaking up its clods,
softening it with showers,
  blessing its yield.

R̸. The seed that falls on good ground will
yield a fruitful harvest.

You have crowned the year with your bounty,
  and your paths overflow with a rich
      harvest;
the untilled meadows overflow with it,
  and rejoicing clothes the hills.

R̸. The seed that falls on good ground will
yield a fruitful harvest.

The fields are garmented with flocks
  and the valleys blanketed with grain.
  They shout and sing for joy.

R̸. The seed that falls on good ground will
yield a fruitful harvest.

Second Reading (Rom 8:18-23)

A reading from the Letter of Saint Paul to
the Romans

Brothers and sisters:
I consider that the sufferings of this present
    time are as nothing
      compared with the glory to be revealed for
        us.
For creation awaits with eager expectation
    the revelation of the children of God;
    for creation was made subject to futility,
    not of its own accord but because of the
      one who subjected it,
    in hope that creation itself
    would be set free from slavery to
      corruption
    and share in the glorious freedom of the
      children of God.

Take your time with this reading by Paul. Even when read well it is not easily understood.

Rehearse it out loud, making sure where the sentences end. Take a nice pause after "glorious freedom of the children of God" before moving into the next section of the reading.

We know that all creation is groaning in labor
   pains even until now;
and not only that, but we ourselves,
who have the firstfruits of the Spirit,
we also groan within ourselves
as we wait for adoption, the redemption of
   our bodies.

If you ever wanted to do a bit of theater with the reading of a gospel, this is a good candidate.

This same parable is featured in the play *Godspell* and it invites a typical acting approach. This approach is easily done with just a few volunteers, and it would certainly provide a different way of visualizing Matthew's Gospel.

As a way to prepare for proclaiming, you as narrator can read the gospel as one volunteer plays the part of the sower. Other volunteers play the part of the "birds that eat up the seed." The same volunteers can play the part of the seeds on rocky ground that spring up quickly but then wither. More volunteers play the part of the seed that springs up but then are choked by thorns played by yet other volunteers. Finally all can play the seed that falls on rich soil.

Gospel   (Matt 13:1-23 [or Matt 13:1-9]; L103A)

A reading from the holy Gospel according to Matthew

[On that day, Jesus went out of the house and
   sat down by the sea.
Such large crowds gathered around him
   that he got into a boat and sat down,
   and the whole crowd stood along the shore.
And he spoke to them at length in parables,
   saying:
"A sower went out to sow.
And as he sowed, some seed fell on the path,
   and birds came and ate it up.
Some fell on rocky ground, where it had little
   soil.
It sprang up at once because the soil was not
   deep,
   and when the sun rose it was scorched,
   and it withered for lack of roots.
Some seed fell among thorns, and the thorns
   grew up and choked it.
But some seed fell on rich soil, and produced
   fruit,
   a hundred or sixty or thirtyfold.
Whoever has ears ought to hear."]

The disciples approached him and said,
   "Why do you speak to them in parables?"
He said to them in reply,

"Because knowledge of the mysteries of
the kingdom of heaven
has been granted to you, but to them it has
not been granted.
To anyone who has, more will be given and he
will grow rich;
from anyone who has not, even what he
has will be taken away.
This is why I speak to them in parables,
because
*they look but do not see and hear but do not
listen or understand.*
Isaiah's prophecy is fulfilled in them, which
says:
*You shall indeed hear but not understand,
you shall indeed look but never see.
Gross is the heart of this people,
they will hardly hear with their ears,
they have closed their eyes,
lest they see with their eyes
and hear with their ears
and understand with their hearts and be
converted,
and I heal them.*

"But blessed are your eyes, because they see,
and your ears, because they hear.
Amen, I say to you, many prophets and
righteous people
longed to see what you see but did not see it,
and to hear what you hear but did not hear it.

"Hear then the parable of the sower.
The seed sown on the path is the one
who hears the word of the kingdom
without understanding it,
and the evil one comes and steals away
what was sown in his heart.
The seed sown on rocky ground
is the one who hears the word and receives
it at once with joy.

But he has no root and lasts only for a time.
When some tribulation or persecution comes
    because of the word,
  he immediately falls away.
The seed sown among thorns is the one who
    hears the word,
    but then worldly anxiety and the lure of
        riches choke the word
    and it bears no fruit.
But the seed sown on rich soil
    is the one who hears the word and
        understands it,
    who indeed bears fruit and yields a
        hundred or sixty or thirtyfold."

Preparing to Proclaim

Key words and phrases: "[G]ather the wheat into my barn."

To the point: The farming and harvest imagery of last week continues with this gospel's parables. The perils of farming are still at play; abundant life is a potential outcome, but so too are weeds that threaten to choke out the long-anticipated good harvest. God has taken a risk on us, on creating humanity and bestowing us with free will. When young people learn about the Fall, they often ask why God gave us free will at all or why God didn't create the world in such a way that evil would not really be an option. We might not fully understand this mystery, but apparently, God thought it was worth the risk. Like farmers who every year take on unpredictable weather and swarming pests and a myriad of fungal diseases, God hopes in us and believes that the fruit we can bear is worth all that can go wrong.

Making Connections

Between the readings: The gospel shows God as a farmer who rather harshly separates the intended harvest from the weeds that are not meant to be there. The first reading balances this image by reminding us that this is a God of forgiveness, known for leniency and repeated mercies. The psalm echoes this theme, praising God for the abounding kindness and never-ending patience that none of us deserves but which we receive anyway.

To experience: We who are adults know that the moral life is not as cut-and-dry as it is in this parable. None of us is fully good or fully evil; judging our hearts is much more complicated than separating us into "children of the kingdom" and "children of the evil one." This is where God's mercy comes in. God knows our hearts deeply and intimately. God knows all of our motivations and our struggles. Still, God is prepared to offer us the utmost generosity in judgment.

Prayer

Reconciling God,
your son took our sins to the cross
that all may be created anew, one in you and
    your love.
Lord, you are good and forgiving.
May we too forgive as you do, love as you do,
and one day bring all to fulfillment
in your merciful presence.
Amen.

Pronunciation
temerity
    tuh-MEH-ruh-tee:
    excessive confidence
    or boldness

Even when you have re-
hearsed this reading, you
dare not go too fast as the
sentence structure is a bit
challenging.

The second part, begin-
ning with "And you
taught your people," is
more easily understood
than the first, and happily,
the message is excellent.
Don't hesitate to deliver
this with a smile on your
face for it is indeed good
news.

First Reading (Wis 12:13, 16-19)

A reading from the Book of Wisdom

There is no god besides you who have the care
    of all,
    that you need show you have not unjustly
        condemned.
For your might is the source of justice;
    your mastery over all things makes you
        lenient to all.
For you show your might when the perfection
    of your power is disbelieved;
    and in those who know you, you rebuke
        temerity.
But though you are master of might, you
    judge with clemency,
    and with much lenience you govern us;
    for power, whenever you will, attends you.
And you taught your people, by these deeds,
    that those who are just must be kind;
and you gave your children good ground for
    hope
    that you would permit repentance for their
        sins.

Responsorial Psalm (Ps 86:5-6, 9-10, 15-16)

R℣. (5a) Lord, you are good and forgiving.

You, O LORD, are good and forgiving,
   abounding in kindness to all who call upon
      you.
Hearken, O LORD, to my prayer
   and attend to the sound of my pleading.

R℣. Lord, you are good and forgiving.

All the nations you have made shall come
   and worship you, O LORD,
   and glorify your name.
For you are great, and you do wondrous
      deeds;
   you alone are God.

R℣. Lord, you are good and forgiving.

You, O LORD, are a God merciful and gracious,
   slow to anger, abounding in kindness and
      fidelity.
Turn toward me, and have pity on me;
   give your strength to your servant.

R℣. Lord, you are good and forgiving.

Second Reading (Rom 8:26-27)

A reading from the Letter of Saint Paul to
the Romans

Brothers and sisters:
The Spirit comes to the aid of our weakness;
   for we do not know how to pray as we
      ought,
   but the Spirit himself intercedes with
      inexpressible groanings.
And the one who searches hearts
   knows what is the intention of the Spirit,
   because he intercedes for the holy ones
   according to God's will.

What a great description of the Spirit Paul gives us here! Don't be afraid to really "punch" the word "Spirit" the first time; if your listeners miss that word, they are missing a good deal of the reading. Hitting the verbs is your next goal, as they tell what the Spirit is doing.

Emphasizing the verbs is always a good way to bring extra energy to a reading. Try reading at least part of this out loud, emphasizing the verbs, and notice the difference.

Gospel (Matt 13:24-43 [or Matt 13:24-30]; L106A)

A reading from the holy Gospel according to Matthew

[Jesus proposed another parable to the
    crowds, saying:
"The kingdom of heaven may be likened
    to a man who sowed good seed in his field.
While everyone was asleep his enemy came
    and sowed weeds all through the wheat,
        and then went off.
When the crop grew and bore fruit, the weeds
    appeared as well.
The slaves of the householder came to him
    and said,
    'Master, did you not sow good seed in your
        field?
Where have the weeds come from?'
He answered, 'An enemy has done this.'
His slaves said to him,
    'Do you want us to go and pull them up?'
He replied, 'No, if you pull up the weeds
    you might uproot the wheat along with
        them.
Let them grow together until harvest;
    then at harvest time I will say to the
        harvesters,
    "First collect the weeds and tie them in
        bundles for burning;
    but gather the wheat into my barn."'"]

He proposed another parable to them.
"The kingdom of heaven is like a mustard seed
    that a person took and sowed in a field.
It is the smallest of all the seeds,
    yet when full-grown it is the largest of plants.
It becomes a large bush,
    and the 'birds of the sky come and dwell in
        its branches.'"

He spoke to them another parable.
"The kingdom of heaven is like yeast
that a woman took and mixed with three
measures of wheat flour
until the whole batch was leavened."

All these things Jesus spoke to the crowds in
parables.
He spoke to them only in parables,
to fulfill what had been said through the
prophet:
I will open my mouth in parables,
I will announce what has lain hidden
from the foundation of the world.

Then, dismissing the crowds, he went into the
house.
His disciples approached him and said,
"Explain to us the parable of the weeds in
the field."
He said in reply, "He who sows good seed is
the Son of Man,
the field is the world, the good seed the
children of the kingdom.
The weeds are the children of the evil one,
and the enemy who sows them is the devil.
The harvest is the end of the age, and the
harvesters are angels.
Just as weeds are collected and burned up
with fire,
so will it be at the end of the age.
The Son of Man will send his angels,
and they will collect out of his kingdom
all who cause others to sin and all
evildoers.
They will throw them into the fiery furnace,
where there will be wailing and grinding
of teeth.
Then the righteous will shine like the sun
in the kingdom of their Father.
Whoever has ears ought to hear."

Preparing to Proclaim

Key words and phrases: "[H]e goes and sells all that he has and buys it."

To the point: This week's series of parables tells us something about how we are to receive the kingdom of God. Finding it and participating in it is like finding a treasure. It probably brings a bit of wonder; how did we get so lucky as to be included in this? But above all it brings joy, the kind of breathtaking joy that leads us to wholehearted pursuit of the thing that brings it. This is the joy of a child who has found an interest that overrides their brain's developmental limits on attention span. This is the joy of someone who has fallen in love. All of these people will find that the object of their interest does not always bring this easy joy. Lovers will find some of their beloveds' flaws hard to live with; children may move on when a new interest fizzles in a challenge they can't overcome; and even God's kingdom makes demands of us and sometimes the sacrifice may seem too much. But the initial joy and wonder tells us something important: this movement of our hearts is how God gets to us.

Making Connections

Between the readings: Solomon asks for something that pleases God: an understanding heart. He pursues wisdom with the wholeheartedness with which we are to pursue the kingdom, which tells us something else about what pursuing the kingdom entails. It is deeply related to this wisdom. The psalm continues this theme, for encountering God's leadership—even his commands—inspires a response of love from us.

To experience: Many of us have some experience of encountering God and responding with the kind of wonder and joy and love that causes the person of the parable to sell all he has in pursuit of it. But the long slog of Christian life in a sinful world often causes these feelings to wear off. Love is not measured by our emotional response to the beloved but by our commitment to living out its demands, with consistency and integrity.

Prayer

Divine Wisdom,
your ways are not our ways,
yet those with understanding hearts,
who earnestly seek you and *love your
    commands*
find joy and hope in you.
Help us always to treasure our relationship
    with you,
and to pursue an ever-deeper love of you,
    with you,
and with all you have created.
Amen.

First Reading (1 Kgs 3:5, 7-12)

A reading from the first Book of Kings

The LORD appeared to Solomon in a dream at
    night.
God said, "Ask something of me and I will
    give it to you."
Solomon answered:
    "O LORD, my God, you have made me, your
        servant, king
    to succeed my father David;
    but I am a mere youth, not knowing at all
        how to act.
I serve you in the midst of the people whom
    you have chosen,
    a people so vast that it cannot be numbered
        or counted.
Give your servant, therefore, an
        understanding heart
    to judge your people and to distinguish
        right from wrong.
    For who is able to govern this vast people
        of yours?"

The LORD was pleased that Solomon made
    this request.

Pronunciation
Solomon   SAH-lo-muhn

This great reading from
the first Book of Kings
explains the wisdom of
Solomon. Rehearse speak-
ing in a different voices
for Solomon and for the
Lord. Tempo can be just
as effective as pitch in
contrasting voices.

Take the same energy that
you have at the beginning
all the way through to the
end.

257

So God said to him:
"Because you have asked for this—
not for a long life for yourself,
nor for riches,
nor for the life of your enemies,
but for understanding so that you may
know what is right—
I do as you requested.
I give you a heart so wise and understanding
that there has never been anyone like you
up to now,
and after you there will come no one to
equal you."

Responsorial Psalm (Ps 119:57, 72, 76-77, 127-128, 129-130)

R̸. (97a) Lord, I love your commands.

I have said, O LORD, that my part
is to keep your words.
The law of your mouth is to me more
precious
than thousands of gold and silver pieces.

R̸. Lord, I love your commands.

Let your kindness comfort me
according to your promise to your servants.
Let your compassion come to me that I may
live,
for your law is my delight.

R̸. Lord, I love your commands.

For I love your commands
more than gold, however fine.
For in all your precepts I go forward;
every false way I hate.

R̸. Lord, I love your commands.

Wonderful are your decrees;
 therefore I observe them.
The revelation of your words sheds light,
 giving understanding to the simple.

R̸. Lord, I love your commands.

Second Reading (Rom 8:28-30)

A reading from the Letter of Saint Paul to the Romans

Brothers and sisters:
We know that all things work for good for
  those who love God,
 who are called according to his purpose.
For those he foreknew he also predestined
 to be conformed to the image of his Son,
 so that he might be the firstborn
 among many brothers and sisters.
And those he predestined he also called;
 and those he called he also justified;
 and those he justified he also glorified.

In the last three lines tie-in the meaning Paul intends by emphasizing the following italicized verbs:

"And those he *predestined* he also *called*;
 and those he *called* he also *justified*;
 and those he *justified* he also *glorified*."

Rehearse the reading out loud so that you can hear it for yourself.

Gospel (Matt 13:44-52 [or Matt 13:44-46]; L109A)

A reading from the holy Gospel according to Matthew

[Jesus said to his disciples:
 "The kingdom of heaven is like a treasure
  buried in a field,
 which a person finds and hides again,
 and out of joy goes and sells all that he has
  and buys that field.
Again, the kingdom of heaven is like a merchant
 searching for fine pearls.
When he finds a pearl of great price,
 he goes and sells all that he has and buys it.]
Again, the kingdom of heaven is like a net
  thrown into the sea,
 which collects fish of every kind.

Any of Matthew's parables in this reading can, of course, stand on their own. Therefore, taking a good pause between each is more than appropriate.

259

When it is full they haul it ashore
    and sit down to put what is good into
        buckets.
What is bad they throw away.
Thus it will be at the end of the age.
The angels will go out and separate the
    wicked from the righteous
    and throw them into the fiery furnace,
    where there will be wailing and grinding
        of teeth.

"Do you understand all these things?"
They answered, "Yes."
And he replied,
    "Then every scribe who has been
        instructed in the kingdom of heaven
    is like the head of a household
    who brings from his storeroom both the
        new and the old."

Preparing to Proclaim

Key words and phrases: "Rise, and do not be afraid."

To the point: On retreats, the story of the transfiguration is often used to charge participants with living out the retreat as they return to the more mundane rhythms of daily life. They may have experienced God in a powerful way, but like the disciples in this story, they must come down from the "mountaintop" of that experience to walk in the valleys below. Talking about their experience might be met with doubt or suspicion, and it is unlikely that the demands of real life will allow them the space and time to have the emotionally powerful experience of God that often occurs in a retreat setting. But, like the disciples, they do not go forth alone. Jesus remains with them—and with us. And our more powerful experiences of intimacy with him can go a long way in enlightening and empowering the more normal parts of our journeys of faith.

Making Connections

Between the readings: Like the gospel, the first reading shows a vision of God as a bright and fiery king in all his glory. It also hints at a trinitarian God; there is at least a Father (the "Ancient One") and a Son here. The second reading, too, speaks of the relationship between the Father and the Son. We see the early church working out its understanding of the three persons of God and how they relate to each other.

To experience: Many of us are blessed at some point with "mountaintop experiences," where God's presence is clear and obvious and stimulates an emotional response commensurate with God's vast goodness. But our lives are not usually lived under conditions that permit constant emotional stimulus. Emotions are part of our human condition—changeable, unpredictable, tied closely to the last time we ate and whether we got enough sleep last night. Walking in the everyday "valleys" of our life calls for staying committed to God when the emotional payoff is low. This is where love becomes a virtue rather than an emotion.

Prayer

Most high over all the earth,
you are light in darkness, glory in gloom.
Each day we may witness your majesty,
if we choose to see with eyes of faith.
Help us change these glimpses of your reign
into real and tangible moments of grace.
We ask this through Jesus Christ, glorious and
    alive.
Amen.

Daniel is describing an extraordinary vision indeed! Read it as such. Take time for a brief pause between the sentences.

The final sentence is very important, so make sure you carry the energy of the reading through to the very end.

First Reading (Dan 7:9-10, 13-14)

A reading from the Book of the Prophet Daniel

As I watched:
    Thrones were set up
        and the Ancient One took his throne.
    His clothing was snow bright,
        and the hair on his head as white as wool;
    his throne was flames of fire,
        with wheels of burning fire.
    A surging stream of fire
        flowed out from where he sat;
    Thousands upon thousands were
            ministering to him,
        and myriads upon myriads attended him.
The court was convened and the books were
        opened.

As the visions during the night continued, I
        saw
    One like a Son of man coming,
        on the clouds of heaven;
    When he reached the Ancient One
        and was presented before him,
    The one like a Son of man received
            dominion, glory, and kingship;
        all peoples, nations, and languages serve
            him.

His dominion is an everlasting dominion
that shall not be taken away,
his kingship shall not be destroyed.

Responsorial Psalm (Ps 97:1-2, 5-6, 9)

℟. (1a, 9a) The Lord is king, the Most High
over all the earth.

The LORD is king; let the earth rejoice;
let the many islands be glad.
Clouds and darkness are round about him;
justice and judgment are the foundation of
his throne.

℟. The Lord is king, the Most High over all
the earth.

The mountains melt like wax before the LORD,
before the LORD of all the earth.
The heavens proclaim his justice;
all peoples see his glory.

℟. The Lord is king, the Most High over all
the earth.

Because you, O LORD, are the Most High over
all the earth,
exalted far above all gods.

℟. The Lord is king, the Most High over all
the earth.

Second Reading (2 Pet 1:16-19)

A reading from the second Letter of
Saint Peter

Beloved:
We did not follow cleverly devised myths
when we made known to you
the power and coming of our Lord Jesus
Christ,
but we had been eyewitnesses of his
majesty.

The first reading describes a vision while this reading describes an eyewitness account by Peter. Give the quote, "This is my Son . . ." the gravity that it deserves!

The poetry of the last sentence is wonderful, so take your time rehearsing it and delivering it.

For he received honor and glory from God the
    Father
    when that unique declaration came to him
        from the majestic glory,
    "This is my Son, my beloved, with whom I
        am well pleased."
We ourselves heard this voice come from
    heaven
    while we were with him on the holy
        mountain.
Moreover, we possess the prophetic message
    that is altogether reliable.
You will do well to be attentive to it,
    as to a lamp shining in a dark place,
        until day dawns and the morning star rises
            in your hearts.

Pronunciation
Elijah   ee-LAI-juh

Daring to state the obvious, what an incredible occurrence Matthew is writing about! So incredible, in fact, that Jesus tells all who were present to not let anyone know about what has just happened until after he is raised from the dead.

Imagine telling someone this story for the first time, as though you actually had been there.

Gospel (Matt 17:1-9; L614)

A reading from the holy Gospel according
to Matthew

Jesus took Peter, James, and his brother, John,
    and led them up a high mountain by
        themselves.
And he was transfigured before them;
    his face shone like the sun
    and his clothes became white as light.
And behold, Moses and Elijah appeared to
    them,
    conversing with him.
Then Peter said to Jesus in reply,
    "Lord, it is good that we are here.
If you wish, I will make three tents here,
    one for you, one for Moses, and one for
        Elijah."
While he was still speaking, behold,
    a bright cloud cast a shadow over them,
    then from the cloud came a voice that said,

"This is my beloved Son, with whom I am
    well pleased;
listen to him."
When the disciples heard this, they fell
    prostrate
and were very much afraid.
But Jesus came and touched them, saying,
    "Rise, and do not be afraid."
And when the disciples raised their eyes,
    they saw no one else but Jesus alone.

As they were coming down from the
    mountain,
    Jesus charged them,
    "Do not tell the vision to anyone
    until the Son of Man has been raised from
        the dead."

Preparing to Proclaim

Key words and phrases: "Take courage, it is I; do not be afraid."

To the point: Peter's emotional trajectory is relatable here; it shows us that having faith is never a one-and-done proposition. His bravado seems to be rewarded when he steps out of the boat and finds himself able to walk on water, but when he encounters new fears, it is as if he never had courage at all. For us, too, the journey of faith is circuitous; it brings moments of courage and confidence as well as moments of doubt and distress. We sometimes find that our most confident moments precede a new experience that throws off everything we thought we knew. All the while, though, Jesus is with us. He goes before us, walking on the water and making it safe; and he stands prepared to catch us when our resolve falters.

Making Connections

Between the readings: In both the first reading and the gospel, God's power is found in calmness and stillness. Elijah expects God's power to be made manifest in wind and earthquake and fire, but God is in fact found in the tiny whispering sound, one that could be missed if Elijah weren't paying attention. The gospel takes this one step further. Not only does Jesus bring stillness, he shows power over the forces of water and wind that so frighten the disciples. God is all-powerful, yes, but God chooses to exercise this power in gentleness.

To experience: There is a group of seabirds called petrels and they earned St. Peter as their eponym because they move their feet in such a way that they appear to walk on water as they feed. Many of our plants and animals were named by people who saw God powerfully present in the natural world. This gospel with its mighty weather imagery and the first reading with its tiny whisper can serve as reminders to pay attention to God's presence in all we encounter—nature, relationships, and even our own gifts.

Prayer

God of Peace,
at times you speak to us not in violent storms
or in fractious earthquakes,
but in calm and gentle whispers.
*Lord, let us see your kindness, and grant us
your salvation.*
When tempests rage and frighten us,
bring us peace, and help us trust in your un-
failing power.
Amen.

First Reading (1 Kgs 19:9a, 11-13a)

A reading from the first Book of Kings

At the mountain of God, Horeb,
Elijah came to a cave where he took shelter.
Then the LORD said to him,
"Go outside and stand on the mountain
before the LORD;
the LORD will be passing by."
A strong and heavy wind was rending the
mountains
and crushing rocks before the LORD—
but the LORD was not in the wind.
After the wind there was an earthquake—
but the LORD was not in the earthquake.
After the earthquake there was fire—
but the LORD was not in the fire.
After the fire there was a tiny whispering
sound.
When he heard this,
Elijah hid his face in his cloak
and went and stood at the entrance of the
cave.

Pronunciation
Horeb   HAWR-ehb
Elijah   ee-LAI-juh

Before the second section of this reading, which starts, "A strong and heavy wind," take a nice pause. Try to imagine what sort of wind would "rend" the mountains—that is, tear them apart. This is some incredibly frightening wind that no one in their right mind would want to experience!

Other terrifying events follow. Each one must stand on its own with each arguably more terrifying than the one before. What is the energy you can call on to deliver this reading accordingly? Then contrast that crescendo of energy with: "After the fire there was a tiny whispering sound."

Responsorial Psalm (Ps 85:9, 10, 11-12, 13-14)

R℣. (8) Lord, let us see your kindness, and grant us your salvation.

I will hear what God proclaims;
    the Lord—for he proclaims peace.
Near indeed is his salvation to those who fear him,
    glory dwelling in our land.

R℣. Lord, let us see your kindness, and grant us your salvation.

Kindness and truth shall meet;
    justice and peace shall kiss.
Truth shall spring out of the earth,
    and justice shall look down from heaven.

R℣. Lord, let us see your kindness, and grant us your salvation.

The Lord himself will give his benefits;
    our land shall yield its increase.
Justice shall walk before him,
    and prepare the way of his steps.

R℣. Lord, let us see your kindness, and grant us your salvation.

In the final section, beginning with, "They are Israelites . . ." recite each attribute slowly and separately as each is very significant.

Conclude with "Christ" and "God," followed by a determined "Amen."

Second Reading (Rom 9:1-5)

A reading from the Letter of Saint Paul to the Romans

Brothers and sisters:
I speak the truth in Christ, I do not lie;
    my conscience joins with the Holy Spirit in
        bearing me witness
    that I have great sorrow and constant
        anguish in my heart.
For I could wish that I myself were accursed
        and cut off from Christ
    for the sake of my own people,
    my kindred according to the flesh.

They are Israelites;
>theirs the adoption, the glory, the
>>covenants,
>the giving of the law, the worship, and the
>>promises;
>theirs the patriarchs, and from them,
>according to the flesh, is the Christ,
>who is over all, God blessed forever. Amen.

Gospel (Matt 14:22-33; L115A)

A reading from the holy Gospel according
to Matthew

After he had fed the people, Jesus made the
>disciples get into a boat
>and precede him to the other side,
>while he dismissed the crowds.
After doing so, he went up on the mountain
>by himself to pray.
When it was evening he was there alone.
Meanwhile the boat, already a few miles
>offshore,
>was being tossed about by the waves, for
>>the wind was against it.
During the fourth watch of the night,
>he came toward them walking on the sea.
When the disciples saw him walking on the
>sea they were terrified.
"It is a ghost," they said, and they cried out in
>fear.
At once Jesus spoke to them, "Take courage,
>it is I; do not be afraid."
Peter said to him in reply,
>"Lord, if it is you, command me to come to
>>you on the water."
He said, "Come."
Peter got out of the boat and began to walk
>on the water toward Jesus.

Don't be afraid to give this reading the energy and drama that it deserves! It is an interesting story as it begins very calmly. Shortly a huge storm kicks up and finally Peter's faith in Jesus is tested. Clearly a crescendo of energy is appropriate here.

But when he saw how strong the wind was he
became frightened;
and, beginning to sink, he cried out, "Lord,
save me!"
Immediately Jesus stretched out his hand and
caught Peter,
and said to him, "O you of little faith, why
did you doubt?"
After they got into the boat, the wind died
down.
Those who were in the boat did him homage,
saying,
"Truly, you are the Son of God."

Preparing to Proclaim

Key words and phrases: "O woman, great is your faith!"

To the point: This is one of the places where the gospels show us Jesus's full humanity; it would seem that his understanding of his own mission is expanded by his encounter with the Canaanite woman. He is the Son of God, and yet he is *moved* here from unresponsiveness to resistance to, finally, realization that perhaps his work is bigger than even he had realized. He begins his life and work within the context of God's pre-established relationship to Israel. In this moment, it is made clear to him and to us that Jesus is for all people. Faith in him is available to all and his healing ministry is not meant to be limited to some pre-approved group. It is very human to draw boundaries and establish groups; we seek to understand what we need to do to be "in." But God's generosity and hospitality are more radical and inclusive than we can ever understand.

Making Connections

Between the readings: The first reading gives a foretaste of what we learn in the gospel: while Israel plays a special role in God's saving work, salvation is for all peoples, regardless of race or origin. The second reading, too, shows Paul striving to resolve the differences between Jews and Gentiles in his community. Both groups have a history of disobedience, but God's greater mercy is also for all.

To experience: Unfortunately, even the church is not exempt from the human tendency to draw exclusive boundaries that name who is in and who is out. Many in the church are excluded because of their gender or income or sexual orientation. On a smaller level, parish activities often unintentionally exclude families whose children don't attend the parochial school and parents who need to work. But God calls us to a more radical inclusiveness, to hospitality that truly loves and receives all.

Prayer

O God,
let all the nations praise you!
You are just, you are welcome, you are love.
Let us never deny your gifts to others,
all created in your image and likeness,
   seeking relationship with you and your holy
      people.
You are unity and healing for all nations.
Amen.

Pronunciation
profanation
   prof-uh-NEY-shun: the
   act of doing or saying
   something terribly of-
   fensive, disrespecting
   someone's religious
   beliefs.

There are only two sen-
tences in this reading. Rehearse out loud the pacing
and punctuation needed
here, particularly of the
second sentence.

First Reading (Isa 56:1, 6-7)

A reading from the Book of the Prophet Isaiah

Thus says the LORD:
Observe what is right, do what is just;
   for my salvation is about to come,
   my justice, about to be revealed.

The foreigners who join themselves to the LORD,
   ministering to him,
loving the name of the LORD,
   and becoming his servants—
all who keep the sabbath free from
      profanation
   and hold to my covenant,
them I will bring to my holy mountain
   and make joyful in my house of prayer;
their burnt offerings and sacrifices
   will be acceptable on my altar,
for my house shall be called
   a house of prayer for all peoples.

Responsorial Psalm (Ps 67:2-3, 5, 6, 8)

R̞. (4) O God, let all the nations praise you!

May God have pity on us and bless us;
   may he let his face shine upon us.
So may your way be known upon earth;
   among all nations, your salvation.

R℣. O God, let all the nations praise you!

May the nations be glad and exult
    because you rule the peoples in equity;
    the nations on the earth you guide.

R℣. O God, let all the nations praise you!

May the peoples praise you, O God;
    may all the peoples praise you!
May God bless us,
    and may all the ends of the earth fear him!

R℣. O God, let all the nations praise you!

Second Reading (Rom 11:13-15, 29-32)

A reading from the Letter of Saint Paul to
the Romans

Brothers and sisters:
I am speaking to you Gentiles.
Inasmuch as I am the apostle to the Gentiles,
    I glory in my ministry in order to make my
        race jealous
    and thus save some of them.
For if their rejection is the reconciliation of
        the world,
    what will their acceptance be but life from
        the dead?

For the gifts and the call of God are
        irrevocable.
Just as you once disobeyed God
    but have now received mercy because of
        their disobedience,
    so they have now disobeyed in order that,
    by virtue of the mercy shown to you,
    they too may now receive mercy.
For God delivered all to disobedience,
    that he might have mercy upon all.

Pronunciation
Gentiles   JEHN-tailz

Paul's writing here is
again rather complex, so
read it slowly, making
sure you totally under-
stand what you are say-
ing. Come to a full stop at
every period.

273

Pronunciation
Tyre   TAI-er
Sidon   SAI-duhn
Canaanite   KAY-nuh-nait

This is such a great account! You have four different voices here. Without being overly dramatic, how can you contrast them for ease of the listeners? Varying tempos and energy is a good place to start.

Gospel (Matt 15:21-28; L118A)

A reading from the holy Gospel according to Matthew

At that time, Jesus withdrew to the region of
Tyre and Sidon.
And behold, a Canaanite woman of that
district came and called out,
"Have pity on me, Lord, Son of David!
My daughter is tormented by a demon."
But Jesus did not say a word in answer to her.
Jesus' disciples came and asked him,
"Send her away, for she keeps calling out
after us."
He said in reply,
"I was sent only to the lost sheep of the
house of Israel."
But the woman came and did Jesus homage,
saying, "Lord, help me."
He said in reply,
"It is not right to take the food of the
children
and throw it to the dogs."
She said, "Please, Lord, for even the dogs eat
the scraps
that fall from the table of their masters."
Then Jesus said to her in reply,
"O woman, great is your faith!
Let it be done for you as you wish."
And the woman's daughter was healed from
that hour.

Preparing to Proclaim

Key words and phrases: "You are the Christ, the Son of the living God."

To the point: Peter is an imperfect, problematic, very human person. Here he shows great faith and insight into the reality of who Jesus is, yet at the passion he will be the first to run away from the frightful scene and will repeatedly deny his connection to Christ. In this scene, he appears to earn his status as first among the disciples by giving the right answer to a tricky question. But in reality, his power and leadership are unearned gifts from God; Jesus even says that it is God who revealed this answer to Peter. Leadership in the church is not earned or deserved. All too often its leaders fail to live out the holiness to which we are all called. But because it is given by God, it still has some level of trustworthiness; the church is never left alone with the imperfection of solely human leadership.

Making Connections

Between the readings: The first reading shows another instance of God delegating power to a human. It is not earned or deserved, but because God gives it, it is real. The key imagery is consistent between these readings, too; key holders have power because they are able to open and shut doors that others cannot. We don't always get to know why certain people have more power than others, and when it comes to church leadership, we are asked to trust that God holds the ultimate power and is really in control.

To experience: When church leadership fails us, it can often cause a crisis of faith. This is absolutely understandable, especially given the ways that we are often miscatechized about the relationship between power and holiness. But the leadership never really belonged to the imperfect humans who failed us. It is, in the end, God who gave the power and who promises to side with the lowly ones.

Prayer

Alpha and Omega,
your love is eternal, without beginning nor end.
We are fearfully, wonderfully made in your
image:
do not forsake the work of your hands.
We know not your mind and your ways;
help us always strive for greater holiness
and a stronger bond with your divine
compassion.
Amen.

Pronunciation
Shebna   SHEB-nuh
Eliakim   I-li'-uh-kim
Hilkaiah   Hill-Ki'-ah
Judah   JOU-duh

Make sure you can recite
the names without any
hesitation. Write their pro-
nunciations on a piece of
paper that you can use as
you proclaim the reading,
if necessary.

First Reading (Isa 22:19-23)

A reading from the Book of the Prophet Isaiah

Thus says the LORD to Shebna, master of the
palace:
"I will thrust you from your office
and pull you down from your station.
On that day I will summon my servant
Eliakim, son of Hilkiah;
I will clothe him with your robe,
and gird him with your sash,
and give over to him your authority.
He shall be a father to the inhabitants of
Jerusalem,
and to the house of Judah.
I will place the key of the House of David on
Eliakim's shoulder;
when he opens, no one shall shut;
when he shuts, no one shall open.
I will fix him like a peg in a sure spot,
to be a place of honor for his family."

Responsorial Psalm (Ps 138:1-2, 2-3, 6, 8)

R⁊. (8bc) Lord, your love is eternal; do not
forsake the work of your hands.

I will give thanks to you, O LORD, with all my
heart,

for you have heard the words of my mouth;
in the presence of the angels I will sing your
     praise;
I will worship at your holy temple.

R̈. Lord, your love is eternal; do not forsake
the work of your hands.

I will give thanks to your name,
     because of your kindness and your truth:
when I called, you answered me;
     you built up strength within me.

R̈. Lord, your love is eternal; do not forsake
the work of your hands.

The LORD is exalted, yet the lowly he sees,
     and the proud he knows from afar.
Your kindness, O LORD, endures forever;
     forsake not the work of your hands.

R̈. Lord, your love is eternal; do not forsake
the work of your hands.

Second Reading (Rom 11:33-36)

A reading from the Letter of Saint Paul to
the Romans

Oh, the depth of the riches and wisdom and
     knowledge of God!
How inscrutable are his judgments and how
     unsearchable his ways!
For who has known the mind of the Lord
or who has been his counselor?
Or who has given the Lord anything
that he may be repaid?
For from him and through him and for him
     are all things.
To him be glory forever. Amen.

The first line is really un-packed by the remainder of the reading. Recite it slowly with conviction. The final line is similar in spirit to the first; deliver it with the same strength.

TWENTY-FIRST SUNDAY IN ORDINARY TIME

Pronunciation
Caesarea
  zeh-suh-REE-uh
Philippi   fil-LIH-pai
Elijah   ee-LAI-juh
Jeremiah
  jehr-eh-MAI-uh

Simon Peter's response hits the jackpot! This is arguably the climax of the reading. How can you best make Peter's answer stand out verbally so that your listeners can say the same?

Gospel (Matt 16:13-20; L121A)

A reading from the holy Gospel according to Matthew

Jesus went into the region of Caesarea
        Philippi and
    he asked his disciples,
    "Who do people say that the Son of Man
        is?"
They replied, "Some say John the Baptist,
        others Elijah,
    still others Jeremiah or one of the
        prophets."
He said to them, "But who do you say that I
        am?"
Simon Peter said in reply,
    "You are the Christ, the Son of the living
        God."
Jesus said to him in reply,
    "Blessed are you, Simon son of Jonah.
For flesh and blood has not revealed this to
        you, but my heavenly Father.
And so I say to you, you are Peter,
    and upon this rock I will build my church,
    and the gates of the netherworld shall not
        prevail against it.
I will give you the keys to the kingdom of
        heaven.
Whatever you bind on earth shall be bound in
        heaven;
    and whatever you loose on earth shall be
        loosed in heaven."
Then he strictly ordered his disciples
    to tell no one that he was the Christ.

Preparing to Proclaim

Key words and phrases: "You are thinking not as God does, but as human beings do."

To the point: Last week Peter answered Jesus's question correctly and was affirmed as a conduit of divine knowledge and received the delegation of divine power. But later in the very same conversation, he messes up. He hears of God's unthinkable plan for Jesus— one that involves a horrific and humiliating death—and he responds as any of us would if a friend started talking like that. He responds with loving protectiveness; but in this case, that is not the right response. God's logic is not our own, and here Jesus introduces the contradictory idea that saving our life causes us to lose it while giving up our life enables us to find it. Mystics reconcile this contradiction by pointing out that much of what we cling to is a superficial self that gives a false sense of what life is. By letting go of all that is not real or permanent, we find our true selves, which are at home with God.

Making Connections

Between the readings: The first reading echoes the idea that human logic is not the same as divine logic; we can feel "duped" by God when our faith brings us humiliation in the eyes of the world. But as Jeremiah finds, God has a way of drawing us back. As St. Augustine famously wrote, our hearts remain restless until they rest in God. The second reading also affirms that the life of faith involves sacrifice. We are not to conform to this world, which means it will often not feel much like home.

To experience: The crosses we are called to take up often seem small in comparison to Christ's. But Christ walks with us even in our smallest sufferings. Even mundane moments of irritation and struggle can become moments in which we practice virtue. We can follow Christ by responding to these frustrations with patience, fortitude, and empathy for others who are involved.

Prayer

God of the Cross,
you created each soul to yearn and pine for you,
even when that road leads to suffering and death.
To you we cry: *My soul is thirsting for you,*
O Lord my God.
We thirst to love like you, serve like you;
help us to empty ourselves in service to your
name.
Amen.

Pronunciation
Jeremiah
    jehr-eh-MAI-uh

This is a great reading!
What is Jeremiah saying?
As an exercise, substitute
"tricked" for "duped." The
writer is almost angry at
the Lord for the situation
in which he finds himself.
Give this reading that sort
of energy.

First Reading (Jer 20:7-9)

A reading from the Book of the Prophet
Jeremiah

You duped me, O Lord, and I let myself be duped;
    you were too strong for me, and you
        triumphed.
All the day I am an object of laughter;
    everyone mocks me.

Whenever I speak, I must cry out,
    violence and outrage is my message;
the word of the Lord has brought me
    derision and reproach all the day.

I say to myself, I will not mention him,
    I will speak in his name no more.
But then it becomes like fire burning in my
        heart,
    imprisoned in my bones;
I grow weary holding it in, I cannot endure it.

Responsorial Psalm (Ps 63:2, 3-4, 5-6, 8-9)

Ry. (2b) My soul is thirsting for you, O Lord
my God.

O God, you are my God whom I seek;
    for you my flesh pines and my soul thirsts
    like the earth, parched, lifeless and without
        water.

R̘. My soul is thirsting for you, O Lord my God.

Thus have I gazed toward you in the
    sanctuary
  to see your power and your glory,
for your kindness is a greater good than life;
  my lips shall glorify you.

R̘. My soul is thirsting for you, O Lord my God.

Thus will I bless you while I live;
  lifting up my hands, I will call upon your
    name.
As with the riches of a banquet shall my soul
    be satisfied,
  and with exultant lips my mouth shall
    praise you.

R̘. My soul is thirsting for you, O Lord my God.

You are my help,
  and in the shadow of your wings I shout
    for joy.
My soul clings fast to you;
  your right hand upholds me.

R̘. My soul is thirsting for you, O Lord my God.

Second Reading (Rom 12:1-2)

A reading from the Letter of Saint Paul to
the Romans

I urge you, brothers and sisters, by the
    mercies of God,
  to offer your bodies as a living sacrifice,
  holy and pleasing to God, your spiritual
    worship.
Do not conform yourselves to this age
  but be transformed by the renewal of your
    mind,
  that you may discern what is the will of
    God,
  what is good and pleasing and perfect.

Let each descriptive in the final line—"what is good and pleasing and perfect"—stand on its own with a slight pause: good (*pause*) and pleasing (*pause*) and perfect.

This powerful reading sums up the passion, crucifixion, and resurrection of Jesus.

"Get behind me, Satan!" is a phrase well known by many. Yet does the younger generation really know or understand what it means? The way in which you say something can easily convey its meaning even if the word or phrase is not totally understood.

Gospel (Matt 16:21-27; L124A)

A reading from the holy Gospel according to Matthew

Jesus began to show his disciples
> that he must go to Jerusalem and suffer greatly
> from the elders, the chief priests, and the scribes,
> and be killed and on the third day be raised.

Then Peter took Jesus aside and began to rebuke him,
> "God forbid, Lord! No such thing shall ever happen to you."

He turned and said to Peter,
> "Get behind me, Satan! You are an obstacle to me.

You are thinking not as God does, but as human beings do."

Then Jesus said to his disciples,
> "Whoever wishes to come after me must deny himself,
> take up his cross, and follow me.

For whoever wishes to save his life will lose it,
> but whoever loses his life for my sake will find it.

What profit would there be for one to gain the whole world
> and forfeit his life?

Or what can one give in exchange for his life?

For the Son of Man will come with his angels in his Father's glory,
> and then he will repay all according to his conduct."

Preparing to Proclaim

Key words and phrases: "For where two or three are gathered together in my name, there am I in the midst of them."

To the point: In this gospel, Jesus gives us some clear directions for the ongoing life in community we are still living out. Sin and offense will never be absent, even within the Christian community; our human tendency to err is too strong. But our unity is too important to let that reality stand alone. Instead, we are to strive to lovingly win back over those who have hurt us; first by ourselves, then with the support of the community. But Jesus does not tell us to withstand endless abuse; he introduces the idea here that setting boundaries can be an acceptable form of loving others. This ought to be discerned within the context of unity as an important value; gathering together in Jesus's name is one way to secure his presence.

Making Connections

Between the readings: In the first reading, there is an even stronger sense of shared responsibility for sins within the community; we owe it to each other to call each other back to the Christian life. But again, our responsibility for others is limited; if they choose not to hear us, we are not called to continuously harp on what we see as their failings. And the second reading rounds out these commands; love is the context for all of this and our ultimate responsibility to each other.

To experience: This gospel implies the need not only for fraternal correction but also for forgiveness; when we inform another of the ways they have hurt us, we are meant to be truly reconciled with them rather than holding it over them or imagining ourselves morally superior. Jesus's instructions here are a recipe for letting go of grudges and moving on to fuller reconciliation.

Prayer

God,
you sent us your Eternal Word
to show us the way to you.
You bid us: *If today you hear his voice, harden
    not your hearts.*
Keep our ears open and our hearts attentive,
and help us to know of your presence in our
    holy community.
Amen.

Pronunciation
Ezekiel   eh-ZEE-kee-uhl

Try emphasizing the
verbs in this reading to
give it the energy it de-
serves. For example:
"Thus says the LORD: You,
son of man, I *have ap-
pointed* watchman . . ."

First Reading (Ezek 33:7-9)

A reading from the Book of the Prophet Ezekiel

Thus says the LORD:
    You, son of man, I have appointed
        watchman for the house of Israel;
    when you hear me say anything, you shall
        warn them for me.
If I tell the wicked, "O wicked one, you shall
        surely die,"
    and you do not speak out to dissuade the
        wicked from his way,
    the wicked shall die for his guilt,
    but I will hold you responsible for his death.
But if you warn the wicked,
    trying to turn him from his way,
    and he refuses to turn from his way,
    he shall die for his guilt,
    but you shall save yourself.

Responsorial Psalm (Ps 95:1-2, 6-7, 8-9)

R̞. (8) If today you hear his voice, harden not
your hearts.

Come, let us sing joyfully to the LORD;
    let us acclaim the rock of our salvation.
Let us come into his presence with
        thanksgiving;
    let us joyfully sing psalms to him.

℟. If today you hear his voice, harden not your hearts.

Come, let us bow down in worship;
    let us kneel before the LORD who made us.
For he is our God,
    and we are the people he shepherds, the
        flock he guides.

℟. If today you hear his voice, harden not your hearts.

Oh, that today you would hear his voice:
    "Harden not your hearts as at Meribah,
    as in the day of Massah in the desert,
where your fathers tempted me;
    they tested me though they had seen my
        works."

℟. If today you hear his voice, harden not your hearts.

Second Reading (Rom 13:8-10)

A reading from the Letter of Saint Paul to the Romans

Brothers and sisters:
Owe nothing to anyone, except to love one
        another;
    for the one who loves another has fulfilled
        the law.
The commandments, "You shall not commit
        adultery;
    you shall not kill; you shall not steal; you
        shall not covet,"
    and whatever other commandment there
        may be,
    are summed up in this saying, namely,
    "You shall love your neighbor as yourself."
Love does no evil to the neighbor;
    hence, love is the fulfillment of the law.

Again, try emphasizing the verbs in this reading to give it the energy it deserves. Notice the "love one another" bookends. Often, Scripture repeats itself to really drive home a point.

As you repeat the opening point at the end of this passage try delivering it with high energy.

TWENTY-THIRD SUNDAY IN ORDINARY TIME

Pronunciation

Gentile   JEHN-tile

Underline all the verbs here and then read this Scripture passage out loud, emphasizing those same verbs. I hope you can hear the difference.

Gospel (Matt 18:15-20; L127A)

A reading from the holy Gospel according to Matthew

Jesus said to his disciples:
"If your brother sins against you,
go and tell him his fault between you and
him alone.
If he listens to you, you have won over your
brother.
If he does not listen,
take one or two others along with you,
so that 'every fact may be established
on the testimony of two or three witnesses.'
If he refuses to listen to them, tell the church.
If he refuses to listen even to the church,
then treat him as you would a Gentile or a
tax collector.
Amen, I say to you,
whatever you bind on earth shall be bound
in heaven,
and whatever you loose on earth shall be
loosed in heaven.
Again, amen, I say to you,
if two of you agree on earth
about anything for which they are to pray,
it shall be granted to them by my heavenly
Father.
For where two or three are gathered together
in my name,
there am I in the midst of them."

Preparing to Proclaim

Key words and phrases: "I say to you, not seven times but seventy-seven times."

To the point: In this gospel, Jesus calls us to radically generous forgiveness, a magnitude of forgiveness far above Peter's guess at what generous forgiveness should be. Again, God's logic is not ours; this is not a transaction that makes sense on human terms. This is one more way that we are called to imitate God, whose mercy is boundless and to whom we owe much more than we are owed. Imitating God in forgiveness is about making us bigger; it expands our hearts so that we may participate more fully in God's life and triumph and joy. But as we saw last week, this call to generous forgiveness doesn't mean we can't have boundaries. While most of us can stand to be more forgiving, God does not will for us to put up with true abuse. Forgiveness in such cases does not mean returning to an abuser with a blank slate and allowing the abuse to happen all over again; it might instead mean coming to a place of understanding even if the relationship cannot be restored.

Making Connections

Between the readings: The first reading makes clear what the gospel hints at: forgiveness is a gift to the one forgiven, but it has an even more powerful impact on the one who forgives. When we refuse to forgive, it is our own hearts that become dry and hardened. Granting others the grace of forgiveness expands our own capacity to live out God's love and thus to become more truly ourselves.

To experience: Even Peter's question is flawed; forgiveness is rarely a discreet, countable act. Granting forgiveness is not always as simple as checking a box to accomplish time number thirteen of the seventy-seven allotted. It can be hard to know when we've "achieved" full forgiveness; old hurts sometimes come back unexpectedly, revealing that they were not as healed as we once thought. More often, it is an ongoing process, one of changing our hearts, embracing humility and compassion, and being willing to be generous with others as God is with us.

Prayer

Caring Savior,
when we are angry, full of wrath and hatred,
remind us that you, holy one, are
*kind and merciful, slow to anger, and rich in
    compassion.*
Help us to forgive one another,
and enable each soul to build your reign
of justice, truth, and love.
Amen.

Pronunciation
Sirach   SAI-rak

Each sentence can stand
alone; therefore, take a
nice pause between each.

The final sentence sums
up the entire reading. Give
it the energy it deserves,
and keep the energy and
diction through to the last
word.

First Reading (Sir 27:30–28:7)

A reading from the Book of Sirach

Wrath and anger are hateful things,
    yet the sinner hugs them tight.
The vengeful will suffer the LORD's vengeance,
    for he remembers their sins in detail.
Forgive your neighbor's injustice;
    then when you pray, your own sins will be
        forgiven.
Could anyone nourish anger against another
    and expect healing from the LORD?
Could anyone refuse mercy to another like
        himself,
    can he seek pardon for his own sins?
If one who is but flesh cherishes wrath,
    who will forgive his sins?
Remember your last days, set enmity aside;
    remember death and decay, and cease from
        sin!
Think of the commandments, hate not your
        neighbor;
    remember the Most High's covenant, and
        overlook faults.

***Responsorial Psalm* (Ps 103:1-2, 3-4, 9-10, 11-12)**

℟. (8) The Lord is kind and merciful, slow to anger, and rich in compassion.

Bless the LORD, O my soul;
 and all my being, bless his holy name.
Bless the LORD, O my soul,
 and forget not all his benefits.

℟. The Lord is kind and merciful, slow to anger, and rich in compassion.

He pardons all your iniquities,
 heals all your ills.
He redeems your life from destruction,
 he crowns you with kindness and
  compassion.

℟. The Lord is kind and merciful, slow to anger, and rich in compassion.

He will not always chide,
 nor does he keep his wrath forever.
Not according to our sins does he deal with
  us,
 nor does he requite us according to our
  crimes.

℟. The Lord is kind and merciful, slow to anger, and rich in compassion.

For as the heavens are high above the earth,
 so surpassing is his kindness toward those
  who fear him.
As far as the east is from the west,
 so far has he put our transgressions from
  us.

℟. The Lord is kind and merciful, slow to anger, and rich in compassion.

Hit the verbs here as well as the proper nouns, "Lord" and "Christ." Underline them and recite the passage aloud. I hope you hear the difference!

Second Reading (Rom 14:7-9)

A reading from the Letter of Saint Paul to the Romans

Brothers and sisters:
None of us lives for oneself, and no one dies
　　for oneself.
For if we live, we live for the Lord,
　　and if we die, we die for the Lord;
　　　so then, whether we live or die, we are the
　　　　Lord's.
For this is why Christ died and came to life,
　　that he might be Lord of both the dead and
　　　the living.

Here is another gospel reading that is easily pantomimed by rehearsed actors while being read. The pantomime will very likely come off in a humorous manner if the actors are well known by the congregation.

Know that humor juxtaposed with a serious message can be very effective. Your listeners will long remember this reading if done in this manner.

Gospel (Matt 18:21-35; L130A)

A reading from the holy Gospel according to Matthew

Peter approached Jesus and asked him,
　　"Lord, if my brother sins against me,
　　how often must I forgive?
As many as seven times?"
Jesus answered, "I say to you, not seven times
　　but seventy-seven times.
That is why the kingdom of heaven may be
　　likened to a king
　　who decided to settle accounts with his
　　　servants.
When he began the accounting,
　　a debtor was brought before him who owed
　　　him a huge amount.
Since he had no way of paying it back,
　　his master ordered him to be sold,
　　　along with his wife, his children, and all his
　　　　property,
　　in payment of the debt.
At that, the servant fell down, did him
　　homage, and said,

'Be patient with me, and I will pay you
    back in full.'
Moved with compassion the master of that
    servant
    let him go and forgave him the loan.
When that servant had left, he found one of
    his fellow servants
    who owed him a much smaller amount.
He seized him and started to choke him,
    demanding,
    'Pay back what you owe.'
Falling to his knees, his fellow servant begged
    him,
    'Be patient with me, and I will pay you
        back.'
But he refused.
Instead, he had the fellow servant put in
    prison
    until he paid back the debt.
Now when his fellow servants saw what had
    happened,
    they were deeply disturbed, and went to
        their master
    and reported the whole affair.
His master summoned him and said to him,
    'You wicked servant!
I forgave you your entire debt because you
    begged me to.
Should you not have had pity on your fellow
    servant,
    as I had pity on you?'
Then in anger his master handed him over to
    the torturers
    until he should pay back the whole debt.
So will my heavenly Father do to you,
    unless each of you forgives your brother
        from your heart."

Preparing to Proclaim

Key words and phrases: "Thus, the last will be first, and the first will be last."

To the point: A common reaction to this gospel is to feel affronted: it really does seem unfair that all the laborers receive the same wage for unequal amounts of work. But Jesus is once again telling us that God's logic does not follow ours. Our sense of justice is too small. God's generosity is always bigger than what we had envisioned, and then is bigger again still. Part of the problem is that most of us identify with the early laborers in the story. We believe we have put in the work and really deserve the good things God gives us and will give us. But none of us really deserves the gifts of God; they are not something that *can* be earned but are by their nature free and gracious gifts. And God promises us the free and undeserved generosity that the latecomers receive in this parable.

Making Connections

Between the readings: The first reading reminds us in no uncertain terms that God's ways are not our ways. God operates on a different kind of logic, one which surpasses everything we would call logical but rather operates out of a love that overflows with lifegiving power. As St. Paul voices in the second reading, we are called to imitate God's ongoing self-gift. We can be united to Christ in both life and death when we strive to follow his example.

To experience: In many ways, it is fair and just that the world does not operate on the divine logic demonstrated in the gospel. Employers should *not* work like the landowner in this parable. A job that paid the same amount for an evening of labor as for a backbreaking dawn-to-dusk day would be what we call a toxic workplace. But the kingdom of heaven does not work like earth; the generosity that awaits us there is beyond our wildest imaginings.

Prayer

Omnipotent God, Immanent God,
you are *near to all who call upon* you,
grace and mercy to each heart in need.
Keep us humble, trusting in the mystery that
    is you;
help us live the paradox that power is service,
Being first is being last, and that in death is
    new life.
Amen.

First Reading (Isa 55:6-9)

A reading from the Book of the Prophet Isaiah

Seek the LORD while he may be found,
    call him while he is near.
Let the scoundrel forsake his way,
    and the wicked his thoughts;
let him turn to the LORD for mercy;
    to our God, who is generous in forgiving.
For my thoughts are not your thoughts,
    nor are your ways my ways, says the LORD.
As high as the heavens are above the earth,
    so high are my ways above your ways
    and my thoughts above your thoughts.

Hit the verbs in the first line, which can easily stand on its own and, therefore, begs a nice pause at its end.

Another pause follows the word "forgiving." The person of the narrator shifts in the next part, for it is now God speaking. How might your tone or tempo (or both!) change at this point?

Responsorial Psalm (Ps 145:2-3, 8-9, 17-18)

R℣. (18a) The Lord is near to all who call upon him.

Every day will I bless you,
    and I will praise your name forever and
        ever.
Great is the LORD and highly to be praised;
    his greatness is unsearchable.

R℣. The Lord is near to all who call upon him.

The LORD is gracious and merciful,
  slow to anger and of great kindness.
The LORD is good to all
  and compassionate toward all his works.

R̶. The Lord is near to all who call upon him.

The LORD is just in all his ways
  and holy in all his works.
The LORD is near to all who call upon him,
  to all who call upon him in truth.

R̶. The Lord is near to all who call upon him.

Pronunciation
Philippians
  fih-LIHP-ih-uhnz

The first sentence of this reading says it all, and it can stand on its own; make sure you provide a nice pause following it. Paul then goes on to explain his first line.

Pause before the final line as well.

Second Reading (Phil 1:20c-24, 27a)

A reading from the Letter of Saint Paul to the Philippians

Brothers and sisters:
Christ will be magnified in my body, whether
  by life or by death.
For to me life is Christ, and death is gain.
If I go on living in the flesh,
  that means fruitful labor for me.
And I do not know which I shall choose.
I am caught between the two.
I long to depart this life and be with Christ,
  for that is far better.
Yet that I remain in the flesh
  is more necessary for your benefit.

Only, conduct yourselves in a way worthy of
  the gospel of Christ.

Gospel (Matt 20:1-16a; L133A)

A reading from the holy Gospel according to Matthew

Jesus told his disciples this parable:
"The kingdom of heaven is like a
landowner
who went out at dawn to hire laborers for
his vineyard.
After agreeing with them for the usual daily
wage,
he sent them into his vineyard.
Going out about nine o'clock,
the landowner saw others standing idle in
the marketplace,
and he said to them, 'You too go into my
vineyard,
and I will give you what is just.'
So they went off.
And he went out again around noon,
and around three o'clock, and did likewise.
Going out about five o'clock,
the landowner found others standing
around, and said to them,
'Why do you stand here idle all day?'
They answered, 'Because no one has hired us.'
He said to them, 'You too go into my
vineyard.'
When it was evening the owner of the
vineyard said to his foreman,
'Summon the laborers and give them their
pay,
beginning with the last and ending with
the first.'
When those who had started about five
o'clock came,
each received the usual daily wage.
So when the first came, they thought that
they would receive more,
but each of them also got the usual wage.

This is a long reading but a great parable. As long as your diction and projection are good, move it along as it is easily understood until about two-thirds of the way through. This is when those who were first hired begin complaining. Here I would slow down a bit, with, of course, the final line providing the climax. Deliver it with determination.

And on receiving it they grumbled against
the landowner, saying,
'These last ones worked only one hour,
and you have made them equal to us,
who bore the day's burden and the heat.'
He said to one of them in reply,
'My friend, I am not cheating you.
Did you not agree with me for the usual daily
wage?
Take what is yours and go.
What if I wish to give this last one the same
as you?
Or am I not free to do as I wish with my own
money?
Are you envious because I am generous?'
Thus, the last will be first, and the first will be
last."

Preparing to Proclaim

Key words and phrases: "He said in reply, 'I will not,' but afterwards changed his mind and went."

To the point: This week's gospel finds us in another parable and another vineyard. We're still talking about the exceeding generosity of God and how it surpasses all our hopes and imaginings. Here, it is about second chances, and it is good news for all of us. Life brings countless opportunities to fail to do right, and all of us fail sometimes. But it is never too late to change course, and we are never too far gone to come back. God's love reaches far beyond what we expect; in fact, our limited imaginations often cause us to exclude daughters and sons with whom God is well pleased. God's love is not limited to those who appear to be living moral and religious lives; it most fully embraces those on the margins of what we and our too-small imaginations have deemed acceptable.

Making Connections

Between the readings: The first reading stresses again that God does not think like us; divine logic is based on love. Our human notions of "fairness" are only marginally related to the true justice that God is bringing about. The second reading takes up a similar theme; we are not only to love others as ourselves but to see them as *more* important than we are. This is illogical and does not fit into the human way of being in the world, but it imitates the lavish love that God offers to all of us.

To experience: In the gospel, neither brother acts with complete honesty or integrity; it would be nice if there were a son who obeyed his father in both word and deed. Perhaps this is pointing to the fact that none of us is perfect, that all of us are in need of God's generous mercy. We don't always think of ourselves as being needy before God; we would like to believe we have merited the good things God gives us. But this gospel challenges us to remember to receive them all as gifts given freely.

Prayer

God of life,
you teach us to empty ourselves,
and not cling to power or influence.
You reach out to sinners,
asking them to transform their hearts,
and return to you.
Remember your mercies, O Lord.
Give us strength to turn away from sin
and to be faithful to your good news.
Amen.

Pronunciation
Ezekiel   eh-ZEE-kee-uhl

This reading begins with
the Lord speaking. Be
sure to make it strong and
direct with a brief pause
after "Thus says the
Lord," and again after
"You say . . ."

The final sentence, which
is very long, should be rehearsed out loud, paying
correct attention to all
punctuation.

First Reading (Ezek 18:25-28)

A reading from the Book of the Prophet
Ezekiel

Thus says the Lord:
You say, "The Lord's way is not fair!"
Hear now, house of Israel:
   Is it my way that is unfair, or rather, are
      not your ways unfair?
When someone virtuous turns away from
      virtue to commit iniquity, and dies,
   it is because of the iniquity he committed
      that he must die.
But if he turns from the wickedness he has
      committed,
   and does what is right and just,
   he shall preserve his life;
   since he has turned away from all the sins
      that he has committed,
   he shall surely live, he shall not die.

Responsorial Psalm (Ps 25:4-5, 6-7, 8-9)

℞. (6a) Remember your mercies, O Lord.

Your ways, O LORD, make known to me;
    teach me your paths,
guide me in your truth and teach me,
    for you are God my savior.

℞. Remember your mercies, O Lord.

Remember that your compassion, O LORD,
    and your love are from of old.
The sins of my youth and my frailties
        remember not;
    in your kindness remember me,
    because of your goodness, O LORD.

℞. Remember your mercies, O Lord.

Good and upright is the Lord;
    thus he shows sinners the way.
He guides the humble to justice,
    and teaches the humble his way.

℞. Remember your mercies, O Lord.

Second Reading (Phil 2:1-11 [or Phil 2:1-5])

A reading from the Letter of Saint Paul to
the Philippians

[Brothers and sisters:
If there is any encouragement in Christ,
    any solace in love,
    any participation in the Spirit,
    any compassion and mercy,
    complete my joy by being of the same
        mind, with the same love,
    united in heart, thinking one thing.
Do nothing out of selfishness or out of
        vainglory;
    rather, humbly regard others as more
        important than yourselves,
    each looking out not for his own interests,
    but also for those of others.

Pronunciation
Philippians
    fih-LIHP-ih-uhnz

Remember to take a nice
pause between sections.
This is Paul's writing, so
rehearse the reading
aloud, paying close attention to the final part.

You will find that paying
attention to the verbs will
help you read this passage
more effectively, especially
the second half.

Have in you the same attitude
    that is also in Christ Jesus,]
        Who, though he was in the form of God,
            did not regard equality with God
            something to be grasped.
        Rather, he emptied himself,
            taking the form of a slave,
            coming in human likeness;
            and found human in appearance,
            he humbled himself,
            becoming obedient to the point of
                death,
            even death on a cross.
        Because of this, God greatly exalted him
            and bestowed on him the name
            which is above every name,
            that at the name of Jesus
            every knee should bend,
            of those in heaven and on earth and
                under the earth,
            and every tongue confess that
            Jesus Christ is Lord,
            to the glory of God the Father.

What an incredible indictment of the chief priests and elders! This is a well-known passage, to be sure, but don't let it slip by without imagining the anger, frustration, and embarrassment of the priests and elders.

The last sentence is the clincher. Keep the energy up and through to the end.

Gospel (Matt 21:28-32; L136A)

A reading from the holy Gospel according to Matthew

Jesus said to the chief priests and elders of
    the people:
    "What is your opinion?
A man had two sons.
He came to the first and said,
    'Son, go out and work in the vineyard
        today.'
He said in reply, 'I will not,'
    but afterwards changed his mind and went.
The man came to the other son and gave the
    same order.

He said in reply, 'Yes, sir,' but did not go.
Which of the two did his father's will?"
They answered, "The first."
Jesus said to them, "Amen, I say to you,
    tax collectors and prostitutes
    are entering the kingdom of God before
        you.
When John came to you in the way of
    righteousness,
    you did not believe him;
    but tax collectors and prostitutes did.
Yet even when you saw that,
    you did not later change your minds and
        believe him."

Preparing to Proclaim
Key words and phrases: *"[B]y the Lord has this been done, / and it is wonderful in our eyes"*

To the point: The image of God as a vineyard keeper continues this week, and the harvest imagery grows stronger as the Northern hemisphere enters more firmly into fall. To Jesus's audience, this parable would have been head-scratchingly mysterious, but for those of us who know the rest of Jesus's story, it foreshadows the passion rather chillingly. But good news still prevails. God's life-giving and saving work does not end when human wickedness tries to stand in its way. Amidst all the pain and brokenness and suffering of this sin-burdened world, God finds ways to continue to give life and bear fruit. God is persistent, not only in carrying out God's plans but also in loving us. God wins and will have final victory, even when it is not apparent. And because God is always on our side, this is very good news.

Making Connections
Between the readings: The first reading echoes the vineyard imagery that has been so strong in the gospels of the past several weeks. Israel is the vineyard that God refuses to give up on; life and love will win out over human failure to participate in them. The second reading balances the anxiety that might be produced by the harsh judgments of the other readings. Paul reassures us that God is a God of peace, who remains with us whenever we choose what is true and good and beautiful.

To experience: This is a parable where it can be hard to identify strongly with any characters. Were it not for Jesus's direct second-person "the kingdom of God will be taken away from you," we might not know what we are supposed to take from it. But yes, even we are prone to rejection of God's messengers and even God's Son. But God never stops trying to reach us, determined to make us partners in bringing forth life.

Prayer

God of the Harvest,
you call us to tend what you have planted,
reminding us that *[t]he vineyard of the Lord
    is the house of Israel.*
May our labors bring your Church to flourish
    and prosper,
and yield much fruit for the building of your
    reign
and the glory of your name.
Amen.

First Reading (Isa 5:1-7)

A reading from the Book of the Prophet Isaiah

Let me now sing of my friend,
    my friend's song concerning his vineyard.
My friend had a vineyard
    on a fertile hillside;
he spaded it, cleared it of stones,
    and planted the choicest vines;
within it he built a watchtower,
    and hewed out a wine press.
Then he looked for the crop of grapes,
    but what it yielded was wild grapes.

Now, inhabitants of Jerusalem and people of
    Judah,
    judge between me and my vineyard:
What more was there to do for my vineyard
    that I had not done?
Why, when I looked for the crop of grapes,
    did it bring forth wild grapes?
Now, I will let you know
    what I mean to do with my vineyard:
take away its hedge, give it to grazing,
    break through its wall, let it be trampled!
Yes, I will make it a ruin:
    it shall not be pruned or hoed,
    but overgrown with thorns and briers;

Pronunciation
Judah   JOU-duh

This is an amazing reading that begins in a gentle, charming, storytelling manner. However, it hardly ends up that way! There are three major shifts in the narrator's story:
1. after "wine press";
2. after "bring forth wild grapes";
3. after "send rain upon it."

Each part becomes darker and more intense, with the final portion, "The vineyard of the LORD . . ." providing the real clincher.

303

I will command the clouds
   not to send rain upon it.
The vineyard of the LORD of hosts is the
      house of Israel,
      and the people of Judah are his cherished
         plant;
he looked for judgment, but see, bloodshed!
   for justice, but hark, the outcry!

Responsorial Psalm (Ps 80:9, 12, 13-14, 15-16, 19-20)

R⁄. (Isaiah 5:7a) The vineyard of the Lord is
the house of Israel.

A vine from Egypt you transplanted;
   you drove away the nations and planted it.
It put forth its foliage to the Sea,
   its shoots as far as the River.

R⁄. The vineyard of the Lord is the house of
Israel.

Why have you broken down its walls,
   so that every passer-by plucks its fruit,
the boar from the forest lays it waste,
   and the beasts of the field feed upon it?

R⁄. The vineyard of the Lord is the house of
Israel.

Once again, O LORD of hosts,
   look down from heaven, and see;
take care of this vine,
      and protect what your right hand has
         planted,
      the son of man whom you yourself made
         strong.

R⁄. The vineyard of the Lord is the house of
Israel.

Then we will no more withdraw from you;
> give us new life, and we will call upon your
> > name.

O Lord, God of hosts, restore us;
> if your face shine upon us, then we shall be
> > saved.

R̸. The vineyard of the Lord is the house of Israel.

Second Reading (Phil 4:6-9)

A reading from the Letter of Saint Paul to the Philippians

Brothers and sisters:
Have no anxiety at all, but in everything,
> by prayer and petition, with thanksgiving,
> make your requests known to God.

Then the peace of God that surpasses all
> understanding
> will guard your hearts and minds in Christ
> > Jesus.

Finally, brothers and sisters,
> whatever is true, whatever is honorable,
> whatever is just, whatever is pure,
> whatever is lovely, whatever is gracious,
> if there is any excellence
> and if there is anything worthy of praise,
> think about these things.

Keep on doing what you have learned and
> received
> and heard and seen in me.

Then the God of peace will be with you.

Pronunciation
Philippians
> fih-LIHP-ih-uhnz

Repetition is a common literary device, as we see here with "whatever is . . ." Your challenge, rather than to rush through the descriptions like a laundry list, is to slow down and deliver each characteristic thoughtfully, according to what they describe.

About two-thirds of the way through this reading, Jesus breaks from his story and asks the chief priests and elders, "What will the owner of the vineyard do to those tenants when he comes?" Before delivering this line, pause, look at the congregation, then read the question slowly to convey a shift in the narration.

The closing lines lose their punch if we are hazy about who Jesus is addressing them to.

Gospel   (Matt 21:33-43; L139A)

A reading from the holy Gospel according to Matthew

Jesus said to the chief priests and the elders
        of the people:
    "Hear another parable.
There was a landowner who planted a
        vineyard,
    put a hedge around it, dug a wine press in
        it, and built a tower.
Then he leased it to tenants and went on a
        journey.
When vintage time drew near,
    he sent his servants to the tenants to obtain
        his produce.
But the tenants seized the servants and one
        they beat,
    another they killed, and a third they stoned.
Again he sent other servants, more numerous
        than the first ones,
    but they treated them in the same way.
Finally, he sent his son to them, thinking,
    'They will respect my son.'
But when the tenants saw the son, they said
        to one another,
    'This is the heir.
Come, let us kill him and acquire his
        inheritance.'
They seized him, threw him out of the
        vineyard, and killed him.
What will the owner of the vineyard do to
        those tenants when he comes?"
They answered him,
    "He will put those wretched men to a
        wretched death
    and lease his vineyard to other tenants
    who will give him the produce at the proper
        times."

Jesus said to them, "Did you never read in the
        Scriptures:
    The stone that the builders rejected
        has become the cornerstone;
    by the Lord has this been done,
        and it is wonderful in our eyes?
Therefore, I say to you,
        the kingdom of God will be taken away
                from you
        and given to a people that will produce its
                fruit."

Preparing to Proclaim
Key words and phrases: "Behold, I have prepared my banquet . . . come to the feast."

To the point: This Sunday, we also begin to see the eschatological themes that will be with us through the end of the church year. They begin on a hopeful note, one in which it is clear that God wants to provide for our needs and have us partake in all that God can offer. In this parable, we see the end game of the lavish generosity the last few weeks' parables have been hinting at. This is more than absurdly recurrent forgiveness and illogical wages. This is a feast, a party. For celebration is the appropriate response when we realize who God is, one whose entire way of being is extravagant, lavish with generosity, and whose whole all-powerful self is constantly spilling forth in self-gift. No one is excluded from this invitation unless they exclude themselves. God's loving abundance is for all.

Making Connections
Between the readings: The first reading gives us a foretaste of the gospel's feast: God provides and God provides abundantly. We are not provided just the bread and water we need to live; this is a tasty, lavish feast. It tends to not just our bare physical needs but to our emotional ones, too: God removes our guilt and wipes away our tears. The second reading also assures us of God's providence; God has all we need (and all we could ever want) and God's "glorious riches" are there to provide for our needs.

To experience: Many of us hesitate to ask God for too much; we strive to pray for the "right" things so that we will not be too disappointed if our desires aren't met. But God already knows all our needs and all our desires and all our thoughts; bringing them to prayer is a way of growing our knowledge of God, not God's knowledge of us. Our neediness before God is an unchangeable and indisputable fact; our acknowledgment of it is simply a way to grow in humility.

Prayer

Good Shepherd,
you provide all that we need,
and sustain us through hunger, sadness,
and our need for redemption.
Seeing you one day face to face, move us to
    exclaim:
*I shall live in the house of the Lord all the
    days of my life.*
The fullness of joys, in your presence, are
    wonderful indeed.
Amen.

First Reading (Isa 25:6-10a)

A reading from the Book of the Prophet Isaiah

On this mountain the LORD of hosts
    will provide for all peoples
a feast of rich food and choice wines,
    juicy, rich food and pure, choice wines.
On this mountain he will destroy
    the veil that veils all peoples,
the web that is woven over all nations;
    he will destroy death forever.
The Lord GOD will wipe away
    the tears from every face;
the reproach of his people he will remove
    from the whole earth; for the LORD has
        spoken.
    On that day it will be said:
"Behold our God, to whom we looked to save
    us!
    This is the LORD for whom we looked;
    let us rejoice and be glad that he has saved
        us!"
For the hand of the LORD will rest on this
    mountain.

Every sentence can stand on its own in this reading. Therefore, do not be afraid to make each sentence a declaration of good news. Take a nice pause after each one.

Responsorial Psalm (Ps 23:1-3a, 3b-4, 5, 6)

R℟. (6cd) I shall live in the house of the Lord all the days of my life.

The LORD is my shepherd; I shall not want.
   In verdant pastures he gives me repose;
beside restful waters he leads me;
   he refreshes my soul.

R℟. I shall live in the house of the Lord all the days of my life.

He guides me in right paths
   for his name's sake.
Even though I walk in the dark valley
   I fear no evil; for you are at my side
with your rod and your staff
   that give me courage.

R℟. I shall live in the house of the Lord all the days of my life.

You spread the table before me
   in the sight of my foes;
you anoint my head with oil;
   my cup overflows.

R℟. I shall live in the house of the Lord all the days of my life.

Only goodness and kindness follow me
   all the days of my life;
and I shall dwell in the house of the LORD
   for years to come.

R℟. I shall live in the house of the Lord all the days of my life.

Second Reading (Phil 4:12-14, 19-20)

A reading from the Letter of Saint Paul to
the Philippians

Brothers and sisters:
I know how to live in humble circumstances;
    I know also how to live with abundance.
In every circumstance and in all things
    I have learned the secret of being well fed
        and of going hungry,
      of living in abundance and of being in
        need.
I can do all things in him who strengthens me.
Still, it was kind of you to share in my
    distress.

My God will fully supply whatever you need,
    in accord with his glorious riches in Christ
        Jesus.
To our God and Father, glory forever and
    ever. Amen.

Gospel (Matt 22:1-14 [or Matt 22:1-10]; L142A)

A reading from the holy Gospel according
to Matthew

[Jesus again in reply spoke to the chief priests
    and elders of the people
    in parables, saying,
    "The kingdom of heaven may be likened to
        a king
    who gave a wedding feast for his son.
He dispatched his servants
    to summon the invited guests to the feast,
    but they refused to come.
A second time he sent other servants, saying,
    'Tell those invited: "Behold, I have prepared
        my banquet,
    my calves and fattened cattle are killed,
    and everything is ready; come to the
        feast.'"

Pronunciation
Philippians
    fih-LIHP-ih-uhnz

Just as in the previous reading, these are all declarative sentences and therefore beg a full stop at all periods.

The climax sentence is, "I can do all things in him who strengthens me." Make sure your listeners know this by your delivery!

It might be helpful to divide this reading into four parts:
1. the first invitation;
2. the second invitation;
3. the third invitation, asking anyone in the streets to attend;
4. the man without a wedding garment.

Giving healthy pauses between the four parts will be helpful for your listeners' understanding.

Finally, of course, there is the kicker: "Many are invited, but few are chosen." This sentence can and should stand on its own.

Some ignored the invitation and went away,
  one to his farm, another to his business.
The rest laid hold of his servants,
  mistreated them, and killed them.
The king was enraged and sent his troops,
  destroyed those murderers, and burned
    their city.
Then he said to his servants, 'The feast is
    ready,
  but those who were invited were not
    worthy to come.
Go out, therefore, into the main roads
  and invite to the feast whomever you find.'
The servants went out into the streets
  and gathered all they found, bad and good
    alike,
  and the hall was filled with guests.]
But when the king came in to meet the guests,
  he saw a man there not dressed in a
    wedding garment.
The king said to him, 'My friend, how is it
  that you came in here without a wedding
    garment?'
But he was reduced to silence.
Then the king said to his attendants, 'Bind his
    hands and feet,
  and cast him into the darkness outside,
  where there will be wailing and grinding of
    teeth.'
Many are invited, but few are chosen."

Preparing to Proclaim

Key words and phrases: "Then repay to Caesar what belongs to Caesar and to God what belongs to God."

To the point: This gospel makes a distinction between the political and the spiritual realms and implies that we have duties to both of them. The church's tradition does not call lay persons to withdraw from secular life; involvement in the political can be part of our partnership with God, how we make the kingdom of heaven present here on earth. It can be an expression of faith, part of how we participate in God's work of love and justice, making this world more holy. But this world, in its current sin-marred state, is not our final home. Political action can be an expression of our faith, but its fruits are only temporary. Political campaigns or candidates or parties can run the risk of becoming idols when we place our hopes in them. In the end, politics leaves us homeless; they will ultimately fail us because our true home is with God. While we are meant to strive for justice, only God can bring about the final justice we seek.

Making Connections

Between the readings: Like the gospel, the first reading makes an important distinction between earthly and divine power. Human leaders may do good work that is willed by God, but God affirms that "I am the Lord and there is no other, there is no God besides me." No other power, no matter how good, can fulfill what is God's to fulfill.

To experience: Political leaders are not the only thing in our lives that run the risk of becoming an idol. Money is a common one; on its own it is a morally neutral tool that can be used for good, but when we pursue it for its own sake it can start to take a place in our hearts that ought to belong to God alone. Security is another; the way we live sometimes betrays that we value our own safety and comfort far above the solidarity to which the gospel calls us.

Prayer

God of Majesty and Might,
there is none like you, kind and understanding,
wise and forgiving.
Therefore, we *give* you *glory and honor,*
we praise your name and your mighty arm,
giving good things to the lowly,
and casting down those who cling to earthly
power.
Amen.

Pronunciation
Cyrus   SAI-ruhs

This reading begins with a sentence that is sixty-one words in length, with thirteen punctuation marks!

Of course, rehearse it aloud, making sure you are familiar and comfortable with all punctuation. "I am the LORD, there is no other" is the point of this reading, being stated twice. Deliver this statement even stronger the second and final time.

First Reading (Isa 45:1, 4-6)

A reading from the Book of the Prophet Isaiah

Thus says the LORD to his anointed, Cyrus,
    whose right hand I grasp,
subduing nations before him,
    and making kings run in his service,
opening doors before him
    and leaving the gates unbarred:
For the sake of Jacob, my servant,
    of Israel, my chosen one,
I have called you by your name,
    giving you a title, though you knew me not.
I am the LORD and there is no other,
    there is no God besides me.
It is I who arm you, though you know me not,
    so that toward the rising and the setting of
        the sun
    people may know that there is none besides
        me.
I am the LORD, there is no other.

Responsorial Psalm (Ps 96:1, 3, 4-5, 7-8, 9-10)

R̸. (7b) Give the Lord glory and honor.

Sing to the LORD a new song;
    sing to the LORD, all you lands.
Tell his glory among the nations;
    among all peoples, his wondrous deeds.

R℣. Give the Lord glory and honor.

For great is the LORD and highly to be praised;
   awesome is he, beyond all gods.
For all the gods of the nations are things of
      nought,
   but the LORD made the heavens.

R℣. Give the Lord glory and honor.

Give to the LORD, you families of nations,
   give to the LORD glory and praise;
   give to the LORD the glory due his name!
Bring gifts, and enter his courts.

R℣. Give the Lord glory and honor.

Worship the LORD, in holy attire;
   tremble before him, all the earth;
say among the nations: The LORD is king,
   he governs the peoples with equity.

R℣. Give the Lord glory and honor.

Second Reading (1 Thess 1:1-5b)

A reading from the first Letter of Saint Paul
to the Thessalonians

Paul, Silvanus, and Timothy to the church of
      the Thessalonians
   in God the Father and the Lord Jesus
         Christ:
   grace to you and peace.
We give thanks to God always for all of you,
   remembering you in our prayers,
   unceasingly calling to mind your work of
         faith and labor of love
   and endurance in hope of our Lord Jesus
         Christ,
   before our God and Father,
   knowing, brothers and sisters loved by
         God,
   how you were chosen.

Pronunciation
Thessalonians
   theh-suh-LO-nih-uhnz
Silvanus   sihl-VAY-nuhs

Daring to state the obvi-
ous, the first sentence is
simply a greeting. Re-
member this is literally a
letter from Paul, Silvanus,
and Timothy written to
build up the Christian
people in Thessalonica.
Go ahead and read it as
such.

For our gospel did not come to you in word
alone,
but also in power and in the Holy Spirit
and with much conviction.

Pronunciation
Pharisees   FEHR-ih-seez
Herodians
    hehr-O-dee-uhnz
Caesar   SEE-zer

I would not shy away
from reading the first part
of this gospel in the hon-
est spirit of the motives
of the Pharisees: evil and
nasty, as they only want
to trap Jesus!

Gospel (Matt 22:15-21; L145A)

A reading from the holy Gospel according
to Matthew

The Pharisees went off
and plotted how they might entrap Jesus in
speech.
They sent their disciples to him, with the
Herodians, saying,
"Teacher, we know that you are a truthful
man
and that you teach the way of God in
accordance with the truth.
And you are not concerned with anyone's
opinion,
for you do not regard a person's status.
Tell us, then, what is your opinion:
Is it lawful to pay the census tax to Caesar
or not?"
Knowing their malice, Jesus said,
"Why are you testing me, you hypocrites?
Show me the coin that pays the census tax."
Then they handed him the Roman coin.
He said to them, "Whose image is this and
whose inscription?"
They replied, "Caesar's."
At that he said to them,
"Then repay to Caesar what belongs to
Caesar
and to God what belongs to God."

Preparing to Proclaim

Key words and phrases: "This is the greatest and the first commandment."

To the point: The Pharisees attempt to entrap Jesus with a trick question: Naming one commandment as the greatest would devalue the others by comparison, making it sound as if he does not value God's word in its fullness. Instead, Jesus shows that he understands God's word far more deeply than those who are tied to reading the law literally. He names not one of the ten commandments but one that comes after them in Deuteronomy. He reveals that fulfilling the law is not about servile deference to what is written, but about love. If our hearts are formed in love, the other commandments will follow, flowing forth from our inner being instead of needing to be forced as outer actions. The second commandment, too, can be named as secondary because it also flows from love of God. If we truly love God, so will we love our neighbor.

Making Connections

Between the readings: The first reading shows that the God of the Old Testament is not some being foreign from the Jesus of the New Testament. The love that Jesus preaches does not *replace* the law. There is continuity here. God's Old Testament commandments are more specific, and make punishment clearer, but they are about the very love for neighbor that Jesus has named as so important. To treat foreigners and widows and orphans with justice is to fulfill the love to which we are called.

To experience: In this life, the moral teachings of the church will always be at times burdensome and challenging. This is simply part of being human; until we are fully united to God in heaven we will not be acting from hearts perfectly formed in love. We can, though, try to reframe our understandings of these teachings; while they are often poorly taught and uncompassionately preached, they are *meant* to help us live in the love Jesus calls us to.

Prayer

God of Wayfarers,
you are welcome to the stranger,
and wonderful bounty to those in need.
May those we meet who need our help
know you through our acts of loving service,
and be compelled, in joy and gratitude,
to praise your name: *I love you, Lord, my
strength.*
Amen.

"Alien" in this reading refers to a foreigner, especially one who is not a naturalized citizen of the country where they are living.

Notice the use of the phrase, "You shall not . . ." These are commandments made by the Lord, just as the Ten Commandments. Deliver them in the same declarative way.

First Reading (Exod 22:20-26)

A reading from the Book of Exodus

Thus says the LORD:
"You shall not molest or oppress an alien,
for you were once aliens yourselves in the
land of Egypt.
You shall not wrong any widow or orphan.
If ever you wrong them and they cry out to
me,
I will surely hear their cry.
My wrath will flare up, and I will kill you with
the sword;
then your own wives will be widows, and
your children orphans.

"If you lend money to one of your poor
neighbors among my people,
you shall not act like an extortioner toward
him
by demanding interest from him.
If you take your neighbor's cloak as a pledge,
you shall return it to him before sunset;
for this cloak of his is the only covering he
has for his body.
What else has he to sleep in?
If he cries out to me, I will hear him; for I am
compassionate."

Responsorial Psalm (Ps 18:2-3, 3-4, 47, 51)

R℣. (2) I love you, Lord, my strength.

I love you, O LORD, my strength,
    O LORD, my rock, my fortress, my deliverer.

R℣. I love you, Lord, my strength.

My God, my rock of refuge,
    my shield, the horn of my salvation, my
        stronghold!
Praised be the LORD, I exclaim,
    and I am safe from my enemies.

R℣. I love you, Lord, my strength.

The LORD lives and blessed be my rock!
    Extolled be God my savior.
You who gave great victories to your king
    and showed kindness to your anointed.

R℣. I love you, Lord, my strength.

Second Reading (1 Thess 1:5c-10)

A reading from the first Letter of Saint Paul
to the Thessalonians

Brothers and sisters:
You know what sort of people we were
    among you for your sake.
And you became imitators of us and of the
    Lord,
    receiving the word in great affliction, with
        joy from the Holy Spirit,
    so that you became a model for all the
        believers
in Macedonia and in Achaia.
For from you the word of the Lord has
    sounded forth
    not only in Macedonia and in Achaia,
    but in every place your faith in God has
        gone forth,
    so that we have no need to say anything.

Pronunciation
Thessalonians
    theh-suh-LO-nih-uhnz
Macedonia
    mas-eh-DO-nih-uh
Achaia   uh-KAY-yuh

Rehearse the pronunciation of "Macedonia" and "Achaia" so you are comfortable with them. If you are not comfortable or show nervousness when reading these words, then the listeners will feel the same.

This is Paul, so be well rehearsed, as he likes to write in complex sentences.

For they themselves openly declare about us
what sort of reception we had among you,
and how you turned to God from idols
to serve the living and true God
and to await his Son from heaven,
whom he raised from the dead,
Jesus, who delivers us from the coming
wrath.

Gospel (Matt 22:34-40; L148A)

A reading from the holy Gospel according
to Matthew

When the Pharisees heard that Jesus had
silenced the Sadducees,
they gathered together, and one of them,
a scholar of the law, tested him by asking,
"Teacher, which commandment in the law
is the greatest?"
He said to him,
"You shall love the Lord, your God,
with all your heart,
with all your soul,
and with all your mind.
This is the greatest and the first
commandment.
The second is like it:
You shall love your neighbor as yourself.
The whole law and the prophets depend on
these two commandments."

Preparing to Proclaim

Key words and phrases: "Whoever exalts himself will be humbled; but whoever humbles himself will be exalted."

To the point: This gospel has one of Jesus's familiar reversals of our expectations for this world. He states that the visible religious leaders of his time are not, in fact, in favor with God. Their misguided love for recognition and honor outweighs their love for God. They seem to hold power—and by earthly standards, they do—but they are not enacting the true power that is available to all of us. This power is God's gift and enables us to enact God's will. It doesn't look much like power, though; it rather looks a lot like servanthood. Jesus tells his followers to humble themselves, because humility is the basis of true exaltation in God's ordering of things. This humility is found in unity, joined as brothers and sisters under one loving teacher and father and master.

Making Connections

Between the readings: Both the psalm and the gospel use images of being cared for as a mother cares for her children; in the psalm it is an image for God's care for us, and in Thessalonians it is an image for how church leaders ought to care for the flock entrusted to them. This is again a reversal of our expectations: the self-giving work of mothers often goes unseen and unacknowledged, yet it is here a mark of leadership.

To experience: We don't always get to see the promise of this gospel played out; too often in this life, it seems that those with power only get more power and those without only fall further and further. Our sinful structures are cyclical by nature, and these cycles can seem insurmountably hard to break. But sometimes cycles are broken: parents can break intergenerational cycles of abuse and trauma, for instance, by sacrificing a power-based relationship for one based on love.

Prayer

Gentle and Compassionate God,
when troubles weigh us down
and storms disturb our well-being,
put this prayer on our lips:
In you, Lord, I have found my peace.
For only you have true peace, that which the
world cannot give.
Grant us humility and rest, and serene hope in
your presence.
Amen.

Pronunciation
Pharisees   FEHR-ih-seez
Sadducees   SAD-joo-seez

Here is another trap set
for Jesus by the Pharisees.
Jesus answers their ques-
tion not only truthfully
but poetically. His answer
should be literally soothing against the agitated
voices of the Pharisees.

First Reading (Mal 1:14b–2:2b, 8-10)

A reading from the Book of the Prophet
Malachi

A great King am I, says the LORD of hosts,
and my name will be feared among the
nations.
And now, O priests, this commandment is for
you:
If you do not listen,
if you do not lay it to heart,
to give glory to my name, says the LORD of
hosts,
I will send a curse upon you
and of your blessing I will make a curse.
You have turned aside from the way,
and have caused many to falter by your
instruction;
you have made void the covenant of Levi,
says the LORD of hosts.
I, therefore, have made you contemptible
and base before all the people,
since you do not keep my ways,
but show partiality in your decisions.
Have we not all the one father?
Has not the one God created us?
Why then do we break faith with one another,
violating the covenant of our fathers?

Responsorial Psalm (Ps 131:1, 2, 3)

R℣. In you, Lord, I have found my peace.

O LORD, my heart is not proud,
　　nor are my eyes haughty;
I busy not myself with great things,
　　nor with things too sublime for me.

R℣. In you, Lord, I have found my peace.

Nay rather, I have stilled and quieted
　　my soul like a weaned child.
Like a weaned child on its mother's lap,
　　so is my soul within me.

R℣. In you, Lord, I have found my peace.

O Israel, hope in the LORD,
　　both now and forever.

R℣. In you, Lord, I have found my peace.

Second Reading (1 Thess 2:7b-9, 13)

A reading from the first Letter of Saint Paul
to the Thessalonians

Brothers and sisters:
We were gentle among you, as a nursing
　　mother cares for her children.
With such affection for you, we were
　　determined to share with you
　　not only the gospel of God, but our very
　　　　selves as well,
　　so dearly beloved had you become to us.
You recall, brothers and sisters, our toil and
　　drudgery.
Working night and day in order not to burden
　　any of you,
　　we proclaimed to you the gospel of God.

And for this reason we too give thanks to God
　　unceasingly,
　　that, in receiving the word of God from
　　　　hearing us,

Pronunciation
Malachi　MAL-uh-kai
Levi　LEE-vai

The Lord is definitely not happy with his priests, and he firmly scolds them in this reading. Let the Lord's anger and curses come through in your voice.

A nice pause before the very last question at the end will heighten the drama.

323

THIRTY-FIRST SUNDAY IN ORDINARY TIME

you received not a human word but, as it
truly is, the word of God,
which is now at work in you who believe.

Pronunciation
Thessalonians
    theh-suh-LO-nih-uhnz

Paul is writing of great
love here. Read the first
sentences with gentleness
and affection.

The part beginning with
"You recall . . ." is a bit
more declarative. Then
the passage concludes
with great joy as the mission is accomplished.

Gospel (Matt 23:1-12; LI5IA)

A reading from the holy Gospel according
to Matthew

Jesus spoke to the crowds and to his disciples,
    saying,
    "The scribes and the Pharisees
    have taken their seat on the chair of Moses.
Therefore, do and observe all things
    whatsoever they tell you,
    but do not follow their example.
For they preach but they do not practice.
They tie up heavy burdens hard to carry
    and lay them on people's shoulders,
    but they will not lift a finger to move them.
All their works are performed to be seen.
They widen their phylacteries and lengthen
        their tassels.
They love places of honor at banquets, seats
        of honor in synagogues,
    greetings in marketplaces, and the
        salutation 'Rabbi.'
As for you, do not be called 'Rabbi.'
You have but one teacher, and you are all
        brothers.
Call no one on earth your father;
    you have but one Father in heaven.
Do not be called 'Master';
    you have but one master, the Christ.
The greatest among you must be your
        servant.
Whoever exalts himself will be humbled;
    but whoever humbles himself will be
        exalted."

Preparing to Proclaim

Key words and phrases: "[S]tay awake, for you know neither the day nor the hour."

To the point: The end of the liturgical year always presents us with Scripture passages that speak of the end times. This theme will continue into Advent's repetitive admonition to stay awake and ready for the ultimate coming of Christ. The Bible's images of this time are sometimes troubling; here, we have a locked door and a Bridegroom who refuses to recognize those who came unprepared for the wedding feast—hardly a reassuring image of Christ's boundless mercy. But this is not a gospel about the mechanics of our preparation; when put into dialogue with the other readings for today, it becomes a gospel about our longing to be with Jesus. Those whose hearts desire him will find ways to prepare their hearts. The specifics of that preparation will look different for all of us, but love and longing are at their core.

Making Connections

Between the readings: The second reading reminds us that, even in the face of all that is dark and scary in the world, we are called to live with hope—hope granted to us through faith in the one who has conquered even death. The first reading tells us more about the wisdom attributed to half the gospel's virgins; this wisdom character is also read as an Old Testament image of Christ. Here, she is not a hardhearted host but is always waiting and preparing for those who seek her. Our love for wisdom—and for Jesus, the wisdom of God—is always met with preexisting love that seeks us first.

To experience: These eschatological November readings are fitting for the month Catholics dedicate to remembrance of the dead. Even as we grieve our losses, this week offers us a reminder to live in hope, not just for ourselves but for all our departed loved ones.

Prayer

Wellspring of Eternal Life,
you who are refreshment and vivification,
our souls are *thirsting for you, O Lord.*
Lead us to drink of you who satisfy all
    desires,
and, revived, keep us watchful and alert for
    your coming.
Make us ready to greet you at your coming.
Amen.

First Reading (Wis 6:12-16)

A reading from the Book of Wisdom

Resplendent and unfading is wisdom,
    and she is readily perceived by those who
        love her,
    and found by those who seek her.
She hastens to make herself known in
        anticipation of their desire;
    whoever watches for her at dawn shall not
        be disappointed,
    for he shall find her sitting by his gate.
For taking thought of wisdom is the
        perfection of prudence,
    and whoever for her sake keeps vigil
    shall quickly be free from care;
because she makes her own rounds, seeking
        those worthy of her,
    and graciously appears to them in the
        ways,
    and meets them with all solicitude.

Responsorial Psalm (Ps 63:2, 3-4, 5-6, 7-8)

℟. (2b) My soul is thirsting for you, O Lord
my God.

O God, you are my God whom I seek;
    for you my flesh pines and my soul thirsts
    like the earth, parched, lifeless and without
        water.

℟. My soul is thirsting for you, O Lord my
God.

Thus have I gazed toward you in the
        sanctuary
    to see your power and your glory,
for your kindness is a greater good than life;
    my lips shall glorify you.

℟. My soul is thirsting for you, O Lord my
God.

Thus will I bless you while I live;
    lifting up my hands, I will call upon your
        name.
As with the riches of a banquet shall my soul
        be satisfied,
    and with exultant lips my mouth shall
        praise you.

℟. My soul is thirsting for you, O Lord my
God.

I will remember you upon my couch,
    and through the night-watches I will
        meditate on you:
you are my help,
    and in the shadow of your wings I shout
        for joy.

℟. My soul is thirsting for you, O Lord my
God.

Each complete sentence can stand on its own. Therefore, take a nice pause between each.

Second Reading (1 Thess 4:13-18 [or 1 Thess 4:13-14])

A reading from the first Letter of Saint Paul to the Thessalonians

[We do not want you to be unaware, brothers and sisters,
about those who have fallen asleep,
so that you may not grieve like the rest,
who have no hope.
For if we believe that Jesus died and rose,
so too will God, through Jesus,
bring with him those who have fallen asleep.]
Indeed, we tell you this, on the word of the Lord,
that we who are alive,
who are left until the coming of the Lord,
will surely not precede those who have fallen asleep.
For the Lord himself, with a word of command,
with the voice of an archangel and with the trumpet of God,
will come down from heaven,
and the dead in Christ will rise first.
Then we who are alive, who are left,
will be caught up together with them in the clouds
to meet the Lord in the air.
Thus we shall always be with the Lord.
Therefore, console one another with these words.

Gospel (Matt 25:1-13; L154A)

A reading from the holy Gospel according
to Matthew

Jesus told his disciples this parable:
"The kingdom of heaven will be like ten
        virgins
    who took their lamps and went out to meet
        the bridegroom.
Five of them were foolish and five were wise.
The foolish ones, when taking their lamps,
    brought no oil with them,
    but the wise brought flasks of oil with
        their lamps.
Since the bridegroom was long delayed,
    they all became drowsy and fell asleep.
At midnight, there was a cry,
    'Behold, the bridegroom! Come out to meet
        him!'
Then all those virgins got up and trimmed
        their lamps.
The foolish ones said to the wise,
    'Give us some of your oil,
    for our lamps are going out.'
But the wise ones replied,
    'No, for there may not be enough for us and
        you.
Go instead to the merchants and buy some for
        yourselves.'
While they went off to buy it,
    the bridegroom came
    and those who were ready went into the
        wedding feast with him.
Then the door was locked.
Afterwards the other virgins came and said,
    'Lord, Lord, open the door for us!'
But he said in reply,
    'Amen, I say to you, I do not know you.'
Therefore, stay awake,
    for you know neither the day nor the hour.'"

Pronunciation
Thessalonians
    theh-suh-LO-nih-uhnz

This is a great reading of
consolation for those who
have lost loved ones. The
second half is made up of
rather complex sentences,
so to avoid confusion re-
hearse aloud until you are
confident of how to use
the punctuation.

Preparing to Proclaim
Key words and phrases: "Come, share your master's joy."

To the point: This gospel introduces an important concept for our life of faith: faithfulness in small matters is how we practice our readiness to be faithful in greater ways. As athletes train through consistent training, we grow in virtue through the discipline of consistent practice whenever the opportunity arises. Small moral choices might seem not to matter, but they do; they are an opportunity to develop our holiness muscles. While the servants deal with their master's money for a limited time, we are responsible for our gifts for the entirety of our lives. This can be an overwhelming proposition, but there is reassurance here: practicing trustworthiness in small ways prepares us for the great joy that God promises. In all the ordinary ways we act with compassion and justice and integrity, we are practicing and preparing for nothing less than heaven.

Making Connections
Between the readings: The first reading echoes the idea that faithfulness in daily labors is how one lives out a lifelong commitment, whether that commitment is to one's spouse or to a life of faith. The second reading has those late fall pre-Advent vibes, when we are reminded of the end times and of our need to stay prepared. In light of the gospel and first reading, we know how to do this: through commitments to our small, daily acts of faith and love.

To experience: Whatever our life circumstances, there are countless opportunities every day to make right or wrong choices. This can seem overwhelming and demanding: why would God ask so much of us? But it can also be seen as an opportunity, one provided by God's endless mercy. We have countless opportunities to do wrong, but we also have boundless chances to correct course, to try again, to participate anew in God's work of making us holy and whole.

Prayer

God of All Good Gifts,
Blessed are those who fear you,
and learn to walk in your ways.
Reward our labors, our service to your holy
    people,
and, at a time only you know,
bring all creation into oneness with each other
    and with you.
Amen.

First Reading (Prov 31:10-13, 19-20, 30-31)

A reading from the Book of Proverbs

When one finds a worthy wife,
    her value is far beyond pearls.
Her husband, entrusting his heart to her,
    has an unfailing prize.
She brings him good, and not evil,
    all the days of her life.
She obtains wool and flax
    and works with loving hands.
She puts her hands to the distaff,
    and her fingers ply the spindle.
She reaches out her hands to the poor,
    and extends her arms to the needy.
Charm is deceptive and beauty fleeting;
    the woman who fears the Lord is to be
        praised.
Give her a reward for her labors,
    and let her works praise her at the city gates.

Responsorial Psalm (Ps 128:1-2, 3, 4-5)

℟. (cf. 1a) Blessed are those who fear the
Lord.

Blessed are you who fear the Lord,
    who walk in his ways!
For you shall eat the fruit of your handiwork;
    blessed shall you be, and favored.

℟. Blessed are those who fear the Lord.

This popular reading lends itself very easily to dramatization. You need: ten children or adults to play the ten virgins; ten paper "lamps" with paper flames that can be folded down to signify "out"; one person to play the bridegroom.

While the five virgins have gone off for more oil, the bridegroom arrives. He leads the five whose lamps have been lit into the wedding feast. The others arrive and call out to be let in, but they are not admitted.

If you dramatize this gospel your listeners will never forget this reading.

Your wife shall be like a fruitful vine
    in the recesses of your home;
your children like olive plants
    around your table.

R⁊. Blessed are those who fear the Lord.

Behold, thus is the man blessed
    who fears the LORD.
The LORD bless you from Zion:
    may you see the prosperity of Jerusalem
    all the days of your life.

R⁊. Blessed are those who fear the Lord.

distaff: a stick or spindle onto which wool or flax is wound for spinning.

There are three basic parts here:
    Part 1 ends with "all the days of her life."
    Part 2 ends with "extends her arms to the needy."
    Part 3 requires a nice pause and a shift in thought, and therefore, in energy and voice.
What do these three parts address, and what might be an appropriate delivery for each?

Second Reading (1 Thess 5:1-6)

A reading from the first Letter of Saint Paul to the Thessalonians

Concerning times and seasons, brothers and
    sisters,
    you have no need for anything to be
        written to you.
For you yourselves know very well that the
    day of the Lord will come
    like a thief at night.
When people are saying, "Peace and security,"
    then sudden disaster comes upon them,
    like labor pains upon a pregnant woman,
    and they will not escape.

But you, brothers and sisters, are not in
    darkness,
    for that day to overtake you like a thief.
For all of you are children of the light
    and children of the day.
We are not of the night or of darkness.
Therefore, let us not sleep as the rest do,
    but let us stay alert and sober.

Gospel (Matt 25:14-30 [or Matt 25:14-15, 19-21]; L157A)

A reading from the holy Gospel according to Matthew

[Jesus told his disciples this parable:
    "A man going on a journey
    called in his servants and entrusted his
        possessions to them.
To one he gave five talents; to another, two; to
    a third, one—
to each according to his ability.
Then he went away.]
Immediately the one who received five talents
    went and traded with them,
    and made another five.
Likewise, the one who received two made
    another two.
But the man who received one went off and
    dug a hole in the ground
    and buried his master's money.

["After a long time
    the master of those servants came back
    and settled accounts with them.
The one who had received five talents came
    forward
    bringing the additional five.
He said, 'Master, you gave me five talents.
See, I have made five more.'
His master said to him, 'Well done, my good
    and faithful servant.
Since you were faithful in small matters,
    I will give you great responsibilities.
Come, share your master's joy.']
Then the one who had received two talents
    also came forward and said,
    'Master, you gave me two talents.
See, I have made two more.'
His master said to him, 'Well done, my good
    and faithful servant.

Pronunciation
Thessalonians
    theh-suh-LO-nih-uhnz

The opening and closing of this reading are the most important parts. They are like bookends that can easily stand on their own. Proclaim them!

Take a nice pause after "like a thief at night" and before "We are not of the night . . ."

Since you were faithful in small matters,
  I will give you great responsibilities.
Come, share your master's joy.'
Then the one who had received the one talent
    came forward and said,
  'Master, I knew you were a demanding
      person,
    harvesting where you did not plant
    and gathering where you did not scatter;
    so out of fear I went off and buried your
      talent in the ground.
Here it is back.'
His master said to him in reply, 'You wicked,
    lazy servant!
So you knew that I harvest where I did not
      plant
    and gather where I did not scatter?
Should you not then have put my money in
      the bank
    so that I could have got it back with
        interest on my return?
Now then! Take the talent from him and give
    it to the one with ten.
For to everyone who has,
    more will be given and he will grow rich;
    but from the one who has not,
    even what he has will be taken away.
And throw this useless servant into the
      darkness outside,
    where there will be wailing and grinding
      of teeth.'"

Preparing to Proclaim

Key words and phrases: "[W]hatever you did for one of the least brothers of mine, you did for me."

To the point: When we envision royalty, we think of glamour and adventure, of triumph and power. Kings and queens are people set apart, people greater than others. In this gospel, Jesus offers us a radically different image. He comes in glory and power, yes, but underlying this is a radical solidarity with the least ones of his kingdom. Christ's power is used to encourage just and compassionate treatment of those we are all too quick to overlook: people who are poor, unfamiliar, and imprisoned. His power lies not primarily in shaming and banishing those who do not obey this command, but in his deep identification with those in need. We would probably claim that we would treat Jesus with the utmost respect, deserving of his unique place in the cosmic kingdom. Here he tells us, though, that we have opportunities to do so all the time. How we treat the least ones we encounter is how we treat Christ, our King.

Making Connections

Between the readings: The first reading also has an image of leadership being turned upside down; shepherds were not people who commanded much respect in the ancient world, but it is them with whom God identifies. In the second reading, Paul affirms that Christ's power does not exist for its own sake. Rather, it is part of God's greater plan to restore us to right relationship with each other, with our world, and with God.

To experience: Even when we know better, we often seek to exert power over those with whom we have been placed in relationship. This can be especially true of the children in our lives, who we often seek to control. But they, too, can bear Christ to us, and as "least ones" in our midst give us an opportunity to enact compassion and justice toward our very King.

Prayer

God who Reigns,
your crown is of thorns, and your throne a
  rugged cross.
Your son's kingship is one of service and
  humility.
Indeed, *[t]he Lord is my shepherd,*
protecting and guiding,
anointing and preserving all life.
Help us all to love as Christ loved us,
finding him in the lowly and least in our midst.
Amen.

The one line that I have often overlooked in this reading is "to each according to his ability." Don't let this line fall through the cracks.

First Reading (Ezek 34:11-12, 15-17)

A reading from the Book of the Prophet
Ezekiel

Thus says the Lord GOD:
  I myself will look after and tend my sheep.
As a shepherd tends his flock
  when he finds himself among his scattered
    sheep,
  so will I tend my sheep.
I will rescue them from every place where
    they were scattered
  when it was cloudy and dark.
I myself will pasture my sheep;
  I myself will give them rest, says the Lord
    GOD.
The lost I will seek out,
  the strayed I will bring back,
  the injured I will bind up,
  the sick I will heal,
  but the sleek and the strong I will destroy,
  shepherding them rightly.

As for you, my sheep, says the Lord GOD,
  I will judge between one sheep and
    another,
  between rams and goats.

Responsorial Psalm (Ps 23:1-2, 2-3, 5-6)

℟. (1) The Lord is my shepherd; there is
nothing I shall want.

The LORD is my shepherd; I shall not want.
  In verdant pastures he gives me repose.

℟. The Lord is my shepherd; there is nothing
I shall want.

Beside restful waters he leads me;
  he refreshes my soul.
He guides me in right paths
  for his name's sake.

℟. The Lord is my shepherd; there is nothing
I shall want.

You spread the table before me
  in the sight of my foes;
you anoint my head with oil;
  my cup overflows.

℟. The Lord is my shepherd; there is nothing
I shall want.

Only goodness and kindness follow me
  all the days of my life;
and I shall dwell in the house of the LORD
  for years to come.

℟. The Lord is my shepherd; there is nothing
I shall want.

Second Reading (1 Cor 15:20-26, 28)

A reading from the first Letter of Saint Paul
to the Corinthians

Brothers and sisters:
Christ has been raised from the dead,
  the firstfruits of those who have fallen
    asleep.
For since death came through man,
  the resurrection of the dead came also
    through man.

Pronunciation
Ezekiel   eh-ZEE-kee-uhl

This reading is so full of
action! Each sentence can
stand alone so again, give
a nice pause after each.
Communicate the par-
ticular action of each sentence with the same
energy that the Lord says
he will use.

For just as in Adam all die,
so too in Christ shall all be brought to life,
but each one in proper order:
Christ the firstfruits;
then, at his coming, those who belong to
Christ;
then comes the end,
when he hands over the kingdom to his
God and Father,
when he has destroyed every sovereignty
and every authority and power.
For he must reign until he has put all his
enemies under his feet.
The last enemy to be destroyed is death.
When everything is subjected to him,
then the Son himself will also be subjected
to the one who subjected everything to him,
so that God may be all in all.

Gospel (Matt 25:31-46; L160A)

A reading from the holy Gospel according
to Matthew

Jesus said to his disciples:
"When the Son of Man comes in his glory,
and all the angels with him,
he will sit upon his glorious throne,
and all the nations will be assembled
before him.
And he will separate them one from another,
as a shepherd separates the sheep from the
goats.
He will place the sheep on his right and the
goats on his left.
Then the king will say to those on his right,
'Come, you who are blessed by my Father.
Inherit the kingdom prepared for you from
the foundation of the world.
For I was hungry and you gave me food,

I was thirsty and you gave me drink,
a stranger and you welcomed me,
naked and you clothed me,
ill and you cared for me,
in prison and you visited me.'
Then the righteous will answer him and say,
'Lord, when did we see you hungry and
feed you,
or thirsty and give you drink?
When did we see you a stranger and welcome
you,
or naked and clothe you?
When did we see you ill or in prison, and visit
you?'
And the king will say to them in reply,
'Amen, I say to you, whatever you did
for one of the least brothers of mine, you
did for me.'
Then he will say to those on his left,
'Depart from me, you accursed,
into the eternal fire prepared for the devil
and his angels.
For I was hungry and you gave me no food,
I was thirsty and you gave me no drink,
a stranger and you gave me no welcome,
naked and you gave me no clothing,
ill and in prison, and you did not care for
me.'
Then they will answer and say,
'Lord, when did we see you hungry or
thirsty
or a stranger or naked or ill or in prison,
and not minister to your needs?'
He will answer them, 'Amen, I say to you,
what you did not do for one of these least
ones,
you did not do for me.'
And these will go off to eternal punishment,
but the righteous to eternal life."

Pronunciation
Corinthians
kawr-IHN-thee-uhnz

Again, be careful with Paul. The third sentence needs to be rehearsed aloud until you are comfortable with all the punctuation. If you don't understand what you are reading, neither will the listeners!

I would caution you not to go through the list of actions like a laundry list. This gospel could easily be likened to an examination of conscience. Deliver it slowly and deliberately.